Contemporary Women Writers Look Back

Also available in the series:

Active Reading by Ben Knights and Chris Thurgar-Dawson
Beckett's Books by Matthew Feldman
Beckett and Phenomenology edited by Matthew Feldman and Ulrika Maude
Beckett and Decay by Katherine White
Beckett and Death edited by Steve Barfield, Matthew Feldman and Philip Tew
Canonizing Hypertext by Astrid Ensslin
Character and Satire in Postwar Fiction by Ian Gregson
Coleridge and German Philosophy by Paul Hamilton
Contemporary Fiction and Christianity by Andrew Tate
English Fiction in the 1930s by Chris Hopkins
Ecstasy and Understanding edited by Adrian Grafe
Fictions of Globalization by James Annesley
Joyce and Company by David Pierce
London Narratives by Lawrence Phillips
Masculinity in Fiction and Film by Brian Baker
Modernism and the Post-colonial by Peter Childs
Milton, Evil and Literary History by Claire Colebrook
Novels of the Contemporary Extreme edited by Alain-Phillipe Durand and Naomi Mandel
Postmodern Fiction and the Break-Up of Fiction by Hywel Dix
Post-War British Women Novelists and the Canon by Nick Turner
Seeking Meaning for Goethe's Faust by J. M. van der Laan
Sexuality and the Erotic in the Fiction of Joseph Conrad by Jeremy Hawthorn
Such Deliberate Disguises: The Art of Phillip Larkin by Richard Palmer
The Palimpsest by Sarah Dillon
The Measureless Past of Joyce, Deleuze and Derrida by Ruben Borg
Women's Fiction 1945–2000 by Deborah Philips

Contemporary Women Writers Look Back
From Irony to Nostalgia

Alice Ridout

BLOOMSBURY
LONDON • NEW DELHI • NEW YORK • SYDNEY

Bloomsbury Academic
An imprint of Bloomsbury Publishing Plc

50 Bedford Square	175 Fifth Avenue
London	New York
WC1B 3DP	NY 10010
UK	USA

www.bloomsbury.com

First published by Continuum International Publishing Group 2010
Paperback edition first printed 2012

© Alice Ridout, 2010

All rights reserved. No part of this publication may be reproduced or transmitted in any form or by any means, electronic or mechanical, including photocopying, recording, or any information storage or retrieval system, without prior permission in writing from the publishers.

Alice Ridout has asserted her right under the Copyright, Designs and Patents Act, 1988, to be identified as Author of this work.

No responsibility for loss caused to any individual or organization acting on or refraining from action as a result of the material in this publication can be accepted by Bloomsbury Academic or the author.

British Library Cataloguing-in-Publication Data
A catalogue record for this book is available from the British Library.

ISBN: HB: 978-1-4411-4744-8
PB: 978-1-4411-3023-5

Library of Congress Cataloging-in-Publication Data
Ridout, Alice.
Contemporary women writers look back : from irony to nostalgia / Alice Ridout.
    p. cm. – (Continuum literary studies)
Includes bibliographical references and index.
ISBN 978-1-4411-4744-8 (hardcover) – ISBN 978-1-4411-3023-5 (pbk.) 1. Literature–Women authors–History and criticism. 2. Authorship. 3. Women and literature. I. Title.

PR116.R54 2012
809'.89287–dc23
                                            2012011826

Typeset by Newgen Imaging Systems Pvt Ltd, Chennai, India
Printed and bound in Great Britain

*This book is dedicated to the memory of
Gwen Valentin (1943–2007)*

Contents

Preface	viii
Acknowledgements	ix
Introduction: *Contemporary Women's Re-writing*	1
Chapter 1. *The Politics of Parody: Toni Morrison's* The Bluest Eye	15
Chapter 2. *'Some books are not read in the right way': Parody and Reception in Doris Lessing's* The Golden Notebook	47
Chapter 3. *Parodic Self-Narratives: Margaret Atwood's* Lady Oracle *and* The Blind Assassin	69
Chapter 4. *Inheritances: Zadie Smith's* On Beauty	103
Chapter 5. *The Politics of Nostalgia: Jane Austen Recycled*	123
Afterword: Belatedness	143
Notes	144
Bibliography	165
Index	183

Preface

I am aware that this book has forced me to enact some of the issues it explores, such as Toni Morrison's confrontation with authority and authorship in *The Bluest Eye* and what it means to be a 'timely' feminist. When reading through the manuscript to kindly cross-check entries in the bibliography, my partner could not resist writing me the note, 'much like this book for you', next to the quotation from Doris Lessing about how traumatic she found the writing experience of *The Golden Notebook*. What enabled me to finish writing was my reading, both of contemporary women's writing and of the inspiring critics working in this field. The very topic of this work – retellings – draws attention to how processes of writing are intimately connected to processes of reading. I have consciously attempted to build my own work upon the contributions of others.

The book offers the narrative of a shift from irony to nostalgia in contemporary women's fiction as a provocative, rather than definitive, story of the changes in contemporary women writers' approaches to their literary pasts. It takes as its starting point Adrienne Rich's famous comment from 1971 in 'When We Dead Awaken: Writing as Re-Vision' that 'Re-vision – the act of looking back, of seeing with fresh eyes, of entering an old text from a new critical direction – is for women more than a chapter in cultural history: it is an act of survival' (35). The critical and literary landscape has changed enormously over the past decade. The two most recently written chapters – one examining Zadie Smith's *On Beauty* and the other looking at retellings of Jane Austen – are attempts to map and address some of these recent changes. As my afterword suggests, the sense of belatedness noted by John Barth and Patricia Waugh (among others) as a defining characteristic of postmodernism seems to have become more, rather than less, pronounced over the past decade. There are a number of reasons for this – the terrorist attacks of 9/11 and 7/7, plus the growing consensus that we are past 'peak oil' and are now living unsustainable life styles are key factors that jump immediately to mind. Thus, I hope Chapters 4 and 5 deliver timely studies of the nostalgia evident in contemporary women's writing. All the chapters in the book focus on how retelling previous stories has been a productive process for contemporary women writers, a strategy both of survival, as Rich suggests, and of creation.

Acknowledgements

This monograph – my first – is the culmination of many years of research and study. During these processes of development and investigation, many scholars have influenced and improved my work. Thank you. I have been extremely lucky in having had my studies supervised by three inspiring feminist scholars: Patricia Waugh, Linda Hutcheon, and Mary Eagleton. I am deeply indebted to all of them. I would also like to thank Mark Levene, Heather Murray, Jill Matus, Russell Brown, and Phyllis Perrakis for their helpful contributions to my development as a scholar. More recently, working closely with Susan Watkins and members of the Contemporary Women's Writing Network has been a wonderful experience for which I am extremely grateful. I would not have got through the last challenging year of this project without the support of all those in BPA120! Thanks to you all, and in particular, to Jo Watkiss, Helen Davies, and James McGrath. I am also very grateful to Emily Marshall and Lucie Armitt for sharing their excellent teaching materials with me this year and, thereby, making it possible for me to complete this book despite a heavy teaching load. Many thanks also to Colleen Coalter and Anna Fleming at Continuum Press for their patience and swift, helpful replies to my queries.

I would like to thank the University of Toronto for the Open Fellowships that supported me through my Ph.D. and Leeds Metropolitan University for the three-year Postdoctoral Research Fellowship that enabled me to complete this project. Thanks are also due to the British Academy, the University of Toronto, Leeds Metropolitan University and the MLA for funding to attend conferences that have assisted me in developing the ideas I present here.

In two chapters I draw on material from previous publications: in Chapter 3, from '"In Paradise there are no stories": Iris Chase Griffen's Textual Revenge in Margaret Atwood's *The Blind Assassin*' in *Margaret Atwood Studies* 2.2 (December 2008): 14–25, and in Chapter 5 from '*Lost in Austen*: Adaptation and the Feminist Politics of Nostalgia' which will appear in a forthcoming issue of *Adaptation*. I am grateful to the editors for permission to use that material here and to the anonymous readers of those submissions for their feedback and suggestions.

Many, many thanks are due to my family for their support of my studies. I am particularly grateful to Paul Gregory for his generous support and endless patience during the final stages of this project. Thanks to Ben Valentin for last minute proof reading and to Emma Parkin for being a constant reminder of just how wonderful sisterhood is. And, finally, of course, to Cali-the-dog, whose persistent demands to be taken for walks kept me sane during book writing and who kept my feet warm during hours of reading!

Introduction

Contemporary Women's Re-writing

This book explores how contemporary women writers have used strategies of parody and retelling to engage with their literary inheritances. I offer the suggestive, rather than prescriptive, narrative of a move from irony to nostalgia as a way of making sense of the shifts in women authors' retellings from 1962 to the present day. Toni Morrison made her literary debut in 1970 with *The Bluest Eye*, Doris Lessing appeared on the literary scene with *The Grass is Singing* in 1950 after her emigration from Rhodesia to London, and Margaret Atwood's first novel was *Surfacing* in 1972. Thus, these three authors have had long literary careers and have themselves reflected this shift from irony to nostalgia in their work. For example, Morrison has claimed in recent interviews that she was motivated to return to pre-America for the setting of her latest novel, *A Mercy* (2008), because of nostalgia for a time before slavery was 'raced.' Doris Lessing, after chastising herself via her protagonist-author Anna in *The Golden Notebook* for her 'lying nostalgia, has published what she claims will be her last novel, *Alfred and Emily* (2008), and it is an account of exactly that – 'lying nostalgia.' She retells the story of her parents' lives but it is an idealized version in which the First World War does not happen.[1] Margaret Atwood's protagonist in *Oryx and Crake* (2003), Jimmy/Snowman, suffers greatly from nostalgia from his lonely position in a post-apocalyptic future. However, this suggestive narrative of a move from irony to nostalgia is not the whole story nor the only story to tell about the developments in these writers' use of the past and of previous texts. In 2005, for example, Atwood rewrote *The Odyssey* from Penelope's point of view, calling it *The Penelopiad*. It is an example of the kind of feminist revision that was popular in the 1960s and 1970s. Toni Morrison's most famous novel, *Beloved* (1987), offers a model of its relationship to past literary texts – slave narratives – that is neither ironic nor nostalgic, but rather imaginatively corrective, what Morrison has termed 're-memory.' These authors have continued to use strategies of parody and irony even as they have adopted and developed other attitudes to the past.

Zadie Smith made her debut with *White Teeth* in 2000 and most of the Austen retellings I examine in the final chapter were published or produced in the twenty-first century. What differentiates these Austen retellings and Smith's

On Beauty from the earlier work of Morrison, Lessing, and Atwood is that these younger authors demonstrate far less anxiety about the woman writer's entry into text. For Morrison, Lessing, and Atwood, writing at all was a challenge and the struggle to write left its mark on their work and informed their relationship to previous literary texts.

Parodists on the Threshold: Toni Morrison, Doris Lessing, and Margaret Atwood

One of the challenges these three writers faced that is no longer relevant to Smith in quite the same way was how to enter their national literary canons. I want to suggest that a more helpful notion than the 'literary canon' for understanding these contemporary women writers' engagement with literary history is the image of the 'house of fiction.' I explore how Toni Morrison, Margaret Atwood, and Doris Lessing all use ironic retellings to create room for their stories in the 'house of fiction.' Zadie Smith demonstrates a much more entitled sense of inheritance in retelling *Howards End* in *On Beauty*. She assumes the 'house of fiction' is her inheritance and she moves confidently in. Finally, the many retellings of Jane Austen's *Pride and Prejudice* that I explore in the final chapter demonstrate nostalgia for Pemberley – the stately home of the desirable Lord Darcy – and a preference for domestic fiction. Many of these retellings seem to enact a kind of 'ventriloquism' of Austen's cultural power.

The house is certainly a contradictory image for women. As Carolyn Steedman argues in *The Tidy House: Little Girls Writing*:

> The house (and as a simple version of it, the nest) has been, for the male theorists and critics who have outlined its inner spaces and detailed its connection with their first dwelling place of the womb, a place of retreat and safety.... But as feminist critics have turned to examine this felicitous inner space, they have discovered in the words of the women who have inhabited the dream houses, in particular those of the nineteenth-century women novelists, only empty rooms, a negative space, madness at the head of the stair. (148)

The domestic space of the house is one in which women historically experienced significantly more power, influence, and freedom than they did in the public and political spheres of life. Glenna Matthews, for example, argues that after the American Revolution, 'the home became crucial to the success of the [American] nation and women – whose education began to be taken much more seriously than ever before – gained the role of "Republican Mother"' (7):

> The home was so much at the center of the culture that historians speak of a 'cult' of domesticity in the early to mid-nineteenth century. Women in their

homes were the locus of moral authority in the society. Further, in the 1850s women could read an outpouring of novels in which housewives figured in highly positive terms.... In short, domesticity was both more elaborate and more valued, and this, in turn meant that the housewife had access to new sources of self-esteem. (6)

However, the house also made extreme demands on women's time and energy. Matthews also points to the negative implications of the housewife's role, providing historical documentation of what she terms 'the sheer onerousness of the housewife's job' (30). In her critique of nostalgia in 'Feminist Fiction and the Uses of Memory,' Gayle Greene suggests that:

Nostalgia is a powerful impulse that is by no means gender specific. Everyone has longings to return home, which is what the word means: *nostos*, the return home.... But nostalgia has different meanings for men and women. Though from one perspective, women might seem to have more incentives than men to be nostalgic – deprived of outlets in the present, they live more in the past, which is why they are keepers of diaries, journals, family records, and photograph albums – from another perspective, women have little to be nostalgic about, for the good old days when then grass was greener and young people knew their place was also the time when women knew their place, and it is not a place to which most women want to return. (295–6)

Discussing contemporary arrangements for managing housework, Pat Mainardi suggests that the tradition of women as housewives has left women with the belief that 'Housework is ultimately my responsibility.' Explicating the hidden meaning of her husband's arguments for not doing half of the housework, Mainardi paraphrases his implied logic: 'if anyone visits and the place *is* a sty, they're not going to leave and say, "He sure is a lousy housekeeper.' You'll take the rap in any case' (163). The 'Guilt over a messy house' Mainardi identifies echoes Woolf's 'Angel in the House.' Woolf described this idealized housewife as so threatening to the woman writer that '[k]illing the Angel in the House was part of the occupation of a woman writer.' In her talk 'Professions for Women,' Woolf justifies this murder as having been entirely out of self-defence: 'Had I not killed her she would have killed me. She would have plucked the heart out of my writing' (276).

The house also frequently marked the limits of women's experience. For example, in Margaret Atwood's *The Blind Assassin*, Iris Chase's grandmother was free to design and decorate her home at will but was unable to travel. This limiting of women's experience to the home directly affected women's literature, as Virginia Woolf explains in 'Women and Fiction':

Even in the nineteenth century, a woman lived almost solely in her home and her emotions. And those nineteenth-century novels, remarkable as they were, were profoundly influenced by the fact that the women who wrote them were excluded by their sex from certain kinds of experience. That experience has a great influence upon fiction is indisputable. The best part of Conrad's novels, for instance, would be destroyed if it had been impossible for him to be a sailor....

Yet *Pride and Prejudice, Wuthering Heights, Villette,* and *Middlemarch* were written by women from whom was forcibly withheld all experience save that which could be met within a middle-class drawing-room. No first-hand experience of war or seafaring or politics or business was possible for them. (143–4; my ellipses)

Indeed, following their extensive research into nineteenth-century writing by women, Sandra Gilbert and Susan Gubar conclude that the confinement of these women to their houses is one of the most influential factors on their lives and writing:

Both in life and art, we saw, the artists we studied were literally and figuratively confined. Enclosed in the architecture of an overwhelmingly male-dominated society, these literary women were also, inevitably, trapped in the specifically literary constructs of what Gertrude Stein was to call 'patriarchal poetry.' For not only did a nineteenth-century woman writer have to inhabit ancestral mansions (or cottages) owned and built by men, she was also constricted and restricted by the Palaces of Art and Houses of Fiction male writers authored. We decided, therefore, that the striking coherence we noticed in literature by women could be explained by a common, female impulse to struggle free from social and literary confinement through strategic redefinitions of self, art, and society. (xi–xii)

This 'female impulse' is evident in the fiction of Toni Morrison, Doris Lessing, and Margaret Atwood and parody is one of the strategies they employ in their attempts to be 'free from social and literary confinement.' Parody expresses both the 'impulse' to freedom and the difficult 'struggle' involved in achieving that freedom.

Given the relationship between women and domestic houses, Henry James's image of the 'house of fiction' is particularly appropriate but also limiting and problematic for women writers.[2] In 'Women and Fiction,' Woolf views women's tendency to write fiction rather than poetry entirely as an effect of the demands and limitations of women's domestic situations:

Fiction was, as fiction still is, the easiest thing for a woman to write. Nor is it difficult to find the reason. A novel is the least concentrated form of art. A novel can be taken up or put down more easily than a play or a poem. George Eliot left her work to nurse her father. Charlotte Brontë put down her pen to pick the eyes out of potatoes. And living as she did in the common sitting-room, surrounded by people, a woman was trained to use her mind in observation and upon the analysis of character. She was trained to be a novelist and not to be a poet. (143)

It would be wrong to assume that feminism had removed these limitations from women writers by the time Toni Morrison was writing *The Bluest Eye* in 1970, Margaret Atwood was publishing *Lady Oracle* in 1976, and Doris Lessing was regarding with disbelief and disapproval the ways in which *The Golden Notebook* was being taken up by the Women's Movement after it appeared in 1962. As Atwood stated in 1981: 'The goals of the feminist movement have not been achieved, and those who claim we're living in a post-feminist era are either sadly mistaken or tired of thinking about the whole subject' (*Second Words* 370). Alice Munro in her 1996 introduction to her *Selected Stories* directly relates her choice of the short story genre to her life as a housewife:

> I did not 'choose' to write short stories. I hoped to write novels. When you are responsible for running a house and taking care of small children...it's hard to arrange for large chunks of time. A child's illness, relatives coming to stay, a pile-up of unavoidable household jobs, can swallow a work-in-progress as surely as a power failure used to destroy a piece of work in the computer. You're better to stick with something you can keep in mind and hope to do in a few weeks, or a couple of months at most. I know that there are lots of women who have written novels in the midst of domestic challenges, just as there are men (and women) who have written them after coming home at night from exhausting jobs. That's why I thought I could do it too, but I couldn't. I took to writing in frantic spurts, juggling my life around until I could get a story done, then catching up on other responsibilities. (x; my ellipses)

Women's 'responsibilities' in the domestic house have certainly influenced the ways in which they have entered the house of fiction and the type of fiction they have written. For example, when asked by Robert Stepto in an interview why her novels have such an 'extraordinary sense of place,' Toni Morrison suggests that most women have a particularly strong sense of place:

> Also, I think some of it is just a woman's strong sense of being in a room, a place, or in a house. Sometimes my relationship to things in a house would be a little different from, say my brother's or my father's or my sons'. I clean them and I move them and I do very intimate things 'in place': I am sort of rooted in it, so that writing about being in a room looking out, or being in a world looking out, or living in a small definite place, is probably very common among most women anyway. (10–11)

Lorna Sage opens her book entitled *Women in the House of Fiction* with the admission that as a teenager what fascinated her about Simone de Beauvoir was that she lived in a hotel. This is certainly understandable given the limitations the house has imposed upon women. 'This single fact,' Sage explains, 'seemed to imply all the rest: domesticity spurned, never cooking for Sartre, living on words and ideas' (viii). For Beauvoir, Sage argues, the house of fiction was 'ramshackle and claustrophobic' mainly because its representations of women and women's writing were so limited (viii). Despite the fact that the image of the 'house of fiction' is James's, Sage implies that it captures the domestic situation in which women have traditionally written – in and about their drawing rooms. Sage goes on to admit that for many women writers demolishing the house and rejecting the traditional feminine novel have not been their response. Indeed, in retrospect, Sage realizes that Beauvoir was far more contradictory and compromised than her hotel residence implied. Sage concludes her 'Preface' to *Women in the House of Fiction* by admitting that '[t]here's no one way of placing the woman novelist – or even of displacing her. The language of domesticity hasn't died, at all. It flourishes alongside street-wise, picaresque writing that embraces mobility and change' (x–xi). Like Woolf, Sage realizes that despite the limitations domesticity has placed on women's writing, the answer is not to pull down the house, but to reimagine women's roles within it. Shakespeare's imaginary sister whose biography Woolf creates in *A Room of One's Own* teaches us the dangers of homelessness: 'Could she even seek her dinner in a tavern or roam the streets at midnight?' (49), asks Woolf. Morrison describes the 'outdoors' of homelessness as 'the real terror of life' in *The Bluest Eye* (17). Getting outside the house can be equally endangering to the woman writer and her work. Instead, women need their own space within the home to themselves – 'a room of one's own,' in Woolf's famous words.

In her series of lectures entitled *Women's Lives: The View from the Threshold*, Carolyn Heilbrun argues that women are intimately connected with liminality and transience:

> In the last decades, writing women have almost entirely determined either to re-examine old habits and loyalties, or to move into a different world, into an as yet unscripted life. But we still have the old forms of family, marriage, parenting, children, solitude, ageing, as well as the old forms of our professions, to cope with. Into these forms we have tried to fit new ideas, and literature is the evidence of this tenuous liminality – that condition where we are always on the threshold, always in between, never accepting the old or quite succeeding in establishing the new. (66)

Imelda Whelehan recognizes that the appeal of the feminist bestsellers by the 'Mad Housewives' (to quote her chapter title) of the Second Wave was that they simultaneously recounted 'life stories which invited women readers to recognize their own lives therein' alongside registering women's desire to cross the threshold by often ending with the protagonist 'on the threshold of a life-changing decision' (65). Heilbrun's argument that 'literature' is 'the evidence of this tenuous liminality' is clear in the novels I explore.

These novels are littered with images of women in a variety of transitional spaces that represent differing degrees of vulnerability and autonomy – Pecola Breedlove in the store front in *The Bluest Eye*, Joan Foster in her rented accommodation on the Other Side in *Lady Oracle*, Iris Chase racing her own death to the finishing line of her life narrative in her house in Port Ticonderoga in *The Blind Assassin* and Anna Wulf writing away in her notebooks in her slightly too big flat waiting for her ex-boyfriend to move in with her in *The Golden Notebook*. Even in the later non-parodic retellings I explore, we see Kiki Belsey living away from her family and inherited house in a secret apartment in town in *On Beauty* and Bridget Jones drinking alone and writing her diary in her London flat in *Bridget Jones's Diary*.

This book argues that in the works by Morrison, Lessing, and Atwood that I explore parody is the textual mark of women's liminality. The parodist's position is also on the threshold, simultaneously within and without, both repeating and critiquing the target text or discourse. Thus parody is a particularly effective strategy for expressing women's position on the threshold. I argue that what has been called women's 'marginal position' is reflected in the parodist's marginal relationship to the target text. A parody almost literally writes in the margins of its target text – repeating but also altering it. Although the margin is a helpful image, I prefer the image of the threshold for several important reasons. First, to say that the parodist writes in the margins of his/her target text echoes the early assessments of parody as being a parasitic, minor genre that lacked creative originality. I will not offer a whole theory of parody here because, since G. D. Kiremidjian's 1969 comment that 'a tradition of systematic aesthetic theory' of parody 'unhappily, does not exist,' it has indeed come into being.[3] Even in 1969, Kiremidjian was able to state that '[t]he nineteenth and twentieth centuries have done much to redeem parody, and its reputation is now a little brighter' (232) and that '[i]t is not possible to see it as a derivative exercise, or at best as one item in the artistic bag of tricks; it possesses its own particular autonomy and integrity, and has shown itself very capable of expressing fundamental modes of experience' (231). Secondly, the margin does not capture a sense of transition in the same way that the image of the threshold does. Transition is not only an important mark of contemporary women's lives but also of parody, which draws attention to the process of writing by taking a finished text and changing it into a new and different text. Thirdly, the image of the margin does not account for the escapist or fantasy elements of women's writing, whereas the image of the threshold understands women's writing as imaginary journeys through the threshold into new possibilities. Lastly, of course, the image of the threshold is particularly pertinent to the fact that women are writing novels that are no longer confined to their drawing rooms and domestic situations, as women's novels of the nineteenth century tended to be.

It is important to remember that the 'house of fiction' not only defined fiction by women in a limiting way, but it also defined literary qualities in a particularly Eurocentric way. While English women writers of the nineteenth century were writing in and about their middle-class drawing rooms, pioneering women in Canada were building log cabins in the bush. African American women were denied their own homes, serving in the homes of their white mistresses or the fields of their white masters. Thus, Atwood and Morrison write in very different national and racial literary traditions. Doris Lessing describes from personal experience the absurdity of her mother's attempt to create a traditional drawing room in their mud hut on the African veld by hanging Liberty curtains in the windows.[4] All three of these writers, therefore, are excluded by a combination of nationality, race, or personal experience from the traditional English house of fiction. Morrison's critical study, *Playing in the Dark*, explores the effect on the 'literary imagination' of the fact that 'readers of virtually all of American fiction have been positioned as white' (xii). She states that: 'My work requires me to think about how free I can be as an African-American women writer in my genderized, sexualized, wholly racialized world' (4). Atwood describes the limiting impression she gained of who can be a writer from her Canadian education: 'The general impression was that to be a poet you had to be English and dead. You could also be American and dead but this was less frequent' (*Second Words* 86). Morrison, Atwood, and Lessing all use parody to reveal their critical awareness of how the literary canon has served to enshrine certain ideologies and preserve the power of the dominant. Their critiques are generated not only by their positions on the threshold as women, but also by their national and racial identities. As Atwood puts it so succinctly in her essay 'On Being a Woman Writer':

> Time after time, I've had interviewers talk to me about my writing for a while, then ask me, 'As a woman, what do you think about – for instance – the Women's Movement,' as if I could think two sets of thoughts about the same thing, one set as a writer or person, the other as a woman. But no one comes apart this easily; categories like Woman, White, Canadian, Writer are only ways of looking at a thing, and the thing itself is whole, entire and indivisible. *Paradox*: Woman and Writer are separate categories; but in any individual woman writer, they are inseparable. (*Second Words* 195)

Thus, I have attempted to read each of these writer's use of parody with an awareness of the other 'categories like Woman, White, Canadian, Writer' that have contributed to her position in the house of fiction.

Defining Parody

Although this study does not offer a new theory of parody, it is pertinent to briefly outline a working definition of parody. My definition of parody is drawn from Linda Hutcheon's *A Theory of Parody*:

> Parody, then, in its ironic 'trans-contextualization' and inversion, is repetition with difference. A critical distance is implied between the background text being parodied and the new incorporating work, a distance usually signaled by irony. But this irony can be playful as well as belittling; it can be critically constructive as well as destructive. The pleasure of parody's irony comes not from humour in particular but from the degree of engagement of the reader in the intertextual 'bouncing' (to use E. M. Forster's famous term) between complicity and distance. (32)

Hutcheon's considerations of the politics of parody and the relationship between parody and postmodernism are especially relevant to my study of women's use of parody as a political strategy.[5] Hutcheon argues in *A Poetics of Postmodernism* that

> it is precisely parody – that seemingly introverted formalism – that paradoxically brings about a direct confrontation with the problem of the relation of the aesthetic to a world of significance external to itself, to a discursive world of socially defined meaning systems (past and present) – in other words, to the political and the historical. (22)

Similarly, I think that it is through their parodies of socially accepted images of women and the traditionally feminine genres of women's fiction that Morrison, Lessing, and Atwood hint at the realities of women's lives. As Hutcheon suggests, parody's

> relationship to the 'worldly' is still on the level of discourse, but to claim that is to claim quite a lot. After all, we can only 'know' (as opposed to 'experience') the world through our narratives (past and present) of it, or so postmodernism argues. (128)

Teresa Ebert might well label this feminist consideration of parody an example of the 'ludic feminism' which she defines as 'a feminism that is founded upon poststructuralist assumptions about linguistic play, difference, and the priority of discourse and thus substitutes a politics of representation for radical social transformation' (3). She opposes this type of feminism to 'historical materialist critique' which she describes as a mode of knowing that inquires into what is not said, into the silences and the suppressed or missing, in order to uncover the concealed operations of power and the socio-economic relations connecting the myriad details and representations of our lives. (7)

What particularly fascinates me in these three women writers' use of parody is exactly the way in which it functions to 'uncover the concealed operations of power' and hints at 'the silences and the suppressed or missing.' By parodying the convention of the framing, authenticating document written by a white person and prefaced to the slave narrative, for example, Morrison manages in *The Bluest Eye* not only to tell Pecola's story but also to reveal the 'operations of power' that have silenced her story until then. Indeed, a focus on these women writers' use of postmodern parody questions the construction of postmodernism as self-referential, apolitical, and disengaged. The texts by Morrison, Lessing, and Atwood that I explore could all be labelled 'postmodern' but every one of them is politically and critically engaged with women's material lives.

Morrison's use of parody to interrogate the traditional place of African American writers in the house of fiction is the focus of my first chapter. Her parody of the white reading primer at the beginning of *The Bluest Eye* draws attention to the difficulties African American writers face in attempting to enter the house of fiction. This parody demonstrates that formal, written English is not Morrison's language. She strives, instead, for 'writing that [is] indisputably black' (afterword, *The Bluest Eye* 211). By echoing the authenticating documents written by white supporters and prefaced to slave narratives, she alerts us to the fact that African Americans have traditionally only gained entry into the house of fiction by complying with the dominant white literary conventions and social ideologies. My first chapter also examines the extent to which Henry Louis Gates Jr.'s theory of 'Signifying' functions as a politicized theory of parody. Morrison's use of formal parody as a way into a thematic exploration of African Americans' 'internalization of assumptions of immutable inferiority originating in an outside gaze' ('Afterword' *The Bluest Eye* 210) offers a helpful corrective to Gates's entirely positive view of 'Signification as parody.'

One fascinating and problematic aspect of parody that I explore in more detail in Chapter 2 on Doris Lessing is the role of the reader in designating a text as parody. Parody cannot fully operate until it is recognized as such by its reader. Joseph Dane makes the point that

> [p]arody is both a critical concept and something in literature to which that concept refers. What we call 'parody' thus can have a variety of literary and critical functions, and those that are of the most interest to me are critical functions: How is literature transformed when it is associated with the label

'parody'? As used here, the word 'parody' is critical shorthand for referring to certain texts and to certain readings of texts. (3)

I am certainly aware that the 'language of parody, however defined, acts to manipulate the literature it is intended to describe' (4), and that to label aspects of these authors' novels 'parodic' is certainly to enact a strategically feminist reading of them, as well as to identify something within the texts themselves. Lessing's concern with the 'misreadings' of *The Golden Notebook* was not limited only to the readers' failure to recognize her use of parody, but her parody of the conventional feminine novel in 'Free Women' did make her particularly vulnerable to such misreadings. I explore the implications of her anger at misreadings of *The Golden Notebook*. I argue that parody has the ability to create (or at least make visible) communities, but also needs specific discursive communities to pre-exist it in order to be recognized.

My third chapter argues that parody functions as a method for writing counter-discursive autobiography in Atwood's explorations of theories of female autobiography in *Lady Oracle* and *The Blind Assassin*. Atwood uses parody to critique the limiting representation of women in popular genres and official history, and to offer glimpses of women's lives that were erased by these discourses. Nancy Walker argues of irony (which functions and is structured like parody and is, indeed, frequently present in parody) that: 'Irony is a mask that the reader is invited to see *as* a mask in order to view simultaneously the reality underneath it' (*Feminist Alternatives* 27). Atwood similarly uses parody in order to offer the reader glimpses of women's autobiographical realities hidden beneath the mask of stereotypical femininity.

Each of the first three chapters in this book thus illuminates a different aspect or use of parody. For all these three women writers, however, parody offers a strategy for avoiding being silenced by their positions on the threshold, 'betwixt and between, neither altogether here nor there, not one kind of person or another, not this, not that' (Heilbrun 8). Parody enables these women writers to express that they are 'not this, not that,' instead of allowing the lack of certainty implicit in this position to silence them. Heilbrun's final paragraph in *Women's Lives* relates women's lived experience on the threshold directly to women's writing:

> There can be no doubt that the stationary, conventional place of women, that place ordained by the patriarchy, by male-founded religions, and protected by women who fear anxiety, uncertainty, and liminality, that place occupied by our mothers, will always be attractive to those who would rather be safe than sorry. Yet a life without danger, with no question about what the future may hold, is not a life, it is a carefully structured drama, a play in which our parts are written for us. The threshold, on the contrary, is the place where as women and as creators of literature, we write our own lines and, eventually, our own plays. (102)

Morrison, Lessing, and Atwood use parody in *The Bluest Eye*, *The Golden Notebook*, *Lady Oracle*, and *The Blind Assassin* to reveal the entry of their female protagonists into storytelling or writing, despite the structures that have attempted to silence them. In all these novels, not only do the authors write from the threshold, they also dramatize the threshold by showing their female protagonists leaving the domestic house and arriving at the threshold of the house of fiction. Claudia MacTeer in *The Bluest Eye* ignores her mother's instructions to visit 'the homes of people she knew or the neighborhoods familiar to us' and 'knocked on all doors, and floated in and out of every house that opened to us' (188), selling flower seeds and making the money that she gives up as a sacrifice for Pecola Breedlove. It is by crossing these other thresholds that Claudia learns the story she later narrates to us of Pecola's rape and pregnancy. Anna Wulf in *The Golden Notebook* gets her own apartment in which to write her notebooks and novel. Iris Chase in *The Blind Assassin* leaves her husband's home to publish a novel and later write her life story. These novels suggest that the threshold of the domestic house can often mark the same place as the threshold of the house of fiction.

Through the Threshold: Zadie Smith and Jane Austen Retellings

The fourth and fifth chapters of this book move on from my exploration of parodic relationships between texts to look at how these daughters' daughters (to extend Heilbrun's use of the generational metaphor) use rewriting. In my chapter on Smith other models of the relationship between her novel and E. M. Forster's *Howards End* emerge. The central one I explore is that of inheritance. Smith seems to inherit *Howards End*, just as Margaret Schlegel inherits the house of that name within Forster's novel. I also look briefly at other models such as indebtedness, ventriloquism, and cannibalism. The focus of this chapter is how Smith's desire to continue Forster's project (rather than ironically critiquing it as the parodist would) enacts 'a practice of the untimely,' to borrow Jane Elliott's phrase. I also explore Smith's other intertextual borrowings from Sam Selvon, Elaine Scarry, and Toni Morrison which complicate the relationship between *On Beauty* and *Howards End* in interesting ways. For Smith, the house does not represent the same threat as it did for earlier women writers. However, it is closely connected to history and the debts and consequences of history. For Kiki, for example, her inherited house is problematic but also enabling.

The final chapter moves into another type of retelling – adaptation – and tries to understand the recent 'Jane Austen Phenomenon' via a close study of the ITV television series *Lost in Austen*. This chapter concludes by trying to tease out the complex feminist politics of the popular nostalgia for Austen-land.

Ironically, sequels to *Pride and Prejudice* return us to the house and the role of housewife. How are we to read the happy housewives of Emma Tennant's *Pemberley*, Linda Berdoll's *Mr Darcy Takes a Wife*, Marsha Altman's *The Darcys and the Bingleys*, and Jane Dawkins's *Letters from Pemberley*?

These final two chapters agree with David James's suggestion in his 2007 essay 'The New Purism' that 'the commonplace tenets of postmodern self-referentiality fall short of explaining how writers choose to advance by adhering to what seems past, contemplating their originality through the lens of inheritance' (687). In the last decade, particularly, writers seem to have moved away from postmodern strategies like parody and metafiction. Smith's 'brazen ahistoricism,' as she calls it in 'On the Beginning,' in revisiting and rewriting Forster cannot be adequately understood as parody.

'Strong Readers'

One thing that all the authors in this book do have in common is that they were readers first. Morrison has repeatedly said that she wrote *The Bluest Eye* because it was a novel she wanted to read and that no one had written yet. Lessing makes a direct connection between growing up in a house full of books and her own writing in her recent Nobel Speech. Margaret Atwood was halfway through an MA in English Literature when she abandoned her studies to pursue her successful writing career. Zadie Smith read English at Cambridge University and discusses her childhood reading a great deal in her non-fiction. Almost all the writers of Austen retellings describe their own writing as an act of homage to Austen, a way of repaying the pleasure they have gained from reading her. Therefore, all of these writers relate interestingly to poststructuralist theories regarding the blurring boundary between writing and reading, between fiction and criticism. Harold Bloom's *Anxiety of Influence* is a good example. He suggests that poetic creation is an act of 'strong reading' of a predecessor. Seán Burke ultimately dismisses the idea that criticism has become literature but not before he convincingly outlines the argument that that is the case:

> This development from strong reader to rewriter to writer has led many post-structuralists to suggest that criticism itself has become a primary discourse. And this notion commands a certain respect, for the weakening boundary between creative and critical is not only a development within criticism, but also a powerful and necessary extension of modernism in general. As the literary text becomes more self-reflexive, as its artifices and narratological structures come to dominate the foreground, as the work of fiction becomes autocritical, autodeconstructive even, it is entirely concinnous that the critical text should become increasingly creative, interpretable, and like the

work of Wilde and Mallarmé, a realm with charms, mazes, and mysteries of its own. (159–60)

Many of these retellings that I examine are metafictional and 'autocritical, autodeconstructive even.' They are all born out of a blurring of the line between critical and creative, between reader and writer.

Chapter 1

The Politics of Parody: Toni Morrison's *The Bluest Eye*

For white middle-class female authors like Virginia Woolf, the house was a threatening image because it represented the limits of women's experience. They were trapped within it. For the working-class black women in Toni Morrison's *The Bluest Eye* (1970) the house is a negative image because it is always accompanied by the threat of 'being outdoors':

> Being a minority in both caste and class, we moved about anyway on the hem of life, struggling to consolidate our weaknesses and hang on, or to creep singly up into the major folds of the garment. Our peripheral existence, however, was something we had learned to deal with – probably because it was abstract. But the concreteness of being outdoors was another matter – like the difference between the concept of death and being, in fact, dead. Dead doesn't change, and outdoors is here to stay.
>
> Knowing there was such a thing as outdoors bred in us a hunger for property, for ownership. The firm possession of a yard, a porch, a grape arbor. Propertied black people spent all their energies, all their love, on their nests. Like frenzied, desperate birds, they overdecorated everything; fussed and fidgeted over their hard-won homes; canned, jellied, and preserved all summer to fill the cupboards and shelves; they painted, picked, and poked at every corner of their houses. And these houses loomed like hothouse sunflowers among the rows of weeds that were the rented houses. (17–18)

When Carolyn Heilbrun describes the threshold as a radical and attractive place for feminists, she is, of course, assuming that these women have houses.[6] As Iris Chase ironically says of the class assumptions behind her Grandfather Benjamin's (the founder of Chase Industries in Atwood's *The Blind Assassin*) declaration 'that conditions for the females in his employ were as safe as those in their own parlours': 'He assumed they had parlours. He assumed these parlours were safe. He liked to think well of everybody' (54). For women who do not own a home, the threshold may well represent a vulnerable space that is too close to the 'concreteness of outdoors,' as the above quotation from *The Bluest Eye* suggests.

This has been a contentious issue in feminism and was famously brought to the academic feminist community's attention by Audre Lorde in her comments at the Second Sex Conference in 1979, which were republished as the essay 'The Master's Tools Will Never Dismantle the Master's House':

> Poor and third world women know there is a difference between the daily manifestations and dehumanizations of marital slavery and prostitution, because it is our daughters who line 42nd Street.... If white american [sic] feminist theory need not deal with the differences between us, and the resulting difference in aspects of our oppression, then what do you do with the fact that the women who clean your houses and tend your children while you attend conferences on feminist theory are, for the most part, poor and third world women? What is the theory behind racist feminism? (99–100)

Morrison's *The Bluest Eye* addresses these difficult issues by exploring the ways in which white ideals of beauty and domesticity are most particularly destructive and alienating for black women and by implicitly suggesting that black women relate differently to their houses than white women. Lorde's comments also draw attention to black women's relationship to 'theory' *per se*. Her criticism suggests that black women's lived experiences – as the mothers of 'daughters who line 42nd street' and as the 'women who clean your houses' – are more meaningful to the situation of black women than 'feminist theory.' This criticism echoes Joyce Ann Joyce's critique of Henry Louis Gates Jr. in her article published in 2008 entitled 'A Tinker's Damn: Henry Louis Gates Jr. and "The Signifying Monkey" Twenty Years Later' in which she returns to her 'discussion' with Gates and Baker in the pages of *New Literary History* in 1987 and his publication of *The Signifying Monkey* in 1988. She concludes that piece by concurring with Lorde that African Americans' material and physical safety is the 'essential point' that poststructuralist theory fails to address:

> Relying on the power of words, the monkey in the tale of *The Signifying Monkey* uses the power of words to manipulate the lion and the elephant so as to secure his own survival. The monkey's survival depends on a common understanding of language that he shares with the lion and the elephant. It is this commonality that the monkey exploits and destabilizes. Moreover, the monkey has to stay in the tree until the lion leaves – that is, until the monkey's environment is safe. This need for safety, in this case the political and social safety of black lives, is the 'essential point' that Gates's poststructuralist ideology will not allow him to explore. (379)

In her contribution to the roundtable in memory of Nellie Y. McKay in the *PMLA* in October 2006, Jane Elliott argues that to a great extent the 'debates about constructionism' have not been resolved, but rather left behind:

It seems as if the aging of the social-construction analysis has made debating its content unnecessary, as if the sheer passage of time has somehow done for us what we could not do for ourselves: moved us beyond a radically skeptical position that for years successfully cast any alternatives to its insights as naïve and politically retrograde. (1698)

Although she sees that putting down these debates over constructionism and essentialism has enabled new work to occur, she does point to one 'problematic aspect' of this positioning of these debates in the past:

As the repeated declarations of feminism's death in the mainstream media and the academy make clear, the production of the new as a signal intellectual value can be used to dismiss uncomfortable insights, which don't have to be disproved as long as they can be made to seem passé. Feminism can be implicated in this same logic itself. For example, the growing tendency to place the debates of the 1980s and 1990s in the past might be seen to offer feminism an all-too-convenient opportunity to shelve the critiques by radical women of color that are also associated with these decades. (1700)

In this chapter I return to these debates of the 1980s and 1990s, in order to examine the politics of postmodern parody and of Gates's attempt to apply poststructuralist theory to African American literature in relation to Morrison's first novel.

At the beginning of *The Bluest Eye* Morrison installs a reading primer's description of the ideal nuclear family in an ideal house: 'Here is the house. It is green and white. It has a red door. It is very pretty. Here is the family. Mother, Father, Dick and Jane live in the green-and-white house' (3). Parody offers a most helpful way to view Morrison's repetition of the reading primer. Morrison 'repeats it with critical distance' (Hutcheon's definition of parody throughout her work) in order simultaneously to critique it and acknowledge its cultural power. Her descriptions of multiple houses in *The Bluest Eye* enable her to introduce the issue of African Americans' complicity with white middle-class ideals as an important theme. Her thematic concern with complicity highlights the repetitive and installing impulse of parody. As Linda Hutcheon has argued, 'parody is doubly coded in political terms: it both legitimizes and subverts that which it parodies. This kind of authorized transgression is what makes it a ready vehicle for the political contradictions of postmodernism at large' (Hutcheon, *The Politics of Postmodernism* 101).

Henry Louis Gates Jr.'s theory of 'Signifyin(g)' is an influential and overtly politicized model of parody. His *The Signifying Monkey* is a sustained attempt to think through African American authors' relationships to their literary pasts by reading their intertextual retellings as examples of the strategy of Signifyin(g). Signifyin(g) is a powerful image and Gates's theory is helpful and provocative. However, this theory fails to acknowledge the necessary repetitive element in parody which allows Gates to make claims for the radical and subversive effects of 'Signification as parody' which ignore its complicit aspects. Morrison's focus on the African American community's complicity with racism offers an important corrective to Gates's theory of Signifyin(g).

The Signifying Monkey and African American Literary History

African American criticism and literature forms a particularly appropriate and helpful context in which to explore the political use of parody. The issue of imitation raised by the use of parody as a political counter-discourse has been extensively debated in the field of African American studies. In her essay, 'Unspeakable Things Unspoken: The Afro-American Presence in American Literature,' Toni Morrison identifies four arguments that 'whitemales'[7] have presented in order to preserve the traditional literary canon and to ensure the absence of African American literature from that canon. One of those arguments concedes that 'Afro-American art exists,' but asserts that it is 'inferior' (208).[8] Many of the adjectives Morrison lists as having been applied to African American literature to support this negative view have also been applied to parody: 'imitative, excessive, sensational, mimetic (merely), and unintellectual' (208). It is significant that many of these adjectives have also been employed to describe literature by women in an attempt to exclude their work from the 'whitemale' canon.

Morrison suggests that African American critics have already developed ways to dispute these pejorative labels: 'strategies designed to counter this lazy labeling include the application of recent literary theories to Afro-American literature so that non-canonical texts can be incorporated into existing and forming critical discourse' (209). Significantly, one of these 'recent literary theories' is a reconsideration of parody. Parody is no longer viewed as simply imitative, derivative, and uncreative, with a limited ridiculing function. As Linda Hutcheon argues, contemporary art itself has taught us to reconsider parody (*Parody* 3). Hutcheon views parody in the twentieth century as 'one of the major modes of formal and thematic construction of texts' and one which 'has a hermeneutic function with both cultural and even ideological implications' (*Parody* 2). The 'cultural and even ideological implications' of parody share interesting similarities with those of early African American literature. Indeed, it is possible to suggest that the re-evaluation of parodic art forms and of African American art are mutually supportive projects. For example, Zora Neale Hurston famously rejected the negative Western devaluing of the black mimic, not by denying that African Americans do mimic but by asserting the 'original,' artistic possibilities of mimicry: 'The Negro the world over is famous as a mimic. But this in no way damages his standing as an original. Mimicry is an art in itself' ('Characteristics of Negro Expression' 301).

Later in 'Unspeakable Things Unspoken,' Morrison suggests three future projects for the Afro-American critic in order to counter the pejorative attitudes she identifies earlier in her essay. One of these counter-discursive projects is 'the development of a theory of literature that truly accommodates Afro-American literature: one that is based on its culture, its history, and the artistic strategies the works employ to negotiate the world it inhabits' (210).[9] This is exactly the project attempted by Henry Louis Gates Jr. in his influential theory of the Signifyin(g) Monkey. In the preface to *The Signifying Monkey*, Gates describes the history of the book: 'The central idea of this book assumed its initial form in a paper that I delivered at a Yale English Department Seminar on Parody' (ix). By basing his theory of African American literature on parody, Gates offers a politicized view of parody which has helpful points of similarity and contrast with the model of parody as a counter-discourse that I wish to explore in Lessing and Atwood's work and which I argue was the dominant model for contemporary women writers' treatment of their literary pasts during the 1960s through to the 1980s.[10]

Instead of directly disputing the claim that African American literature has tended to be imitative and repetitive, Gates offers a history of African American literature to demonstrate why early black writers may well have been motivated to write *like* white writers. Many early slave narrators were literally writing for their lives. Viewing itself as the human norm, Western culture read African American texts for signs of similarity to itself that would prove the humanity of black authors, or for differences in order to confirm that racial difference was irreducible and that the black race was not human. If similarities were found between black and white literary texts, however, this similarity was often recast as 'imitation' and also read as evidence that the black race was not capable of creative thought. It was assumed that writing could mark the transformation that so many of the slave narratives described, from being an illiterate object of exchange to a literate subject:

> The recording of an 'authentic' black voice, a voice of deliverance from the deafening discursive silence which an enlightened Europe cited as proof of the absence of the African's humanity, was the millennial instrument of transformation through which the African would become the European, the slave become the ex-slave, the brute animal become the human being. (63)

For the black slave, *writing the self* often recorded the *loss of that self*, as the illiterate African slave became the literate, Western subject. Given this early history of African American writing, in *The Signifying Monkey*, Gates argues that the issues of imitation and authenticity were inevitably complex and contradictory for the African American writer:

> Blacks, as we have seen, tried to write themselves out of slavery, a slavery even more profound than mere physical bondage. Accepting the challenge of the

great white Western tradition, black writers wrote as if their lives depended upon it – and, in a curious sense, their lives did, the 'life' of 'the race' in Western discourse. But if blacks accepted this challenge, we also accepted its premises, premises in which perhaps lay concealed a trap. (66)

Gates expresses one of these dangerous premises in the question 'how can the black subject posit a full and sufficient self in a language in which blackness is a sign of absence?' (65). The difficulties and contradictions of critiquing from within have led many writers and critics of African American literature to argue, in the famous words of Audre Lorde, that 'the master's tools will never dismantle the master's house.' Lorde argues that those who have been excluded from 'the master's house' need to redefine social structures rather than fight to gain access to the current structures:

> Those of us who stand outside the circle of this society's definition of acceptable women; those of us who have been forged in the crucibles of difference; those of us who are poor, who are lesbians, who are black, who are older, know that *survival is not an academic skill.* It is learning how to stand alone, unpopular and sometimes reviled, and how to make common cause with those other identified as outside the structures, in order to define and seek a world in which we can all flourish. (99)

Gates's own career as a critic follows the movement he maps in the African American literary tradition from imitation of white forms to the search for an authentic black voice. He describes how his own initial desire to enter and engage with the Western canon has been replaced by his search for a black vernacular:

> The Western critical tradition has a canon, just as does the Western literary tradition. Whereas I once thought it our most important gesture to *master* the canon of criticism, to *imitate* and *apply* it, I now believe that we must turn to the black tradition itself to arrive at theories of criticism indigenous to our literatures. (67)

This statement of intent points to a paradox that is at the heart of Gates's work. Gates states a need to return to 'the black tradition itself'; however his brief outline of African American literature implies there is no such thing. The written black literary tradition was always implicated in and reacting to the white Western tradition. As Gates himself argues, 'Any one who analyzes black literature must do so as a comparativist, by definition, because our canonical texts have complex double formal antecedents, the Western and the black' (*The Signifying Monkey* xxiv).

In *The Signifying Monkey*, Gates tries to negotiate this contradiction between his desire for an indigenous theory of literature and the imitative nature of

African American literary texts by suggesting that repetition and imitation are themselves authentically 'black':

> Free of the white person's gaze, black people created their own unique vernacular structures and relished in the double play that these forms bore to white forms. Repetition and revision are fundamental to black artistic forms, from painting and sculpture to music and language use. I decided to analyze the nature and function of Signifyin(g) precisely because it is repetition and revision, or repetition with a signal difference. Whatever is black about black American literature is to be found in this identifiable black Signifyin(g) difference. (*The Signifying Monkey* xxiv)

However, Gates largely fails to operate as a comparativist in his analysis of specific literary texts in *The Signifying Monkey*, ignoring the fact that black literary texts were rarely 'free of the white person's gaze' but, in fact, usually relied on a sympathetic white person's gaze in order to get into print. He suppresses the interesting contradictions inherent in the notion of an 'identifiable black Signifyin(g) difference,' by focusing his close readings on the ways African American writers signify on other African American texts, rather than on white texts. Therefore, the 'voice'[11] being parodied is another African American one, not a 'whitemale' one, which would introduce the attendant dangers of complicit repetition, linguistic re-colonization of the black voice and the implication of a white literary 'master.'[12] I wish to offer a critique of certain aspects of Gates's theory of Signifyin(g) and to show how his theory falls prey to the contradictions inherent in using parody as a counter-discourse.[13]

Signifyin(g)'s Complicit Repetition

Perhaps one of the reasons why Gates has drawn some very personal criticism for his methods from certain colleagues is that he imitates white critics and theories extensively in publications produced for an academic community that valorizes originality and punishes plagiarism.[14] Gates suggests that in writing about Signifyin(g) in academic discourse, he is translating from one language to another. What concerns me is whether he is translating from the black vernacular into Western academic discourse or vice versa.[15] I have already noted Gates's comment that his theory of the Signifying Monkey grew out of a paper on parody. Critics of Gates's work have suggested other sources for his theory of the Signifying Monkey.[16] To rewrite other critics' theories in an academy that so values originality, without appearing self-conscious about that contradiction or theorizing it adequately, has certainly left Gates open to attacks from his colleagues. As Hutcheon argues of parody generally,

> Parody also contests our humanist assumptions about artistic originality and uniqueness and our capitalist notions of ownership and property. With

parody – as with any form of reproduction – the notion of the original as rare, single, and valuable (in aesthetic or commercial terms) is called into question. (*Politics* 93)

As my later chapter on Zadie Smith's *On Beauty* explores in more detail, parody and retellings inevitably draw our attention to issues of cultural capital and questions of ownership, inheritance and indebtedness. Gates could do more to overtly and self-consciously critique the 'humanist assumptions' and 'capitalist notions of ownership' upheld by the academy in which he publishes his Signifyin(g) criticism.

However, I am more concerned that this contradiction points to a more fundamental contradiction in Gates's theory – one that is at the centre of Morrison's *The Bluest Eye*. In stating that 'Whatever is black about black American literature is to be found in this identifiable black Signifyin(g) difference' (xxiv), Gates is attempting to erase the problematic complicity inherent in his theory of the Signifyin(g) Monkey. 'Blackness' cannot lie only in the 'Signifyin(g) *difference*' between a Signifyin(g) text and its target, but it is also in the *repetition* necessary for parodic Signifyin(g) to be recognized and to function as Signifyin(g) or parody. Several times Gates states that the importance of the Signifyin(g) Monkey developed under slavery.[17] The monkey is not a central character in the original myths of Esu-Elegbara that Gates explores.[18] The Signifyin(g) Monkey expresses the black slave's desperate need to *appear complicit* even as he constructs a counter-discourse. Timothy Powell recognizes Signifyin(g)'s inherent relation to slavery when he points out that the indirect expression of Signifyin(g) was a necessary element of slaves' covert communication under the Master's gaze:

> Forced to live in a state of incarceration, wherein they could not express themselves explicitly, the earliest black Americans were impelled to adopt a dualistic and duplicitous form of the white man's language that would allow black meanings to be secretly imbued in the language of the Master. (46)

This recognition reminds us of Lorde's statement that '*survival is not an academic skill*' (99) and Joyce Ann Joyce's concern for the 'safety of black lives' (379). For both these black female critics, the literary qualities of black Signifyin(g) are secondary to their success as strategies for survival. These are strategies historically forced upon black Americans by very real material threats to life. Gates attempts, at times, to erase the enforced nature of Signifyin(g)'s complicity, which Powell expresses here in phrases and words such as 'forced,' 'could not express themselves explicitly,' 'impelled to adopt a dualistic and duplicitous form', and 'secretly imbued.' Instead, Gates celebrates Signifyin(g), defining it as inherently radical and different, and as essentially 'black.' This contradicts the model of subjectivity and 'blackness' he expresses elsewhere, in which 'blackness' is a discursive construct constituted in each particular text and context. Diana Fuss theorizes this contradiction in her chapter '"Race" Under Erasure?: Poststructuralist Afro-American Theory' in *Essentially Speaking* by suggesting that Gates and Houston Baker both demonstrate a 'romanticism of the vernacular':

> A powerful *dream* of the vernacular motivates the work of these two Afro-Americanists, perhaps because, for the professionalized literary critic, the vernacular has already become irrevocably lost. What makes the vernacular (the language of 'the folk') so powerful a theme in the work of both Gates and Baker is precisely the fact that it operates as a phantasm, a hallucination of lost origins. It is in the quest to recover, reinscribe, and revalorize the black vernacular that essentialism inheres in the work of two otherwise anti-essentialist theorists. The key to blackness is not visual but *auditory*; essentialism is displaced from sight to sound. (90)

This essentialism is evident in Gates's statement in the introduction to *The Signifying Monkey* that 'The mastery of Signifyin(g) creates *homo rhetoricus Africanus*, allowing – through the manipulation of these classic black figures of Signification – the black person to move freely between two discursive universes' (75). Gates links the mastery of Signifyin(g) directly to an African identity. The figures of Signifyin(g) are described as 'classic black figures' and it is the 'black person' who acquires linguistic freedom by learning them. Signifyin(g) is presented as a distinct 'discursive universe' from Western language. It is interesting to note that Fuss links this '*dream* of the vernacular' directly to nostalgia by suggesting that the vernacular functions as a 'hallucination of lost origins' in Gates and Baker's work. Thus, Gates's 'dream' that Signifyin(g) can create *homo rhetoricus Africanus* can be read as a desire for a vicarious 'homecoming' through the auditory. As Svetlana Boym explains, 'Nostalgia (from *nostos* – return home, and *algia* – longing) is a longing for a home that no longer exists or has never existed. Nostalgia is a sentiment of loss and displacement, but it is also a romance with one's own fantasy' (xiii).

Gates later attempts to erase his essentialism by arguing that 'Signifyin(g), of course, is a principle of language use and is not in any way the exclusive province of black people, although blacks named the term and invented its rituals' (90). How, then, does its 'mastery' result in '*homo rhetoricus Africanus*'? Gates goes on to offer some examples of what he terms 'Signification as parody.' The first example is a white racist parody of black language (92). I fail to see how it is strategically helpful to label this Signifyin(g). It is unclear to me how this white racist parody of the black vernacular which is demeaning to African Americans is related to the African American tradition of Signifyin(g). This seems to imply that the white Western world does not have its own traditions of indirect speech. Given that the white Western world clearly does have its own traditions of parody and satire, it would be more accurate and appropriate to read the white racist's parody of black speech in relation to these Western language practices rather than African. This is not to suggest that black slaves' Signifyin(g) practices could not have influenced their white masters' linguistic strategies, but rather that it seems to compromise Gates's repeated assertions concerning the authenticity and 'blackness' of Signifyin(g) to read this racist parody as an example of Signifyin(g). In this instance the 'Signifyin(g) difference' indicates a white racist presence rather than 'whatever is black.' The example of the white racist using Signifyin(g) as a rhetorical strategy is an attempt to de-essentialize his theory of Signifyin(g) as the black man's vernacular. However, if there is not something particularly 'black' about Signifyin(g), how are we to understand the relevance of the myths of Esu-Elegbara Gates so diligently recounts in the opening chapters? Furthermore, positioning Signifyin(g) as not inherently a 'black' language contradicts his claim that: 'Teaching one's children the fine art of Signifyin(g) is to teach them about this model of linguistic circumnavigation; to teach them a second language that they can share with other black people' (76). The notion that Signifyin(g) constitutes a 'second language' shared among 'black people' implies both community building and an exclusionary boundary that contradicts his example of the white racist Signifyin(g) on black people. In his example, the white racist has gained easy access to the black vernacular 'language' and then used it to link this very black 'language' to Western stereotypes of the black person's limited intellectual abilities. Gates's example demonstrates what Christopher Douglas has suggested that *The Bluest Eye* reveals: 'structurally, racial or cultural concepts of group identity are no different from the typologies and stereotypes that they might promise to replace' (157). I will return to Douglas's view that Morrison's use of the word 'funk' is an example of this in my reading of the novel below.

I have focused on Gates's discussion of 'Signification as parody' because it is most relevant to contemporary women writers' use of parody as a strategy for negotiating their literary pasts which the first chapters of this book will explore. It is also parody or 'formal revision' that Gates renames 'critical signification, or formal Signifyin(g)' and takes as his 'metaphor for literary history' (*The Signifying Monkey* 107). Therefore, it is a particularly privileged mode of Signifyin(g) within Gates's theory. However, Gates does define Signifyin(g) as including many rhetorical strategies or tropes. In differentiating between different terms within the African American vernacular, I find Claudia Mitchell-Kernan's categorizations more helpful and clear. In her definitions of several related terms, 'sounding' and 'playing the dozens' act as specific genres of verbal interaction, whereas Signifyin(g) is the rhetorical strategy of indirect communication:

> When I was a child in the Chicago area, my age group treated signifying and sounding as contrasting tactics. Signifying at that time was a fairly standard tactic which was employed in sounding (as a verbal insult game). That is, the speech event sounding could involve either direct insults (sounds) or

indirect insults (signifying), but they were mutually exclusive tactics. Closely related was the activity of playing the dozens, which then involved broadening the target of the insults to include derogatory remarks about the family of the addressee, particularly his mother. In playing the dozens, one could either sound on the addressee's ancestors or signify about them. Sounding and playing the dozens categorically involve verbal insult; signifying does not. It may be that what these folk categories have in common has obscured what are felt by many to be crucial differences and moreover, functions which are more diverse than have been assumed. (310–11)

This careful categorization of differences is in direct contrast with Gates's listing of these terms under the umbrella term, 'Signifyin(g)': 'The black rhetorical tropes, subsumed under Signifyin(g), would include marking, loud-talking, testifying, calling out (of one's name), sounding, rapping, playing the dozens, and so on' (52). Mitchell-Kernan's phrases, such as 'in the Chicago area,' 'my age group,', and 'at that time,' suggest the context-specific nature of her definitions. Definitions of these black vernacular terms are arrived at in specific black communities. So, it is not that Gates's definitions should be viewed as 'wrong,' but rather we need to assess how useful his categories are. Clearly, he is attempting to find a metaphor for the African American literary tradition, rather than identify specific types of language use as Mitchell-Kernan is. However, there is a difficulty with Gates's use of this terminology. He is forced to use subcategories, such as 'signification as parody,' in order to talk about specific rhetorical strategies. Indeed, the 'signification as parody' that he privileges in his theory is the closest to Mitchell-Kernan's definition of Signifyin(g). She argues that Signifyin(g) is characterized by 'its indirect intent or metaphorical reference' (320) and is interpretable only if the addressee realizes that 'dictionary entries for words are not always sufficient for interpreting meanings or messages, or that meaning goes beyond such interpretations' (311).

Mitchell-Kernan suggests that one of the 'latent advantages' of Signifyin(g)'s indirection is that criticisms can be made while confrontation is avoided because 'indirect messages' 'structure interpretation in such a way that the parties have the option of avoiding real confrontation.' She also suggests that Signifyin(g) can 'provoke confrontations without at the same time unequivocally exposing the speaker's intent.' In both cases, she views the speaker as the one with power because he has 'control of the situation at the receiver's expense' (316; see also 316–17 for specific examples). Surely, however, the receiver also has the power to choose not to acknowledge the implicit message. That this can disempower the speaker is clearly evident in my chapter on Doris Lessing's *The Golden Notebook* as a 'misread' parody. Indeed, although Mitchell-Kernan does identify some strategies and words which the speaker uses to alert his/her listener to the fact that s/he is Signifyin(g), it is possible that the speaker's implicit message (that which he expresses through Signifyin(g)) is simply not recognized by the addressee. The possibility of being misinterpreted, of having the 'implicit message' ignored, is also present in parody. As Hutcheon argues in *The Politics of Postmodernism*, 'there exists a very real threat of elitism or lack of access in the use of parody in any art. This question of accessibility is undeniably part of the politics of postmodern representation' (105). In the case of Signifyin(g), it is less a threat of intellectual elitism, so much as one of exclusion due to being outside of a particular community. One needs to know the rules of Signifyin(g) within that particular black community to be able to interpret its texts; hence, Gates's sense that he is 'translating' from the black vernacular into Western discourse. To what extent, however, does the need for this 'translation' limit Signifyin(g)'s political usefulness? Can Signifyin(g) be used to express an emancipatory black politics? There is a need for other communities to be able to interpret what Mitchell-Kernan terms the 'implicit message' of Signifyin(g), if it is to have a political effect on the community as a whole. As Doris Lessing so succinctly puts it concerning gendered identities in *The Golden Notebook*, 'What's the use of [women] being free if [men] aren't? I swear to God, that every one of them, even the best of them, have the old idea of good women and bad women' (404). Changing the dominant discourse's 'old idea[s]' is an important precursor to social change. No matter what changes individual women, African Americans or members of any 'marginal' group achieve in their own lives, it is only by challenging and changing the representation of these groups in the dominant discourse that broad social changes can occur.

The solution to the problem of access to parody is also its limitation as a politically subversive strategy. As Hutcheon states, 'it is the complicity of postmodern parody – its inscribing as well as undermining of that which it parodies – that is central to its ability to be understood' (105). Asked by Kathleen O'Grady in an interview whether she sees parody as a 'defining feature of contemporary feminist work,' Hutcheon offers a helpful answer that identifies the advantages of using parody as a political strategy:

> It seems to me that, like Canadians, women are often in the position of defining themselves AGAINST a dominant culture or discourse. One way to do that, a way with great subversive potential, is to speak the language of the dominant (which allows you to be heard), but then to subvert it through ironic strategies of exaggeration, understatement, or literalization. Parody is the mode that allows you to mimic that speech, but to do so through re-contextualizing it and therefore without subscribing to its implied ideals and values. Women writers (witness Jane Austen) have known of this transgressive power of parody for a long time. ('Theorizing' 3–4)

However, 'speak[ing] the language of the dominant' in order to be heard creates another predicament for counter-discursive parody. If the black artist must more clearly inscribe that which he/she signifies upon in order to increase the accessibility of his/her text, the radical nature of his/her politics is compromised by this conservative repetition. In the same interview, Hutcheon also discusses the political limitations of postmodern parodic strategies for feminists:

> I happen to think that postmodernism is political, but not in a way that is of much use, in the long run, to feminisms: it does challenge dominant discourses (usually through self-consciousness and parody), but it also re-instates those very discourses in the act of challenging them. To put it another way, postmodernism does deconstruct, but doesn't really reconstruct. No feminist is happy with that kind of potential quietism, even if she (or he) approves of the deconstructing impulse: you simply can't stop there. This important issue of agency has become central not only to feminism, of course, but to 'queer theory' and to postcolonial theory. (3)

As she argues in her conclusion to *The Politics of Postmodernism*,

> Complicity is perhaps necessary (or at least unavoidable) in deconstructive critique (you have to signal – and thereby install – that which you want to subvert), though it also inevitably conditions both the radicality of the kind of critique it can offer and the possibility of suggesting change. (152)

Gates's Signifyin(g) certainly seems to be a form of 'deconstructive critique' which requires a degree of complicity. Gates attempts to erase this contradiction by placing 'blackness' only in the 'difference' generated by the practice of Signifyin(g) on previous literary texts. In his close readings of specific texts, his focus on relations between African American authors enables him to avoid the problematic nature of the complicity inherent in his model of Signifyin(g). The issue of complicity becomes far more urgent when the text being Signified upon by the African American writer is by a white author. Gates also erases the historically *enforced* nature of black practices of indirect communication under slavery. He fails to address the limitations of such practices if they always require a cross-cultural speaker like himself to 'translate' them.

The dangers of complicity and the political potential of parody are two central concerns of Morrison's in *The Bluest Eye*. In this novel she Signifies upon a white reading primer. Recognizing that Signifyin(g) involves the same repetition and installing of its target text as parody does, enables us to attend to Morrison's message concerning the dangers and inevitability of complicity. Indeed, this recognition of the problematic, yet necessary, complicity of parodic counter-discourses is the main difference between postmodern parody and Gates's theory of Signifyin(g). There are, however, some important similarities that I wish to identify before moving on to a reading of parody in *The Bluest Eye*. The first is Gates's suggestion that Signifyin(g) is a helpful strategy in creating 'a new narrative space for representing the recurring referent of Afro-American literature, the so-called Black Experience' (111). For many contemporary writers faced with a postmodern feeling of belatedness, revising past literary forms has been an effective way to clear 'a new narrative space' while acknowledging their position at the end of a long literary tradition. John Barth captures this contemporary sense that parody can create 'a new narrative space' in his famous revision of his title 'The Literature of Exhaustion' (1967) into 'The Literature of Replenishment' (1980). In 'The Literature of Replenishment' Barth addresses the fact that his earlier essay was misread as arguing that literature was dead and that parody was a sign of its exhaustion:

> The simple burden of my essay ['The Literature of Exhaustion'] was that the forms and modes of art live in human history and are therefore subject to used-upness, at least in the minds of significant numbers of artists in particular times and places: in other words, that artistic conventions are liable to be retired, subverted, transcended, transformed, or even deployed against themselves to generate new and lively work. I would have thought that point unexceptional. But a great many people...mistook me to mean that literature, at least fiction, is *kaput*; that it has all been done already; that there is nothing left for contemporary writers but to parody and travesty our great predecessors in our exhausted medium – exactly what some critics deplore as postmodernism. (205; my ellipses)

Reading 'The Literature of Exhaustion' with this warning in mind, it is clear that even in that earlier essay, Barth viewed parody and irony as useful tools for the postmodern artist faced with the challenge of 'confront[ing] an intellectual dead end and employ[ing] it against itself to accomplish new human work' (69–70). The 'intellectual dead end,' Barth explains in 'The Literature of Replenishment,' was that of Modernism, rather than literature, the novel or language. He concludes 'The Literature of Replenishment' with the hope that contemporary parodic literature, 'what is gropingly now called postmodernist fiction...might also be thought of one day as a literature of replenishment' (206; my ellipses).

A second important similarity between postmodern theories of parody and Signifyin(g) is the importance of wit and the comic. While I would disagree with Margaret Rose that 'the creation of comic incongruity or discrepancy' is a 'significant *distinguishing* factor in parody' (31, emphasis added), certainly the incongruity between the target text and the parody can often create comedy. Similarly, in African American linguistic games such as 'sounding' and 'playing the dozens' it is often the ability to make the audience laugh that marks a successful player. As Mitchell-Kernan argues, Signifyin(g) is 'clearly thought of as a kind of art – a clever way of conveying messages' (317). Paul Lewis discusses the social functions of humour in his book *Comic Effects*: 'Sociological studies have shown that, because it expresses shared values, humor can be a social lubricant and a tool or force in the exercise of power in social groups' (36). This comment suggests important reasons why humour is often used by parodists and Signifiers. Humour reinforces the values and knowledge that the interpreter must share with the parodist or Signifier in order to recognize the 'implied message' of their texts and utterances. In 'playing the dozens,' if a speaker can make the audience laugh by Signifyin(g) upon his verbal opponent, then the speaker has exercised power over his opponent. As Lewis states even more clearly elsewhere:

> because the presentation of a particular image or idea as a fitting subject for humor is based on value judgments, the creation and use of humor is an exercise in power: a force in controlling our responses to unexpected and dangerous happenings, a way of shaping the responses and attitudes of others, and a tool in intergroup and intra-group dynamics. (13)

Therefore, when a parodist makes his audience laugh at his target text, then he has shaped 'the responses and attitudes' of his audience towards that target text. He has offered a specific text 'as a fitting subject for humor' and by laughing, the audience has demonstrated that they agree with his implied 'value judgments.' The parodist can be said to have used humour as 'a rhetorical ploy, a more or less hidden persuader' (67). When using parody as a counter-discourse, the parodist's aim is to persuade his audience to share his critical attitude towards the target text (even if the target may be him/herself). Lewis's analysis of the social functions of humour clarifies why parodists do frequently enlist it to help them achieve this goal. However, I would argue that while humour can increase a parody's effectiveness, humour is not a *defining* characteristic of either parody or Signifyin(g).

The last similarity I wish to discuss between parody and Signifyin(g) is that they can both be used to express the constructed nature of the self while still asserting political agency. This is one of the debates that Elliott suggests feminism has simply left behind rather than resolved. As Robert Phiddian argued in 1997 in 'Are Parody and Deconstruction Secretly the Same Thing?' parody 'has already seen its way out of the deconstructive impasse that treats language as an endless and odorless play of differences' by recognizing that 'reference occurs, *despite language*' (691). Parody demonstrates more clearly than Gates's model of 'Signifyin(g) difference' that the subject is written by the discourses in which it is situated but it also points to a way out of that potential impasse. Kim Worthington offers a useful summary of the postmodern discursive subject: 'Subjectivity, in short, is understood to derive from intersubjectivity. That is, our conceptions of selfhood are deemed to be constituted by, not merely reflected in, the terms of language, which is social and public' (5). By speaking 'the language of the dominant,' as Hutcheon puts it, the repetitive, complicit aspect of parody acknowledges the fact that the self is 'constituted by, not merely reflected in, the terms of language' (Worthington 5). Clearly, if 'the language of the dominant' has posited you as invisible, absent or non-human, to admit that you have been constructed by that discourse is severely to limit the emancipatory possibilities of your text; hence, Gates's reluctance to admit the complicit and repetitive aspect of Signifyin(g) and his nostalgic desire to see Signifyin(g) as a 'second language' which links African Americans directly to their lost African origins (rather than as a specific use of the English language). As Worthington goes on to point out, one of the possibilities a poststructuralist understanding of the subject 'forces us to confront is the idea that personal authenticity and subjective agency are impossible, given their constitution in the terms of social discourse' (8). However, the difference or critical distance parody achieves from its target text or discourse implies that the self *is* capable of critique and agency. This difference is also the mark of parody's creativity. Significantly, it is through '*creative deviancy*' that the subject asserts 'personal authenticity and subjective agency' in Worthington's model of the self (102).

Despite Gates's reluctance to acknowledge the ways in which Signifyin(g) repeats 'the language of the dominant' and his attempt to posit Signifyin(g) as a completely different language, he has been keen to deconstruct the irreducible difference 'race' has come to signal.[19] Morrison has expressed concern at what she perceives as a call to deconstruct 'the ideas of difference inscribed in the trope of race' if that means erasing 'race.'[20] Although Morrison does not subscribe to an essentialist notion of 'race,'[21] she suggests that those who wish to wholly erase the category of 'race' are blind to both culture and history:

> Suddenly (for our purposes, suddenly) 'race' does not exist. For three hundred years black Americans insisted that 'race' was no usefully distinguishing factor in human relationships. During those same three centuries every academic discipline, including theology, history, and natural science, insisted 'race' was *the* determining factor in human development. When blacks discovered they had shaped or become a culturally formed race, and that it had specific and revered difference, suddenly they were told there is no such thing as 'race', biological or cultural that matters and that genuinely intellectual exchange cannot accommodate it. (203)

Morrison's point echoes one made by Worthington concerning the constructed nature of the self as narrative. Just because something is linguistically constructed or narrated does not mean it 'does not exist' or is unreal. As Worthington says, in calling selfhood a narrative, 'this is in no way to suggest that selfhood is a fiction, if fiction is understood as something that is untrue, fallacious, opposed to fact, but rather to suggest that selfhood is an active interpretative process' (13). More recently in a 2009 essay for *Eurozine* entitled '"I Am Not a Woman Writer": About Women, Literature and Feminist Theory Today,' Toril Moi discusses some of the reasons why 'feminist theory stopped being concerned with women and writing' (3). She identifies poststructuralist theory – especially theories of the 'death of the author' and Judith Butler's influential work, *Gender Trouble* – as a major reason for this silence. She points out, however, that Butler and Beauvoir's work constitute '*theories of origins*' but these theories '*simply do not tell us what we ought to do once gender has come into being*' (4; original emphasis). In *The Bluest Eye*, Morrison explores this notion that 'self' and 'race' are cultural constructions or narratives *that really do exist*. Her parody of the white reading primer acknowledges what Worthington terms the 'determining force' of 'language and the discursive processes which structure social interaction' and demonstrates how gender and race 'come into being' (to borrow Moi's phrase). In the character of Pecola Breedlove, Morrison confronts the 'disturbing notion...that personal authenticity and subjective agency are impossible, given their constitution in the terms of social discourse' (Worthington 8; my ellipsis). However, the changes Morrison makes to the reading primer's grammar and spacing, Claudia MacTeer's self-conscious and resistant study of the dominant ideology, and the different images of houses throughout *The Bluest Eye* are all examples of Worthington's notion of 'creative deviancy' that suggest ways in which the dominant ideology can be challenged and changed. These are all things that Morrison and her narrator, Claudia, do to disrupt the processes that bring gender and race into being and to react to those constructed identities once they have been brought into being. Claudia's MacTeer's 'peripheral existence' (*The Bluest Eye* 17) enables her to occupy the position of the parodist. She is situated both within and without the community she describes, and like the parodist, she both repeats and critiques it.

'Here is the house': Toni Morrison's *The Bluest Eye*

The first version of what Morrison terms in her 'Afterword' the 'barren white-family primer' (215) appears on the page like this:

> Here is the house. It is green and white. It has a red door. It is very pretty. Here is the family. Mother, Father, Dick, and Jane live in the green-and-white house. They are very happy. See Jane. She has a red dress. She wants to play. Who will play with Jane? See the cat. It goes meow-meow. Come and play. Come play with Jane. The kitten will not play. See Mother. Mother is very nice. Mother, will you play with Jane? Mother laughs. Laugh, Mother, laugh. See Father. He is big and strong. Father, will you play with Jane? Father is smiling. Smile, Father, smile. See the dog. Bowwow goes the dog. Do you want to play with Jane? See the dog run. Run, dog, run. Look, look. Here comes a friend. The friend will play with Jane. They will play a good game. Play, Jane, play. (3)

After this version, Morrison repeats the primer three more times. From the second version of the reading primer Morrison removes all punctuation but leaves the spaces between the words and the double-spacing. The third version runs all the words together without any punctuation or spaces and is single-spaced.[22] The final repetition of the primer appears in fragments before each chapter that describes the Breedlove family. Morrison alters the primer even more radically in this repetition as she capitalizes the text, runs the words all together, and repeats those words that are most ironically relevant to the chapter they precede. Thus the chapter describing Pecola Breedlove's ugly home in a storefront is preceded by this excerpt of reading primer:

> HEREISTHEHOUSEITISGREENANDWH
> ITEITHASAREDDOORITISVERYPRETT
> YITISVERYPRETTYPRETTYPRETTYP (33)

The repetition of 'pretty' points to the word's powerfully destructive effect on Pecola. It simultaneously functions as a sign of Morrison's critique because in this fragmentary repetition – 'PRETTYPRETTYPRETTYP' – she turns the word into irrelevant nonsense. Morrison's parody of the white reading primer focuses our attention on three central issues: the educational processes through which the dominant ideology is taught, the primary social structure of the family in which that ideology is expressed or resisted, and the complex issues of authority, language and subjectivity raised by Morrison's entry into authorship as an African American.

'Education, Education, Education'

Morrison's implied warning concerning the dangers of education is crucially important to the novel as a whole. Donald Gibson discusses how Morrison's use of the reading primer as a preface to her novel focuses our attention on the processes of education: 'It reveals the role of education in both oppressing the victim – and more to the point – teaching the victim how to oppress her own black self by internalizing the values that dictate standards of beauty' (160). Gibson argues that Morrison reveals 'the cost of learning to read and write carries with it the necessity to submit to values beyond and other than literary *per se*, for words do not exist independently of value' (160–1).[23] In an interview with Thomas LeClair, Morrison stated that: 'The primer with white children was the way life was presented to the black people. As the novel proceeded I wanted that primer version broken up and confused, which explains the typographical running together of the words' (127). Discerning the individual words in the third version of the reading primer is a difficult and alienating experience, which mirrors how children struggle with this text as they learn to read. The poor, black children of this novel, Claudia and Frieda MacTeer, and Pecola Breedlove, are alienated from the primer not only by their inexperience as readers, but also by its cultural and ideological assumptions.

Morrison has repeatedly suggested that what motivated her to *write The Bluest Eye* was that it was a novel she wanted to *read* that had not been written yet – the story of a poor black girl.[24] It is ironic and appropriate that Merle Hodge's *Crick Crack, Monkey* – also the story of a poor black girl – was published in exactly the same year as *The Bluest Eye* (1970). Hodge uses a similar technique to Morrison's blurring of the words of the primer together to relate the children's inability to understand them. She presents the poor black girl, Tee, reciting what is clearly supposed to be the Lord's Prayer:

> Our father (*which was plain enough*)
> witchartin
> heavn
> *HALLE*
> Owèdbethyname
> *THY*
> Kingdumkum
> *THY*
> willbedunnunnert
> azitizinevn... (29)

Hodge uses comic parody in *Crick Crack, Monkey* to enact the same political critique of education as Morrison does more tragically in *The Bluest Eye*.

One of Morrison's key points in looking at the reading primer and the movie industry in *The Bluest Eye* is that a text or cultural artefact does not need to be *overtly* racist to 'teach' racism. In 'Unspeakable Things Unspoken,' Morrison suggests that the status quo always attempts to portray itself as natural and invisible:

> the status quo sees itself as not – as though the term '*a*political' were only its prefix and not the most obviously political stance imaginable since one of the functions of political ideology is to pass itself off as immutable, natural and 'innocent'. (207)

Morrison's concern is with how 'political ideology' renders itself invisible while continuing to do its social and cultural work. Race is not directly mentioned once in the reading primer. One effect of exploring the processes by which black subjects learn the status quo is that the status quo is revealed not to be 'immutable, natural and "innocent"'. As Gibson says, Morrison 'undercuts the validity of the proposition of the dominant culture that blue eyes and cleanliness are inherently valuable by historicizing social value. Claudia "learned" to worship Shirley Temple just as she "learned" to delight in cleanliness' (163). Indeed, more recent work on the novel has emphasized its historical context. For example, Jennifer Gillan's article published in 2002, for example, reads the novel as a critique of the 1965 Department of Labor report *The Negro Family: The Case for National Action* by Patrick Moynihan. Christopher Douglas's 2006 article positions the novel alongside the legal and cultural debates about race in the 1940s and 1950s suggesting that '*The Bluest Eye* is an inaugural text of U.S. multiculturalism' (161). These more recent readings of the novel suggest that Morrison's 'historicizing of social value' is one of the novel's most enduring contributions.

Morrison's removal of the punctuation from the reader can also be viewed as a positive sign that the status quo the primer describes is not 'immutable,' but can be changed.[25] Similarly, in Hodge's *Crick Crack, Monkey* Tee's alteration of 'which art in heaven' to 'witchartin' can be read as 'witch-artin(g)' implying the practice of Voodoo, and thereby undercutting the Christianity of the Lord's Prayer with Trinidad's local beliefs. The fragments of the reading primer that Morrison places at the beginning of the chapters are followed by descriptions of Pecola's home and family that are so different from the reading primer that they function further to undermine the notion that the primer is a 'natural and "innocent"' version of the American family.

The target of much of Morrison's critique in *The Bluest Eye* is the black community itself. What frustrates Morrison is the extent to which the black community assists in the process of teaching its members that they are inferior instead of protecting them from this racist assumption. As Morrison asks of the 'reclamation of racial beauty in the sixties' in the 'Afterword' to *The Bluest Eye*: 'Why, although reviled by others, could this beauty not be taken for granted within the community? Why did it need wide public articulation to exist?' (210). Morrison's argument is that the popular 1960s slogan 'Black is beautiful' reveals a history of black people believing they are not beautiful, even as it challenges the dominant white ideology. As Jill Matus explains:

> However self-affirming assertions such as 'black is beautiful' were in the 1960s and 1970s, they were too simple to redress the complex and long-prepared effects of valuations based on colour. Morrison commented on the movement's assertion of racial beauty: 'If the best thing happened in the world and it all came out perfectly in terms of what the gains and goals of the *Movement* were, nevertheless nobody was going to get away with that; nobody was going to tell me that it had been that easy. That all I needed was a slogan: "Black is Beautiful"' (Naylor 199). Focusing on the complex formations of subjectivity in a racialised country, Morrison's first novel implicitly takes on assertions of racial pride – black is beautiful – and scrutinises the historical backlog of self-devaluation that such assertions cannot magically erase. (37–8)

Morrison's frustration at the black community's 'historical backlog of self-devaluation' and internalization of dominant white values helps to explain why Morrison's critique of members of the black community such as Geraldine in *The Bluest Eye* is so fierce. They have internalized white ideals and notions of beauty and the symbols of this internalization are their houses.

The issue of beauty is central here and has received a great deal of attention recently, as I explore in Chapter 4 in relation to Zadie Smith's *On Beauty*. Anne Anlin Cheng has suggested that, 'From Plato to Mao Tse-Tung, from George Eliot to Toni Morrison, beauty has always provoked unrest' (191). Cheng argues that, 'The idea that beauty's adverse function in racial politics duplicates beauty's debilitating role in gender politics, however, has been more assumed than theorized' (192). Cheng places a helpful focus *not* on the object of beauty but on 'whether the very process of pleasure might be inherently objectifying and whether such so-called objectification might compromise – or constitute – the observer's own subject position more than the viewer would like or can afford to acknowledge' (203). Cheng points out that Morrison's anecdote about her friend which prompted her to write *The Bluest Eye* draws as much attention to Morrison's own discomfort with beauty as her friend's. Morrison describes in her afterword 'the harm she was doing to *my* concept of the beautiful' (211). For Morrison, as for Claudia, the 'moment of seeing through beauty...is also, curiously, the moment of finding beauty' and this 'shock' is 'ambiguous, marking either an instant of critical separation or psychical identification (or both) between the young girls' (202). Here, Cheng is referring to Morrison and her school friend, but the relationship between Claudia and Pecola (or even Claudia and her doll) is similar.

The Nuclear Family: 'an isolated horror'

Morrison parodies the reading primer's ideal house and the nuclear family that lives in it throughout *The Bluest Eye* thereby drawing our attention to the ways in which families also teach ideology. Her parodies vary in the degree to which they repeat or subvert the ideal expressed in the reading primer. In this way she uses parody to introduce the important theme of African Americans' complicity with white middle-class ideals. The houses described in *The Bluest Eye* offer a critique of Dick and Jane's house that succeeds in destabilizing, if not wholly inverting, the value system implied by the clean house of the reading primer. Morrison encourages us to associate cleanliness with emotional sterility, and disordered, messy houses with loving (if contradictory and complex) family relationships.

Although Claudia's house is green like the Dick-and-Jane house, it is 'old, cold, and green' rather than 'green and white' and 'very pretty.' The windows of Claudia's bedroom are stuffed with rags against the cold and 'it is too cold to lie stockingless' (10). Claudia goes on to outline the specific hardships of being a child in her community. She describes the anger with which adults respond to their children's illnesses: 'When we catch colds, they shake their heads in disgust at our lack of consideration' (10).[26] Claudia recalls one specific cold she had caught when she went out to gather tiny pieces of coal that had been dropped along the railway tracks without wearing a hat. The narrative focalizer shifts from the younger Claudia, who is humiliated and upset by her mother's anger at her, to the older Claudia who looks back on this experience and realizes that her mother was 'not angry at [her], but at [her] sickness'(11). After describing her illness, shame, and sorrow, the older Claudia asks, 'But was it really like that? As painful as I remember?' (12):

> Only mildly. Or rather, it was a productive and fructifying pain. Love, thick and dark as Alaga syrup, eased up into that cracked window. I could smell it – taste it – sweet, musty, with an edge of wintergreen in its base – everywhere in that house. It stuck, along with my tongue, to the frosted windowpanes. It coated my chest, along with the salve, and when the flannel came undone in my sleep, the clear, sharp curves of air outlined its presence on my throat. And in the night, when my coughing was dry and tough, feet padded into the room, hands repinned the flannel, readjusted the quilt, and rested a moment on my forehead. So when I think of autumn, I think of somebody with hands who does not want me to die. (12)

Her answer to her own question concerning the accuracy of her painful memories reveals that, despite the economic deprivations she suffered as a child, her 'old, cold, and green' house is held together by a fiercely protective love.

Geraldine's house, in contrast, attempts to repeat the ideal house of the reading primer as is evident in the way the colours of her house echo the green, white and red of the house in the reading primer. That Morrison is parodying Geraldine's attempt to comply with the middle-class ideal of the reading primer is evident in her excessive description. When Pecola enters Geraldine's house she notices the 'big red-and-gold Bible,' the '[l]ittle lace doilies,' the 'big lamp with green-and-gold base and white shade,', and the 'rug on the floor, with enormous dark-red flowers' (89). When Geraldine throws Pecola out of her house, 'Pecola backed out of the room, staring at the pretty milk-brown lady in the pretty gold-and-green house' (92). Geraldine's black cat with the blue eyes is, of course, a symbol of both Geraldine and Pecola's internalization of the dominant gaze. Its death can certainly be read as a symbol of the danger inherent in Pecola's desire for blue eyes in her black face.

Morrison describes how Geraldine and women like her have been taught to conform to white ideals of beauty:

> They wash themselves with orange-colored Lifebuoy soap, dust themselves with Cashmere Bouquet talc, clean their teeth with salt on a piece of rag, soften their skin with Jergens Lotion. They smell like wood, newspapers, and vanilla. They straighten their hair with Dixie Peach, and part it on the side. (82)

By offering a generalized description of 'these sugar-brown Mobile girls' (82) before introducing Geraldine in particular, Morrison widens the target of her social critique. She describes the process these girls undergo in learning 'how to behave':

> The careful development of thrift, patience, high morals, and good manners. In short, how to get rid of the funkiness. The dreadful funkiness of passion, the funkiness of nature, the funkiness of the wide range of human emotions.
> Wherever it erupts, this Funk, they wipe it away: where it crusts, they dissolve it; wherever it drips, flowers, or clings, they find it and fight it until it dies. They fight this battle all the way to the grave. (83)[27]

Morrison's use of 'Funk' instead of 'mess' gives it a positive value and, by using a black vernacular term, she associates it with blackness. This is a racial identity Geraldine attempts to deny. Despite herself being a victim of the 'line between' black and white, Geraldine constantly polices the 'line between colored and nigger' (87). Geraldine's son, Junior, is 'bored and frightened at home' (88) as his mother imposes upon him her belief that 'colored people were neat and quiet; niggers were dirty and loud' (87). Even as a child, Junior is forbidden to make a mess. As Christopher Douglas points out, 'funky' was originally a bad smell associated with tobacco which became racialized in the twentieth century. The term's negative connotations were subverted in the 1950s when it was used to describe jazz positively. Douglas suggests that 'funk's history involves fascination with the bodies of black people, and it's this fascination that Morrison's typology restores' (156) – the typology of the 'these sugar-brown Mobile girls.'[28] Thus, for Douglas, Morrison's use of this word 'funk' returns us to debates about essentialism and communal racial identity that Jane Elliott (referring to feminism rather than African American criticism) suggests the academy is attempting to move on from by positioning them as 'out-of-date' (qtd above; 1700). In contrast, Douglas positions Morrison's novel as 'representative of our current paradigm of literary multiculturalism' and argues that it 'shows us, at the dawn of multiculturalism, that there is no real difference between the type (or stereotype) and a notion of culture. Both are ideal forms that are created by the elimination of a certain amount of alterity' (161). As I mentioned above, Douglas's analysis is also pertinent in relation to Gates's example of the white racist Signifyin(g). Common practices and identities are, Douglas demonstrates, intimately connected to negative stereotypes. The case of Signifyin(g) is itself exemplary. Read negatively as a stereotypical behaviour, it demonstrates the racist assertion that African Americans are capable only of mimicry, not creation. In Gates's positive reading Signifyin(g) is a shared African American practice which builds and reflects community. Thus we see how any act of deconstructive critique or counter-discursive reversal is haunted by that which it is attempting to reject or replace.

Morrison's parody of houses is accompanied by a parallel critique of the families within them. Asked in 'The Salon Interview' by Zia Jaffrey whether she wanted to get remarried or whether her failed marriage had changed her thinking about 'the notion of marriage,' Morrison replied:

> No, I like marriage. The idea. I think it's better to have both parents totally there, and delivering something for the children. Where it's not preferable is if that's all there is, if it's just a mother and a father. That's an isolated horror. I would much rather have a large – a connection – with all of the members of the family, rather than... Because, usually, marriage, you think, that little atomic family, which I deplore. (2)

Susan Willis views Morrison as 'writing against the privatized world of suburban house and nuclear family' (309). Pecola's family echoes the structure of Dick and Jane's nuclear family: 'Mother, Father, Dick, and Jane live in the green-and-white house' (*The Bluest Eye* 3). The repetition of fragments of the reading primer as epigraphs to chapters describing Pecola's family in *The Bluest Eye* encourage the reader to see specific intertextual relations between the white reading primer and the narrative of Pecola's family and life. Reading in the tradition of Gates's claim that 'Whatever is black about black American literature is to be found in this identifiable black Signifyin(g) difference' (Gates, *The Signifying Monkey* xxiv), critics have focused almost exclusively on the important contrasts between these two texts.[29]

The contrasts between the reading primer and Morrison's narrative are, of course, extremely important. The 'pretty' house of the reading primer is replaced by the 'ugly' storefront the Breedloves occupy and from which they are then ejected. 'Mother' of Dick and Jane's family becomes 'Mrs. Breedlove,' who is referred to by the formal and distancing title of 'Mrs. Breedlove' by all her family (43). Jane's 'big strong' father is replaced by the ineffectual, drunk, and violent Cholly. The pet cat and dog in the reading primer belong to Dick and Jane's family. Pecola's family cannot afford pets. The cat and dog in Pecola's narrative belong to others and she unintentionally kills both.[30] Reading *The Bluest Eye* as parodying the reading primer – and, therefore, repeating as well as subverting it – encourages us to recognize the double-pronged nature of Morrison's attack. It is through the similarities between Pecola's family and Jane's family that Morrison manages 'to hit the raw nerve of racial self-contempt, expose it' (Dittmar 211).

The most obvious similarity between Jane's family and Pecola's is that both are examples of the nuclear family. Through her parodic inversion of the Dick-and-Jane's family in describing Pecola's family, Morrison expresses her sense that the 'little atomic family' is 'an isolated horror.' Pauline's original family is in direct contrast to this. Her family was part of a network of 'neighbours and kin' and it migrated within that network '[i]n shifts, lots, batches, mixed in with other families' (111).[31] However, when Pauline and Cholly marry they live in accordance with the ideal family model described in the reading primer:

> They agreed to marry and go 'way up north, where Cholly said steel mills were begging for workers. Young, loving, and full of energy, they came to Lorain, Ohio. Cholly found work in the steel mills right away, and Pauline started keeping house. (116)[32]

As a man who left the house to work, Cholly 'had no problem finding other people and other things to occupy him – men were always climbing the stairs asking for him, and he was happy to accompany them, leaving her alone' (118). The economic difference between their situation and that of the family in the reading primer makes the nuclear family an inappropriate model for Pauline and Cholly: 'In her loneliness, she turned to her husband for reassurance, entertainment, for things to fill the vacant places. Housework was not enough; there were only two rooms, and no yard to keep or move about in' (117). Pauline does not have the middle-class ideal home with many rooms to clean and a yard to maintain to occupy her time. As a poor farm girl, she cannot fit into the urban, increasingly middle-class society around her: 'The women in the town wore high-heeled shoes, and when Pauline tried to wear them, they aggravated her shuffle into a pronounced limp' (117–18). Willis diagnoses the cause of the black woman's alienation in the capitalist, industrial north as 'the result of striving to achieve the white bourgeois social model (in which she worked but did not live)' (310). When Pauline starts spending money on clothes to try to fit in with the town's women, she and Cholly begin to argue. Their arguing increases, as does Cholly's drinking, until he comes to the house where Pauline works as a house maid, 'drunk wanting some money' (120). Pauline's employer refuses to pay Pauline unless she leaves Cholly. Pauline is reduced to begging her employer for money:

> Then I got so desperate I asked her if she would loan it to me. She was quiet for a spell, and then she told me I shouldn't let a man take advantage over me. That I should have more respect, and it was my husband's duty to pay the bills, and if he couldn't, I should leave and get alimony. All such simple stuff. What was he gone (sic) give me alimony on? I seen she didn't understand that all I needed from her was my eleven dollars to pay the gas man so I could cook. (120–1)

This incident was an important warning to Pauline that the ideology that supports the Dick-and-Jane household does not lend equal support to a poor, black household. This is the focus of Jennifer Gillan's reading of the novel as a critique of the Moynihan Report:

> In shifting blame from systematic inequality to the structural equality of the black social structure, the Moynihan Report ignored several obstacles

in postwar America to the black community's adoption of the gendered divisions of the nuclear family model: the exclusion of black males from breadwinner roles and the corresponding re-channeling of black females into domestic servant roles, the de facto exclusion of black families from the commodity culture through which families publicly display their success at achieving economic power through consumerism, and the need for black families to pool resources in order to consolidate their economic weakness and maintain some semblance of economic and social stability. (288)

Pauline's pregnancy returns her and Cholly to their original hope that they will be able to live out the middle-class ideal of a nuclear family:

They eased back into a relationship more like the early days of their marriage, when he asked if she were tired or wanted him to bring her something from the store. In this state of ease, Pauline stopped doing day work and returned to her own housekeeping. But the loneliness in those two rooms had not gone away. When the winter sun hit the peeling green paint of the kitchen chairs, when the smoked hocks were boiling in the pot, when all she could hear was the truck delivering furniture downstairs, she thought about back home, about how she had been all alone most of the time then too, but that this lonesomeness was different. (121–2)

One of the signs of 'ease' is that Cholly offers to buy Pauline things from the store which demonstrates the extent to which the nuclear family is dependent on black males being able to play the 'breadwinner roles,' as Gillan puts it, and demonstrates Cholly and Pauline's desires to be complicit with white middle-class ideologies of consumerism and family. The ironic echo of the 'green and white' ideal house of the reading primer in the 'peeling green paint of the kitchen chairs' points to the difference in economic power of the two households, while simultaneously alerting us to similarity. The women remain isolated at home, 'housekeeping.' Pauline's decision not to insist on returning to her original family, which would have offered what Morrison calls 'a large – a connection – with all of the members of the family,' results in Pauline and Cholly's isolation. This isolation increases with their worsening poverty. There is as much irony in the contrast between the Breedloves' public situation in a storefront window and their private isolation, as there is in the contrast between the shabbiness of the storefront and the 'pretty' house of the reading primer.

We have seen how Morrison's parodic descriptions of houses point to the black community's varying degrees of complicity with the reading primer's ideals and thereby enables her to raise the difficult issue of racism *within* the black community. Similarly, the parodic relationship between Pecola's family and the reading primer's family allows Morrison to show how Pecola falls victim to her own family's internalization of a family model they cannot afford to uphold. Barbara Rigney has suggested that: 'What most wrenches the heart about Pecola in *The Bluest Eye* is not her poverty and her madness, but her motherlessness and her silence' (13). Indeed, Morrison implies that Pauline's treatment of Pecola is as psychologically damaging as Cholly's incestuous rape. One of the novel's most disturbing scenes occurs in the Fishers' kitchen. This scene reveals how complicit Pauline is with the ideology of the reading primer, reiterates the important dichotomy between mess and cleanliness set up by the reading primer's clean house described in proper English, and suggests how the novel's multiple narrative layers, voices and frames relate to each other. The colour imagery is especially important in this scene and is used throughout the novel to identify parallels between the many narratives and frames Morrison employs. Unlike the 'peeling green paint' (121) of Pauline's kitchen chairs, the green in the Fishers' part of town is described as 'velvet green' (105). The 'large white house' (105) repeats the white of the house in the reading primer. The colourful 'wheelbarrow full of flowers' ironically echoes the dandelions Pecola enjoys earlier in the novel, but contrasts with the marigolds that refuse to grow. Pecola's 'light red sweater and blue cotton dress' (106) relate ironically to Jane's 'red dress' in the reading primer and the Fisher girl's 'pink sunback dress and pink fluffy bedroom slippers' (108).[33] This colour imagery connects this scene with the reading primer and with the narrative structured by the seasons.

Pecola has come to collect the laundry in order to assist her mother, but she accidentally knocks over Pauline's berry cobbler creating a 'mess.'[34] Instead of valuing her daughter's attempt to make a practical contribution to her family, Pauline abuses Pecola for spilling the berry cobbler. She knocks Pecola to the floor and yells at her to '"Pick up that wash and get on out of here"' (109). Meanwhile, she hushes and soothes the 'little pink-and-yellow girl' who far from assisting Pauline, requests 'another pie.'[35] Pauline is completely complicit with the 'very nice' Mother of the reading primer, but only in the clean, white house of the Fisher family. She has so internalized the values of the dominant ideology that she rejects her own child in order to maintain the dominant values – 'get on out of here, so I can get this mess cleaned up,' she says (109). The 'beauty, order, cleanliness, and praise' (127) Pauline discovers in the Fisher house is threatened by her messy, clumsy daughter. Pauline despaired at the mess of the storefront (127) and her daughter's ugliness (126), and

> kept this order, this beauty, for herself, a private world, and never introduced it into her storefront, or to her children. Them she bent toward respectability, and in so doing taught them fear: fear of being clumsy, fear of being like their father, fear of not being loved by God, fear of madness like Cholly's mother's. (128)

The fact that Pauline teaches her children the value system that has victimized her, thereby acting as their oppressor (and teaching her children to act as their own oppressors), is one of the many 'abuses and betrayals' that Linda Dittmar points to when she argues that the 'novel does seem overwhelmingly pessimistic' (140). Pecola is born into her mother's belief that she is ugly, whereas Claudia describes how she and her sister, Frieda, have to learn that society values them less:

> We were sinking under the wisdom, accuracy, and relevance of Maureen's last words. If she was cute – and if anything could be believed, she *was* – then we were not. And what did that mean? We were lesser. Nicer, brighter, but still lesser. Dolls we could destroy, but we could not destroy the honey voices of parents and aunts, the obedience in the eyes of our peers, the slippery light in the eyes of our teachers when they encountered the Maureen Peals of the world. What was the secret? What did we lack? Why was it important? And so what? Guileless and without vanity, we were still in love with ourselves then. We felt comfortable in our skins, enjoyed the news that our senses released to us, admired our dirt, cultivated our scars, and could not comprehend this unworthiness. (74)

The 'fraudulent love' Claudia later learns for Shirley Temple repeats the dominant ideology but with a critical distance: 'I learned much later to worship [Shirley Temple], just as I learned to delight in cleanliness, knowing, even as I learned, that the change was adjustment without improvement' (23). In contrast, Pecola has never experienced what it feels like to be 'in love with [herself].'

Morrison's Parody of the Slave Narrative: 'an enabling act'

Morrison's use of parody in *The Bluest Eye* does enable to her to raise some particularly important issues, even if it also limits the radical potential of her critique. Perhaps the most complex of these issues are those raised by Morrison's own entry into authorship as an African American. For example, installing this primer at the start of her first novel allows Morrison to point to the dangers of Western language for African Americans attempting to destabilize its values. Timothy Powell has described this as 'the struggle to depict the black figure on the white page' (45). It is ironic, Powell argues, that 'Morrison's quest for the black *logos* begins with the consummate example of the *white* text – the Dick-and-Jane reader' (47). Powell focuses on how important this Signifyin(g) confrontation with the *white* text is for the black writer:

> [The Dick-and-Jane reader] is, however, a highly significant beginning, since it points to the fact that all Afro-American writers have, willingly or not,

been forced to begin with the Master's language. The Dick-and-Jane reader comes to symbolize the institutionalized ethnocentrism of the white logos, of how white values and standards are woven into the very texture of the fabric of American life. (48)

And, one might add, American *language*. Certainly, Morrison's afterword to *The Bluest Eye* seems to imply that the exploration of how the dominant white ideology has affected black communities, subjects and culture is part of her attempt to create 'writing that [is] indisputably black':

> The other problem, of course, was language. Holding the despising glance while sabotaging it was difficult. The novel tried to hit the raw nerve of racial self-contempt, expose it, then soothe it not with narcotics but with language that replicated the agency I discovered in my first experience of beauty. Because that moment was so racially infused (my revulsion at what my school friend wanted: very blue eyes in a very black skin; the harm she was doing to *my* concept of the beautiful), the struggle was for writing that was indisputably black. I don't yet know quite what that is, but neither that nor the attempts to disqualify an effort to find out keeps me from trying to pursue it. (211)

'[S]abotaging' the 'despising glance' is presented here as an important stage in the 'struggle for writing that was indisputably black.' Donald Gibson's reading of Morrison's parody as an 'enabling act' is pertinent here. He suggests that Morrison parodies the authenticating document that traditionally introduced slave narratives by starting her novel with the white reading primer, but she does not simply reject the authority implied by the 'act of authentication,' she actually 'seizes' that authority for herself. He sees the gesture as 'the obverse of what in the slave narrative was the act of authentication' because '[t]he superiority assumed by Charles Sumner and Wendell Phillips as authenticators of Frederick Douglass's *Narrative*, for example, is assumed by Morrison herself in her text' (161). Thus, Morrison parodies the way in which African American literature has traditionally been presented in *The Bluest Eye* by prefacing her text with the white reading primer. Although the reading primer repeats the convention of framing the African American's text with authenticating documents by white supporters, friends, and editors,[36] the message of Morrison's frame is entirely different from the intent expressed by the authenticating documents of slave narratives. L. Maria Child, Linda Brent's (pseudonym for Harriet Ann Jacobs) authenticator and editor, assumes the book's readers will be white and urges them to realize the relevance of this slave's narrative to their lives.[37] She hopes it will arouse 'conscientious and reflecting women at the North to a sense of their duty in the exertion of moral influence on the question of Slavery' (4).

Similarly, Lloyd Garrison urges the readers of Frederick Douglass's *Narrative* to realize their affinity with his cause against the un-Christian slaveholders:

> Reader! are you with the man-stealers in sympathy and purpose, or on the side of the down-trodden victims? If with the former, then you are the foe of God and man. If with the latter, what are you prepared to do and dare on their behalf? Be faithful, be vigilant, be untiring in your efforts to break every yoke and let the oppressed go free. (10–11)

In contrast to these prefaces by white authors, which urge the readers to see the common morality between themselves and the slaves, Morrison's preface by a white author – the reading primer – emphasizes the disjunction, difference, even irrelevance of white ideals and society to the black community, while allowing the parallels to show though in full irony. Whereas the authenticating documents by Child and Garrison stress the moral and religious beliefs that the white audience *shares* with the black slave, Morrison stresses the economic *difference* between these groups. Of course, Morrison's most famous refunctioning of slave narratives is her notion of 're-memory' in *Beloved*. As she explains in 'The Site of Memory,' she wanted to 'rip that veil drawn over "proceedings too terrible to relate"' by telling the story that she perceived to be missing from the slave narratives – 'their interior life' (2293). Given just how important her interaction with slave narratives would be for her future writing career, that Morrison started that career by parodying the way they were presented to the public is highly significant.

Morrison's afterword, which she added in 1993, further parodies the extratextual apparatus that was frequently published with early slave narratives. The important contrasts between the slave narrative's authenticating documents and Morrison's afterword reveal her parodic effect. First, the afterwords of slave narratives were usually documents such as letters attesting to the veracity of the slave's account, whereas Morrison's afterword draws attention to the fictional status of her text and to her artistic use of language. Furthermore, Morrison describes her 'struggle . . . for writing that was indisputably black' (211), whereas the ex-slaves apologized for the differences between their language and their white, middle-class audience's language. They frequently requested their audiences to 'excuse deficiencies in consideration of circumstances' (Jacobs 1), and their white editors 'pruned excrescences a little' (Jacobs 2). Morrison's afterword also contrasts with the extra-textual documents of early slave narratives because it asserts the importance of the individual victims of racism. In contrast, many slaves did not want attention for their own individual story but rather wanted their story to excite more general anti-slavery sentiments in its reader. Brent, for example, claims that she does not want to 'attract attention to myself' or 'excite sympathy for my own sufferings' (Jacobs 1). In her afterword, Morrison describes how Claudia's childhood perspective links the marigold seeds' failure to grow with Pecola's stillborn child, drawing the connection between a minor destabilization in seasonal flora and the insignificant destruction of a black girl. Of course 'minor' and 'insignificant' represent the outside world's view – for the girls, both phenomena are earthshaking depositories of information they spend a whole year of childhood (and afterward) trying to fathom, and cannot. (214)

Morrison rejects the outside world's devaluing of Pecola's individual story.

A final difference between Morrison's afterword and the extra-textual apparatus of early slave narratives is that instead of pleading with her reader to feel implicated and involved, as Brent, Child, and Garrison did, Morrison assumes the reader is already and unavoidably implicated:

If [the girls] have any success [trying to fathom the events in the novel], it will be in transferring the problem of fathoming to the presumably adult reader, to the inner circle of listeners. At the least they have distributed the weight of these problematical questions to a larger constituency, and justified the public exposure of a privacy. If the conspiracy that the opening words announce [i.e. 'Quiet as it's kept'] is entered into by the reader, then the book can be seen to open with its close: a speculation on the disruption of 'nature' as being a social disruption with tragic individual consequences in which *the reader, as part of the population of the text, is implicated*. (214; my emphasis)

Morrison's parody of the slave narrative's various appendices attempts to revise how we read African American literature. By drawing attention to the fictional status of her text and to the multiple artistic problems she attempted to solve in the novel, she requires that her reader not treat her text as a simple realistic account of her 'black experience,' but rather as an artistic endeavour, which may or may not, of course, have political and social effects.

To show how Morrison uses parody in *The Bluest Eye* in order to address the theme of African Americans' complicity is not, of course, the same thing as examining Morrison's own complicity as a parodist with the dominant discourse. Donald Gibson argues that Morrison's implication is that complicity is unavoidable:

The implication of the novel's structure is that our lives are contained within the framework of the values of the dominant culture and subjected to those values. We have all (there is reason to believe the author does not exclude herself nor anyone else) internalized those values, and to the extent that we have, we are instruments of our own oppression. (162)

However, Morrison also, to borrow Patricia Yaeger's words, sets 'beside the metaphors that tell us that language is the medium of women's oppression and suffering, images of women who seize words and use them for their own purposes' (6). The very existence of Claudia's narrative implies some degree of success in this attempt to 'seize words.'[38] As we shall see in the following two chapters, this novel is exemplary of the kind of ironic and critical repetition of previous literary texts that is common to women writers of the postmodern period. The next chapter will read Doris Lessing's *The Golden Notebook* as another consummate example of this kind of critical and politically motivated parody. Just as we have seen in *The Bluest Eye,* parody inevitably raises questions about authorial authority. In the case of Lessing's *The Golden Notebook,* the paratexts (to borrow Gérard Genette's word for 'those liminal devices and conventions, both within the book (*peritext*) and outside it (*epitext*), that mediate the book to reader' (xviii)) that have been the focus of the last part of this chapter again emerge as crucial to an understanding of the issues of authority and authorship posed by parody.

Chapter 2

'Some books are not read in the right way':[39] Parody and Reception in Doris Lessing's *The Golden Notebook*

As the previous chapter examining Toni Morrison's parody of the white reading primer in *The Bluest Eye* argued, parody introduces issues of authorship, authority and intention. Nowhere have those issues been more vigorously contested, nor more clearly connected to the workings of parody, than in the reception of Doris Lessing's *The Golden Notebook* (1962) and the preface she added to the novel in 1971. It is a wonderful irony that the reception of *The Golden Notebook* upholds a comment made by its own protagonist, 'that something had happened in the world which made parody impossible' (389). Central to Lessing's intervention in the reception of her novel in her 1971 preface was her desire to make it clear that 'this novel was not a trumpet for Women's Liberation' (8). As Barbara Ellen comments in her 2001 interview with Lessing, 'The interesting thing about Doris Lessing is not that she's not a feminist, but how insistent she is that she's not a feminist' (www.guardian.co.uk). Her repeated public declarations (some of which Ellen describes in her article) that she is not a feminist force us to ask the questions Toril Moi raises in a 2009 article for *Eurozine*: 'Why are some women writers reluctant to acknowledge that they are women writers? How are we to take the claim that "I am not a woman writer"?' (1). Lessing's repeated public statements that she is not a feminist writer echo this claim. This chapter explores Lessing's anger at what she sees as the *mis*readings of her novel. These *mis*readings were related to both her use of parody and her problematic relationship to her feminist readers. Parody, like irony, requires a pre-existing community within which it can be recognized. However, Lessing's relationship to the feminist community of readers who recognized in her a spokesperson for their concerns is one of misunderstanding and mutual frustration.

The Golden Notebook: 'Failure' or 'Masterpiece?'

In *Doris Lessing: Border Crossings*, Susan Watkins and I identify the 'centrality of the metaphor of border crossings to Lessing's life and work' (3). This is what

Lorna Sage in her work on Doris Lessing has termed the 'colonial metaphor' (11) and what Carolyn Heilbrun identifies as 'liminality' in her lecture series *Women's Lives: The View from the Threshold*. Although perhaps transition and liminality can be read as central to all of Lessing's work, it is *The Golden Notebook* that has been positioned by her critics as a particularly transitional work in her *oeuvre*. For example, Ruth Whittaker focuses on the fact that Lessing interrupted her *Children of Violence* series in order to write *The Golden Notebook*. For Whittaker, the most important product of the process of writing *The Golden Notebook* is not *The Golden Notebook* itself, so much as the tools and techniques Lessing acquired from it that would enable her to complete the *Children of Violence* series:

> *The Golden Notebook* is a transitional novel, more about processes than finished products. It is an arduous, painfully creative book, like labour and giving birth, and it marks a distinct change in Lessing as a novelist.... What is born from *The Golden Notebook* are the techniques which will enable Lessing to portray Martha's new growth, which is inaccessible through the conventions of realism. (7; my ellipses)

Thus Whittaker positions *The Golden Notebook* as an exercise in experimentation rather than a successful literary product. Indeed, Lessing herself, asked by Minda Bikman whether she has a favourite novel, describes *The Golden Notebook* as 'the most useful to me personally, as a sort of education' (*Putting the Questions Differently* 63). The negative vocabulary Whittaker uses, such as 'arduous, painfully creative', and her identification of 'a distinct change in Lessing as a novelist' are echoed in Lessing's own comments in the preface concerning her experience of writing the novel:

> I was involved not merely because it was hard to write – keeping the plan of it in my head I wrote it from start to end, consecutively, and it was difficult – but because of what I was learning as I wrote. Perhaps giving oneself a tight structure, making limitations for oneself, squeezes out new substance where you least expect it. All sorts of ideas and experiences I didn't recognize as mine emerged when writing. The actual time of writing, then, and not only the experiences that had gone into the writing, was really traumatic: it changed me. (10)

Lessing's vocabulary, such as 'it was difficult', and 'traumatic', shares the negative tone of Whittaker's analysis.[40] Her image of how a limiting structure 'squeezes out new substance' echoes Whittaker's image of the novel being 'like labour and giving birth'. Lessing also acknowledges that the novel marks a transition in her life and writing.[41]

Whittaker's analysis points to another way in which critics have positioned *The Golden Notebook* as a transitional text. Many view it as the novel in which

Lessing rejects her earlier belief that 'the realist novel, the realist story, is the highest form of prose writing' ('The Small Personal Voice' 8). In this reading, *The Golden Notebook* marks the transition from realism to space fiction in Lessing's *oeuvre*.[42] In the 1980s, critics came to view *The Golden Notebook* as a transition into postmodernism.[43] In focusing on these ways in which *The Golden Notebook* is a transitional text, many of these critics have been more interested in what *The Golden Notebook* transitions from and to than in the liminal space it creates and occupies. Indeed, few critics have explored the paradox that Lessing captures transition and process in a finished literary product.

An interesting result of this positioning of *The Golden Notebook* as a liminal or transitional text has been a number of critical pronouncements that the novel is a failure. Patricia Waugh, for example, has argued that the reader's experience of *The Golden Notebook* parallels Anna's own Laingian 'breakthrough' but that the novel fails to show what is being broken into:

> Through the stylistic dislocation, the parody of social and fictional convention, [the reader] experiences the enlightenment and creative release provided by all successful parody. On one level, of course, the novel is a failure. Doris Lessing has not yet formulated a viable alternative to the traditional novel, nor a viable alternative politics to the male-defined discourses of the Communist Party. She does, however, 'lay bare' their inadequacies and thereby achieves a measure of release which breaks her own writer's block. (77)[44]

Waugh makes a direct link between *The Golden Notebook*'s success as a parody and its failures as a novel. Kate Fullbrook argues that,

> By remaining firmly within what still remains the dominant literary mode, the texture of Lessing's writing gains enormously in its capabilities to communicate with large numbers of readers who are comfortably at home within realist strategies, but it fails to embody the radical questioning that it discursively proposes. (145–6)

Indeed, Fullbrook's final assessment of Lessing's subversive effect is negative: 'In the end, this alliance to the realist temper, if not to realist subject matter, becomes the single most limiting factor undermining Lessing's unarguably impressive and courageous writerly programme' (146).

Lessing herself has promoted this kind of reading of *The Golden Notebook*: that while it is exactly its liminality that results in *The Golden Notebook*'s success as a parody, this liminality is also the mark of its 'failure' as a novel. Lessing states, 'I like *The Golden Notebook* even though I believe it to be a failure because it at least hints at complexity' (*A Small Personal Voice* 88). Similarly, in an interview with Michael Dean, she repeats this idea of the novel's failure: '*The Golden Notebook* was a failure in a formal sense, because as usual I take on too much. It was so ambitious, it couldn't help but fail' (*Putting the Questions Differently* 90).

However, when Dean points out that the novel 'became a great deal more than what you intended it to be', Lessing's reply suggests that the formal 'failure' of the novel is also its success:

> Oh, it spilled all over the place, didn't it? I don't mind because I don't believe all that much in perfect novels. What's marvellous about novels is they can be anything you like. That is the strength of the novel. There are no rules. (*Putting the Questions Differently* 90–1)

Thus, Lessing seems to imply that *The Golden Notebook* only fails according to formal criteria that she actually rejects. Indeed, this is what I find fascinating about the reception of *The Golden Notebook*. As Sarah Crown stated in *The Guardian*'s announcement of Doris Lessing's receipt of the 2007 Nobel Prize, she 'is best known for her 1962 postmodern feminist masterpiece *The Golden Notebook*' (guardian.co.uk). Here we have a Nobel Laureate whose 'masterpiece' is a widely considered a 'failure'. This chapter will argue that understanding *The Golden Notebook* as a parody illuminates this paradox and moves us away from categorizing this novel as the complex, messy afterbirth of Lessing's creation of the new forms of space and science fiction that would dominate her writing for the two decades after its publication. Instead, I will argue with Nick Bentley, that *The Golden Notebook* is 'outside this model of Lessing's writing as linear progression; rather, it stands on its own, as a more radically experimental novel than what comes before or after it' (44). Bentley's positioning of this 'critical fiction' alongside the Marxist literary theories and ideologies of form of the 1950s focuses on precisely the metafictional elements that my focus on the function of parody in the novel attempts to elucidate.

Mainly because most critics see Lessing's use of parody in *The Golden Notebook* as marking the route she took away from realism to her later postmodern narrative strategies and space fiction, parody is rarely viewed as an important mode in itself in Lessing's *oeuvre*. In 1969, G. D. Kiremidjian argued that there had been a reassessment of parody:

> It is not possible to see [parody] as a derivative exercise, or at best as one more item in the artistic bag of tricks; it possesses its own particular autonomy and integrity, and has shown itself very capable of expressing fundamental modes of experience. This reassessment of parody in our own era has led also to a revaluation of the form in relation to the various genres, with the result that we have a sharper appreciation of the pervasive parodism of *Don Quixote*, which stands at the head of the European tradition in the novel. (231)

Despite Kiremidjian's claim, many Lessing scholars have indeed seen parody as 'one more item in the artistic bag of tricks'. Critics have largely failed to recognize the ways in which *The Golden Notebook* is structured by parody's 'own particular autonomy and integrity'. Thus, although critics have often pointed out that 'Free Women' is a parody,[45] the implications of that parodic frame require further exploration.

Doris Lessing's *The Golden Notebook*: A Parody

Lessing creates the sense of having captured process in finished artistic product through the parodic structure of her novel. Her own description of the 'shape of this novel' in her preface is a helpful and concise explanation of its complex structure:

> There is a skeleton, or frame, called *Free Women*, which is a conventional short novel, about 60,000 words long, and which could stand by itself. But it is divided into five sections and separated by stages of the four Notebooks, Black, Red, Yellow, and Blue. The Notebooks are kept by Anna Wulf, a central character of *Free Women*. She keeps four, and not one because, as she recognizes, she has to separate things off from each other, out of fear of chaos, of formlessness – of breakdown. Pressures, inner and outer, end the Notebooks; a heavy black line is drawn across the page of one after another. But now that they are finished, from their fragments can come something new, *The Golden Notebook*. (7)

It is important to note that *The Golden Notebook* opens and closes with sections of 'Free Women' so that the notebooks are indeed 'framed' by 'Free Women'. We do not realize that Anna wrote 'Free Women' until the end of *The Golden Notebook*. This realization forces the reader to reinterpret 'Free Women' with this retrospective knowledge. This circular structure contributes greatly to *The Golden Notebook*'s sense of process. The content of the notebooks also emphasizes the process of writing. They include an unfinished novel, 'The Shadow of the Third', crossed out writing exercises, discussions of Anna's previously published novel, *Frontiers of War*, and parodies of different genres and plots.

As Lessing's preface makes clear, 'Free Women' and the notebooks are juxtaposed against each other in a contradictory relationship which makes the parodic nature of 'Free Women' clear and generates paradoxes. Magali Michael has explored the ways in which Lessing strategically uses the concepts and literary methods that her novel as a whole critiques and rejects.[46] Of 'Free Women', for example, Michael argues that it 'functions both as parody of the conventional novel and as a basis or organizing principle for *The Golden Notebook*' (97). Michael sees Lessing's critique of the conventional feminine novel as separate from her complicit and strategic use of it. As the above consideration of Gates and Hutcheon's theories of parody demonstrated, repetition is a necessary component of parody. Thus, it is helpful to read Lessing's simultaneous *critique* and *use* of the conventional realist novel as two inherent aspects of her parody. The repetition and complicity that are necessary for 'Free Women' to function as a parody are exactly what simultaneously enable it to assist the reader as an organizing principle in *The Golden Notebook*. *The Golden Notebook* demonstrates this paradoxical nature of parody and reveals both the strategic usefulness and the limitations of parody's doubleness.

The notion that the notebooks contain the 'raw material' that is omitted from the conventional novel has been encouraged by Lessing's own comments. For example, in the preface Lessing describes 'Free Women' as 'a summary and condensation of that mass of material' which is presented in the notebooks (13). Similarly, in an interview with Michael Dean, Lessing contrasts the 'five bits of conventional novel' with the notebooks' 'chaos in the middle' and explains: 'One thing I was saying was this feeling of despair, which every writer feels when they've finished a novel, that you haven't been able to say it because life is too complex ever to be put into words' (*Putting the Questions Differently* 90). Lessing's comment does not address the problem that the notebooks are also attempts to put life 'into words'. In contrast, throughout the notebooks Anna constantly addresses this issue. This leads us to the crucial significance of what Mary Eagleton has termed the 'figure of the woman author who appears so frequently and in a number of guises as a character in contemporary fiction' (1).

'Free Women' places a parodic frame around the entire *The Golden Notebook*, thereby raising important questions about the novelist's project and the limitations of language's ability to express experience. As Bentley argues, 'the text does not represent Lessing's working out of a changing attitude to realism but is a critical and philosophical investigation into the nature of fiction itself and the relationship between literary form and politics' (44) and, I would add, the relationship between literary form and lived experiences. As Mary Eagleton argues of the figure of the woman author, although 'one would not want to present all fiction as merely veiled autobiography, the figure of the woman author provides the living author with the opportunities to explore, to some extent at least, her own situation, her aspirations and anxieties' (5). Mark Curie's comments regarding metafiction are pertinent here. In his introduction to his edited collection on *Metafiction*, he questions the accepted definition of metafiction as 'fiction with self-consciousness, self-awareness, self-knowledge, ironic self-distance'. 'It is not enough that metafiction knows that it is fiction; it must also know that it is metafiction if its self-knowledge is adequate, and so on in an infinite logical regress' (1). Therefore, he offers an alternative definition of metafiction that defines it as a 'borderline discourse, as a kind of writing which places itself on the border between fiction and criticism, and which takes that border as its subject' (2). Thus, metafiction can be read, like parody, as a liminal, border crossing genre. Defining metafiction in this way, Currie argues, 'gives metafiction a central importance in the projects of literary modernity, postmodernity and theory' (2). This reading of metafiction echoes very closely Bentley's positioning of *The Golden Notebook* as 'critical fiction'. Indeed, one of the things that Currie sees metafiction taking from criticism is 'a fixation with the relationship between language and the world' (2).[47] This is a central aspect of the examination of the 'nature of fiction itself' that Bentley sees the novel enacting.

Kiremidjian's point that parody has often played a central role in the 'novelist's creative and imaginative processes' (231) is a central theme of the notebooks. Anna produces several set pieces of parody in her notebooks as she tries to work through the relationship between experience and fiction. She seems to turn to parody as a way out of her tendency towards a 'lying nostalgia' she is particularly self-critical of. For example, she writes a parodic synopsis of her own previously published novel (72–4); she parodies a young American's journal (384–6); she also parodies the diary of 'a lady author of early middle-age' and has it accepted by her editor as her own diary (387–9); she includes parodic plot synopses based on her relationship with Saul (467–75); and the aborted novel entitled 'The Shadow of the Third' which dominates the early part of the yellow notebook uses language that is as conventional as that used in 'Free Women'. The cumulative effect of these parodies is that the reader is left highly suspicious of any attempt to express experience through language. The parodies show that all genres have literary conventions that shape and distort the material they are supposed to 'express'. Anna's parody of a lady writer's diary, which is misread as her own, most particularly alerts the reader not to accept Anna's notebooks as straightforward mimetic accounts of reality. This parody highlights the fact that even private genres like diaries and notebooks have conventions that impose themselves upon the experiences the author is trying to convey, and change or falsify them. The notebooks that Lessing describes as the 'chaos in the middle' or a 'mass of material' are narrativized, edited, ordered, and, therefore, falsified accounts of Anna's experiences, just as 'Free Women' is.

Reluctance to recognize the central importance of parody to what Kiremidjian terms 'the novelist's creative and imaginative processes' and the 'denigration' of parody which Linda Hutcheon outlines in the introduction to *A Theory of Parody* (4) have resulted in the negative assessments of Lessing's literary and political achievement in *The Golden Notebook* which I have outlined above. However, if we accept Kiremidjian's claim that parody 'possesses its own particular autonomy and integrity', then parody itself can be seen to be the 'viable alternative to the traditional novel' that Patricia Waugh called for her in her critique of *The Golden Notebook*'s failures (77; qtd above). Indeed, the point Kiremidjian makes about *Don Quixote*'s 'pervasive parodism' forces us to question whether Lessing isn't actually using subversive strategies derived from within the literary canon of the 'traditional novel' itself.

By parodying the conventional realist novel, Lessing positions herself on its threshold. She remains within the tradition of the novel even as she critiques its ideological and aesthetic assumptions. Catherine Belsey argues in *Critical Practice* that: 'To challenge familiar assumptions and familiar values in a discourse which, in order to be easily readable, is compelled to reproduce these assumptions and values, is an impossibility' (4–5). Paradoxically, it appears to be an impossibility that Lessing achieves. *The Golden Notebook* reminds us time and again that, as Belsey argues, '[t]he transparency of language is an illusion' (4), and yet Lessing is still able to use this language to install within her novel a sense of the 'real world'. It is important to acknowledge the ways in which Lessing's position within (even if she is, simultaneously, also without) the realist novel is a compromising one. Fullbrook's negative assessment of this simultaneously critical and complicit position is derived from the assumption that realism is inherently a conservative mode politically, an assumption that Belsey did much to promote and Bentley encourages us to question.

Throughout the novel, the *way* in which Anna tells her story in her notebooks is foregrounded. Her handwriting is described, the annotations and scribblings are noted, and she frequently comments on her own writing. When the inner 'Golden Notebook' informs us that she is the author of 'Free Women' (the conventional novel that frames her notebooks) a further metafictional layer is revealed.[48] One could go as far as to suggest that its main subject matter is itself, its own existence, production, problems, and implications and, indeed, Bentley's essay and Currie's definition of metafiction imply this may be the case.

It is easy to assume that 'Free Women' is an 'objective' account of what 'really happened' by an omniscient narrator, until we learn in the inner 'Golden Notebook' that it was written by Anna herself. As Lessing says in her 2008 online interview with John Mullen, 'Free Women' was 'supposed to be sarcastic'. However, unlike Margaret Atwood's excessive and flamboyant parodies of Gothic novels in *Lady Oracle*, 'Free Women' identifies itself as a parody by being so conventional and limiting. The juxtaposition of Lessing's short conventional sentences in 'Free Women' against the complex mess of Anna's notebooks alerts the reader to the authorial intention to parody. When Lessing does transcribe the less orderly language of conversation in 'Free Women', she always marks it off with inverted commas and repeatedly uses the phrase 'she said' (and variations of it) to indicate who is speaking.

That 'Free Women' is a parody only slowly becomes clear as *The Golden Notebook* progresses. As Patricia Meyer Spacks puts it, 'Five sections of the book bear the title "Free Women", a phrase surrounded by invisible inverted commas of steadily increasing emphasis' (96). An event that is central to 'Free Women' but does not occur in the notebooks is Tommy's attempted suicide. This event illustrates how easy it is to miss the 'invisible inverted commas' around 'Free Women' when reading its early sections. It occurs in 'Free Women 2' when the reader is already halfway through *The Golden Notebook*, and it is not until the next sections of the notebooks that we start to question whether it 'really' occurred. 'Free Women' echoes the novel about the young man attempting suicide that Ella is trying to write in 'The Shadow of the Third'. In the Blue Notebook, Anna records Molly's reaction to Tommy's 'series of lectures on the Life of the Coal-miner' and his marriage to a petit-bourgeois socialist academic who would 'do beautifully as the wife of a provincial businessman with slightly liberal leanings that he uses to shock his Tory friends' (480). Molly says, 'I feel as if I'm living inside a sort of improbable farce' (522). Conversely, in 'Free Women' Molly describes Tommy after his blinding as being 'like he was before, only – confirmed' and 'all in one piece for the first time in his life' (335). Thus the life Tommy leads in the 'true' notebooks appears inauthentic and improbable, while the 'fictional' story of his attempted suicide and blinding in 'Free Women' confirms him and puts him together.[49] Roberta Rubenstein offers a very helpful account of how a similar blurring of the boundaries between 'fictionalized and autobiographical versions of her experiences' is evident in Lessing's fictional and autobiographical accounts of her own experiences in *Home Matters* (17). As Lessing, herself, states in *Under My Skin*: 'There is no doubt fiction makes a better job of the truth' (314). The textual layers in *The Golden Notebook* – 'Free Women', Ella's planned novel in 'The Shadow of the Third', and the Blue Notebooks – confuse the notion of truth and its representation in just the same ways as Lessing's non-fictional and fictional accounts of her own life do in Rubenstein's analysis. Although the headings of the five sections of 'Free Women' are clearly parodic throughout,[50] Lessing does invest this realist novel with a certain degree of truth-telling power. Given that Lessing implies that some aspects of 'Free Women' are more 'true' than what 'really happened', it is not surprising that many critics failed to see Lessing's parodic intent in 'Free Women'.

Lessing's anger in her 1971 preface with the critics who did not 'so much as notice this central theme' of breakthrough (8) and her opinion that 'for the most part the criticism was too silly to be true' (14) has motivated several critics to explore those duplicitous aspects of the novel that encouraged what Lessing identifies as *mis*readings. Clearly, Lessing's preface refers to misreadings of the novel's themes and structure as well as its use of parody. However, parody's ironic strategy of saying what it does not mean did, I believe, particularly encouraged what Lessing viewed as misreadings. Claire Sprague has argued that the opening line immediately confronts the reader with a deception:

> The novel's opening sentence, 'The two women were alone in the London flat', is a perfect example of Lessing simplicities and mysteries. To those who withdraw from her realistic style, the sentence says, 'This is ordinary realism; I can stop reading here; the rest is predictable, without surprises'. *That reading is wrong.* Readers who go on discover how much surprise and unpredictability, how much doubletalk and doubles talk the opening sentence and the novel as a whole contain. Its deceit is most richly apparent when the reader looks back after having read the entire novel. ('Doubletalk and Doubles Talk' 181, my emphasis)[51]

Although Sprague acknowledges that 'misreadings' occurred,[52] she does not clarify whether they were Lessing's fault or the reader's. For example, in the above quotation, she implies that the misreadings were Lessing's fault when she uses the negative word 'deceit' to describe the opening line of the novel. 'Deceit' implies a deliberate motivation on Lessing's part to mislead her readers. Lessing's frustration and regret at the misreadings of her novel in the preface clearly demonstrate that 'deceit' was not her motivation. Sprague also seems to be holding Lessing responsible for encouraging the wrong kind of reader to her novel. The novel opens with a section of 'Free Women'. Therefore, it sets itself up as a realist novel and discourages readers who 'withdraw from her realistic style' from reading any further. However, Sprague's phrase 'That reading is wrong' suggests that errors were made in the *reading* rather than the *writing*. Patrocinio Schweickart clearly 'blames' Lessing for these 'misreadings', suggesting that the failure of critics to consider the shape of the novel is due to the fact that the novel is '*readable* in spite of the odd arrangement of the text' (265).[53] Schweickart focuses on Lessing's failure to take 'effective measures to prevent' misreadings:

> [Lessing] objects vehemently to the misreadings of her novel, but she has not taken effective measures to prevent them. Indeed, she seems to delight in laying traps for her readers. Has she naively miscalculated our predilection to naivete or is she cynically manipulating it? It is also good to remember that Lessing's heroine is keenly aware that the vocation of the writer is suspect, that writing may very well put her in complicity with a contemptible system, that writing and publishing amount to making herself into a commodity to be bought and sold in the marketplace. (276–7)

As Mary Eagleton concludes in her book, the 'figure of the woman author that' emerges from her study 'continues to be caught up in old problems about access to cultural production and anxiety about the kind of values she might be forced either to forfeit or to embrace in the process' (153–4). As we shall see in more detail below, when Anna presents her parody of a synopsis to the film company, she is trying to draw critical attention to these 'old problems' and the 'kind of values' the marketplace upholds. However, the film company does not demonstrate the self-conscious critical distance from itself required to recognize itself as a target of parody. It is certainly a significant irony that Doris Lessing's protagonist in *The Golden Notebook* decides 'that something had happened in the world which made parody impossible' (389), given that *The Golden Notebook* itself is a parody that was initially not read as such.

In *The Golden Notebook* and its preface, Lessing explores how the repetitive element of parody can result in its total mis-recognition. Roberta Rubenstein's ambiguous comment that '*The Golden Notebook* begins conventionally enough, with two women alone in a London flat' is pertinent here (*The Novelistic Vision of Doris Lessing* 73). Of course, Rubenstein's description of this opening line begs the question: 'conventionally enough' for what? I assume that Rubenstein means 'conventionally enough' to be misread as realism in just the way that

Sprague describes – 'This is ordinary realism; I can stop reading here; the rest is predictable, without surprises' (181). Perhaps, therefore, we have to disagree with Rubenstein and say that 'Free Women' does not start 'conventionally enough' to signal the parodic intent of the author. It is only in 'Free Women 5' that the narrative becomes exaggeratedly conventional and therefore clearly parodic. The sentence, 'He was there five days with her, sleeping in her bed at night' (573) in 'Free Women 5' is clearly an inadequate summation of the anxiety, extensive role-playing, and mental breakdown Anna and Saul play out together. Anna's prediction of what Molly will say – 'Not the most sensible thing you ever did' (543) – which is repeated when Molly does 'actually' say it (576), is another clear marker of parody. Saul tells Anna that if Molly does 'button this one up' in this way 'it won't be true', to which Anna replies, '"Possibly not. But I'd like to hear it, all the same"' (543). 'Free Women', therefore, emerges from this interplay between the inner 'Golden Notebook' and 'Free Women 5' as Anna's distorted wish-fulfilment.

The Golden Notebook forces us to question the very possibility of narration and of truth. Having been 'deceived' into reading the opening sections of 'Free Women' as mimetic and truthful accounts of what happened, the reader only slowly becomes aware that 'Free Women' is actually a parody. Lessing means something quite different from what she says. Of course, this question of whether it is possible to narrate the truth is posed as much by Lessing's use of metafiction as by her use of parody. 'Words. Words. I play with words', Anna tells us in 'The Golden Notebook',

> hoping that some combination, even a chance combination, will say what I want. Perhaps better with music? But music attacks my inner ear like an antagonist, it's not my world. The fact is, the real experience can't be described. I think, bitterly, that a row of astericks, like an old-fashioned novel, might be better. Or a symbol of some kind, a circle, perhaps, or a square. Anything at all, but not words. (549)

Critics have taken Anna at her word, explicating the squares of her four notebooks and the circle created by the opening line of the novel. But what does it mean to be told that the 'old-fashioned novel' that orientates and explains the chaos of *The Golden Notebook* to the reader is as meaningless as a 'row of astericks?'

Lessing's use of referential language in *The Golden Notebook* is paradoxical and contradictory. Caryn Fuoroli argues that referential language is 'a limiting but stabilizing element' in the novel, claiming that Lessing accepts the 'paradoxical nature of referential language, that it can be used as a means of overcoming its own simple naming function'. Although Anna moves beyond referential language in the final sections of her notebooks, Fuoroli believes that '*The Golden Notebook* itself never abandons its source in referential language' (146). For Robert Phiddian, although 'it is true that parody, generically in its forms and linguistically in its textuality, works on fundamental assumptions about the nonreferentiality of language and form' what has made it so attractive to contemporary authors is that 'it normally does so cannily, knowing that language *does* connect with the world, mimesis, and intention, however messily' (691). Fuoroli goes on to claim that the referential model of language is the basis of Lessing's control over *The Golden Notebook*: 'it is this firm basis in referential language which provides Lessing with the necessary authorial control over the novel's style and structure' (147). Tommy's use of the word 'good' in his pivotal discussion with Anna in 'Free Women' is a clear example of Lessing's use of referential language as 'a limiting but stabilizing element':

'I know you despise my father. It's because he is not a good man'.
At the word good, Anna involuntarily laughed, and saw his frown. She said, 'I'm sorry, but it's not a word I use'.
'Why not? It's what you mean? My father's ruined Marion and he's ruining those children. Well, isn't he?' (240)

Although Anna laughs at the naivety of the word 'good', Tommy's questions insist that the phrase 'not a good man' says something meaningful and truthful about his father. This moment is a perfect example of parody's canny awareness that 'language *does* connect with the world, mimesis, and intention, however messily' (Phiddian 691). Lessing's continued investment in the referential possibilities of language, even as she joins Anna in laughing at them, is a further demonstration of the way in which *The Golden Notebook* plays out the 'particular autonomy and integrity' (Kiremidjian 231) of parody's doubleness and liminality.

'I have nothing in common with feminists'[54]: Authorship and Authority

The position of Lessing in relation to *The Golden Notebook* has been extensively debated. Fuoroli's image of Lessing in 'authorial control over the novel's style and structure' is an example of those readings that view the complex structure of the novel as evidence of Lessing's ability to control and organize her material.[55] Other readings focus on the chaos created by the complex form of this novel and on the displacement of Lessing's voice by the multiple framing devices and narrators in the novel.[56] Lessing's own lament in her 1972 preface indicates that she does not feel in 'authorial control' of her novel at all. Lessing notes with surprise and dismay that while she may have 'as author, such a clear picture of a book', her readers have seen it 'so very differently' (20).[57] Lessing's reaction to the misreadings of her parody is surprising and ironic given that she explores just such misreadings in *The Golden Notebook* itself. For example, there is the story '[b]y a comrade living somewhere near Leeds' which Anna cannot decide whether to read as 'parody, irony or seriously':

> When I first read it, I thought it was an exercise in irony. Then a very skilful parody of a certain attitude. Then I realized it was serious – it was at the moment I searched my memory and rooted out certain fantasies of my own. But what seemed to me important was that it could be read as parody, irony or seriously. It seems to me this fact is another expression of the fragmentation of everything, the painful disintegration of something that is linked with what I feel to be true about language, the thinning of language against the density of our experience. (273)[58]

Anna's parody of a young American's journal (384) similarly reads uncomfortably like Saul's diary, and is accepted by 'an American little review as the work of a friend too shy to send it himself' rather than as a parody (386). As we have seen, Anna's parody of her own journal is accepted by the editor, Rupert, despite Anna's feeling that it was 'a bit thick'. She has to write to him in the same parodic tone to cancel its publication: 'but unfortunately my rare sensibility overcame me at the last moment and I decided to keep my privacy. Rupert sent me a note saying that he so understood, some *experiences* were too personal for print' (389). Indeed, the editors' repeated failure to recognize that Anna and her friend James are writing parodies leads them to decide 'that something had happened in the world which made parody impossible' (389). That this was Lessing's own experience with *The Golden Notebook* is the fascinating irony which this chapter attempts to illuminate.'

The failure of these parodies to be read as such reveals the dangers for the parodist of the necessary repetitive element of parody. Lessing's position as parodist is fraught with paradoxical advantages and disadvantages. The failure to recognize that a text is parody can result in the total misreading of authorial intention, gravely compromising 'authorial control' (Fuoroli 147). Lessing's preface implies that this is exactly what happened with *The Golden Notebook*. The addition of the preface radically alters the reader's experience of *The Golden Notebook*. When Anna sits down to review her own novel, *Frontiers of War*, 'as if it had been written by someone else' (74), she finds herself writing two completely different reviews. The first describes the novel as it would have been read in 1951, when it was first published. That review points to the 'novelty of its setting' and the 'novelty of its story' (74). In contrast, Anna realizes that if she had reviewed it in 1954, she would have started her review with the sentence, 'The spate of novels with an African setting continues' (75). Criticism of *The Golden Notebook* reveals a similar change from pre- to post-1971. The popularity of metafiction and postmodern notions of the decentred subject, along with Lessing's own statements in the preface concerning the novel's structure and themes, altered readings of *The Golden Notebook* dramatically.

Lessing's anger at the early 'misreadings' of her novel may well have arisen from the ideological implications of such misreadings. *The Golden Notebook* explores the ideological dangers of readers failing to recognize parody when Anna's parodic synopsis of *Frontiers of War* (now retitled *Forbidden Love*) is read as a straightforward proposal by the 'man at the synopsis desk' (74). Anna's parodic intent is marked by linguistic excess and repetition. For example, Peter Carey is 'dashing', 'idealistic and inflammable'; his scholarship at Oxford is described as a 'brilliant scholastic career'; Mrs. Boothby is 'neglected by her hard-drinking, money-loving husband'; and the Cook's wife is 'neglected by her politics-mad husband'.[59] However, the 'man at the synopsis desk' states that it is 'a perfectly good synopsis and written in their terms' (74), meaning that Anna uses the sentimental language preferred by the movie industry. The fact that the 'man at the synopsis desk' is known only by his job title implies a critique of the movie industry's annihilation of individuality. It is the 'terms' that are important, not the experiences that Anna is trying to describe. Anna's attempt to use parody to subvert the sentimental, conservative values of the film industry fails as she is seen to be complicit with its 'terms'. This failure, which she views entirely as a failure of her *reader* (just as Lessing blamed her critics for their misreadings), forces her to become the *reader* of her own novel:

> I came home, conscious of a feeling of disgust so much more powerful than usual, that I sat down and made myself read the novel for the first time since it was published. As if it had been written by someone else. (74)

The result of this reading experience is that Anna is forced to realize that a novel is an incomplete process until it is read and that each reading creates a different interpretation. She realizes that *Frontiers of War* is (at least) two different novels. As noted above, she sees that the novelty that was its strength in 1951 is entirely lost by 1954. Anna realizes the extent to which the position of the reader dictates how the novel is read. Her experience of reading *Frontiers of War* only confirms how difficult it would be to persuade a reader positioned as 'the man at the synopsis desk' to read an overly sentimental synopsis as a parody. He is unable to gain critical distance from what he calls 'their terms' and simply consumes her synopsis uncritically. The text, Anna learns, is limited by the position of its reader. It is strange that Lessing documents her heroine learning this lesson while it took *The Golden Notebook* to teach the same lesson to Lessing herself.

The 'man at the synopsis desk' demonstrates that parody – like irony – requires a particular relationship between the writer and reader. They need to share the knowledge that what is meant is different from what is being said. Feminists wanted to believe they had this kind of relationship with Lessing when they recognized 'Free Women' as a parody. Although Lessing acknowledges that she put 'into print' 'many female emotions of aggression, hostility, resentment' (8–9), she angrily and clearly states, 'this novel was not a trumpet for Women's Liberation' (8). Lessing, therefore, was in what she describes as 'a false position' (8). Those who assumed themselves to be in the community of readers who recognized her parodic intent in *The Golden Notebook* actually failed to notice what Lessing identified as her 'central theme' of breakdown. They 'belittled' her novel by labelling it as being 'about the sex war' or claiming it 'as a useful weapon in the sex war' (8). Lessing's preface demonstrates the complex relationship between the writer and reader of a parody. In *The Golden Notebook*, this relationship is further complicated by the 'figure of the woman author', Anna, who encourages a sense of community with the reader by sharing with us her private notebooks, writing processes and authorial intentions. The shared knowledge required for a text intended as parody to be recognized and read as such indicates the existence of a community. It is not entirely clear, however, whether that community is *created* by the recognition of an intended parody or is a *prerequisite* for this recognition to occur.

Irony requires the same reader recognition as parody does to function successfully, and Linda Hutcheon argues of irony that community pre-exists the recognition of irony:

> No theorist of irony would dispute the existence of a special relationship in ironic discourse between the ironist and the interpreter; but for most, it is irony itself that is said to *create* that relationship. I want to turn that around here, and argue instead that it is the community that comes first and that, in fact, enables the irony to happen. (*Irony's Edge* 89)

To some extent Lessing's comments concerning the reception of *The Golden Notebook* support Hutcheon's argument. She suggests that she made certain assumptions in *The Golden Notebook*, such as 'a woman's way of looking at life has the same validity as the filter which is a man's way' (11). These assumptions were too unusual or radical to remain in the background of the novel. Instead, they were read as the novel's central themes. Lessing suggests that had *The Golden Notebook* been pre-dated by a feminist community that had already changed social assumptions concerning gender, her novel would not have been read as a novel 'about the sex war' (8):

> Some books are not read in the right way because they have skipped a stage of opinion, assume a crystallization of information in society which has not yet taken place. This book was written as if the attitudes that have been created by the Women's Liberation movements already existed. It came out first ten years ago, in 1962. If it were coming out now for the first time it might be read, and not merely reacted to: things have changed very fast. Certain hypocrisies have gone. (9)

Here Lessing implies that the community required to read (as opposed to 'react' to or 'misread') her novel simply did not exist in 1962. However,

Lessing's other comment, that she had put 'into print' 'many female emotions of aggression, hostility, resentment' and that 'what many women were thinking, feeling, experiencing, came as a great surprise' (8–9), suggests that the recognition of Lessing's parodic intent *did* help to create a sense of feminist community. Just as Lessing did not bring these female experiences into being but rather, as she says, 'put them into print' (9), so too did she not so much *create* a feminist community as much as make it more visible. Hence why reading the novel was a 'consciousness raising' experience for so many 1960s readers. However, Lessing's relationship with that community of feminist readers has always been fraught as Susan Brownmiller's account of a talk she gave at the Lexington YMHA in 1969 makes clear:

> When a cult writer is introduced to his/her cult, is it necessarily a painful encounter? An encounter full of surprise and misunderstanding took place last Thursday evening at the Lexington YMHA when Doris Lessing met some vociferous Doris Lessing fans at her first New York public appearance. The expectations of fan and writer collided in a drama that was not without irony.... Prepared to crown a leader, a delegation from the women's liberation movement was thrice refused.... In three separate attempts, an effort was made to have the writer declare herself as a champion of feminism. Lessing, who had previously declared that she was not Martha Quest (the heroine of her quintet of novels, 'The Children of Violence', of which the new book is the final volume), was having none of it. Perplexity gave way to exasperation and then to irony as the women questioners pursued their theme. (218; my ellipses)

Lessing greatly disappointed the feminist community that came out to claim her as their spokeswoman by telling them, 'I'm sorry there are so many unhappy women. But there are a lot more important battles than the sex war' (Brownmiller 219). Lessing's reception seems to confirm Hutcheon's claim that a *pre-existing* community enables irony and parody to happen but the ongoing conflict between Lessing and her feminist readers raises interesting questions about authorial authority and intention. As Barbara Ellen documents in her 2001 article following an interview with Lessing, she has continued to assert that she has 'nothing in common with feminists' (1).[60]

What Lessing seems most upset about in the preface is that the communities that did believe they understood her intent in *The Golden Notebook* were responding only to certain aspects of the novel. As Hutcheon explains of irony's discursive communities:

> The important thing to realize is that we all live in many discursive communities at one and the same time: simultaneously I am Italian Canadian, a teacher, a lapsed Catholic, white, female, middle-class, a spouse but not a

parent, an inept but enthusiastic pianist, an avid cyclist, an opera lover. Any of these could be the basis for a discursive community that would allow me to share with someone else enough background and information to decide on the appropriateness as well as the existence and interpretation of irony. That these different communities might offer conflicting decisions (especially about appropriateness) is part of the complexity of the reception of irony. (*Irony's Edge* 100–1)

What disappointed Lessing was that those who shared one of her many discursive communities – women – were able to read her parody only within their particular discursive community:

Ten years after I wrote it, I can get, in one week, three letters about it, from three intelligent, well-informed, concerned people, who have taken the trouble to sit down and write to me.... But one letter is entirely about the sex war, about man's inhumanity to woman, and woman's inhumanity to man, and the writer has produced pages and pages all about nothing else, for she – but not always a she, can't see anything else in the book.

The second is about politics, probably from an old Red like myself, and he or she writes many pages about politics, and never mentions any other theme.

These two letters used, when the book was as it were young, to be the most common.

The third letter, once rare but now catching up with the others, is written by a man or a woman who can see nothing in it but the theme of mental illness.

But it is the same book.

And naturally these incidents bring up again questions of what people see when they read a book, and why one person sees one pattern and nothing at all of another pattern, and how odd it is to have, as author, such a clear picture of a book, that is seen so very differently by its readers. (20; my ellipses)

Lessing felt that the 'essence of the book, the organization of it, everything in it, says implicitly and explicitly, that we must not divide things off, must not compartmentalize' (10). What Lessing seems to have wished she had in 1962 was a reader who shared the totality of her experiences and discursive communities. Looking back, ten years later, on her anger at the novel's initial reception, Lessing admits that 'over this novel...I lost it' and acknowledges that she was, indeed, wishing for the impossible:

...writers are looking in the critics for an *alter ego*, the other self more intelligent than oneself who has seen what one is reaching for, and who judges you only by whether you have matched up to your aim or not. I have never met a writer who, faced at last with that rare being, a real critic, doesn't lose all paranoia and become gratefully attentive – he has found what he thinks he needs. But what he, the writer, is asking is impossible. Why should he expect this extraordinary being, the perfect critic (who does occasionally exist), why should there be anyone else who comprehends what he is try to do? After all, there is only one person spinning that particular cocoon, only one person whose business it is to spin it.

It is not possible for reviewers and critics to provide what they purport to provide – and for which writers so ridiculously and childishly yearn. (14)

As I have been hinting throughout this chapter, the relationship between the parodist and the reader is an important theme within *The Golden Notebook* itself. In the novel, as we have seen, Anna concludes 'that something had happened in the world which made parody impossible' (389). Her condescending attitude towards her editor Rupert and the man at the synopsis desk who fail to 'get' her parodies supports Mrs. Marks's judgement of Anna: '"My dear Anna, your attitude to art is so aristocratic that you write, when you do, for yourself only"' (417). Lessing's claim 'that writers are looking in the critics for an *alter ego*, the other self more intelligent than oneself' implies a similarly 'aristocratic' attitude to art. Her statement that the writer should not expect there to 'be anyone else who comprehends what he is try to do' echoes John Duvall's critique of how identity politics have tended to function in Toni Morrison studies as a way of limiting who has the authority to read and teach Morrison. Duvall argues that the assumption in Morrison studies is that African American women can understand Morrison's work more accurately than other readers. He goes on to point out that 'the absolute horizon of such a perspective must posit that the only critic who can truly understand Toni Morrison is Toni Morrison. Whatever is political in identity politics would dissolve into the literalized and tantological moment of identity' (7). Lessing's preface is in danger of doing exactly this: implying that the only critic who can truly understand *The Golden Notebook* is herself. As a white male critic of Morrison, Duvall is keen to point out that '[b]eing an African-American woman critic of Morrison may create obstacles as well as advantages to a reading of Morrison and does not ensure correct interpretation' (7). It is important to recognize that this is equally true of a writer's ability to be his/her own critic.

The preface places Lessing's readers in 'a false position' similar to that she found herself in with Women's Liberation movements. The effect of the preface is similar to that of Anna's rejection and correction of her long, detailed account of 15 September 1954. In an attempt to record her life accurately, Anna writes a full account of one day that includes all her emotions and thoughts, as well as events. At the end of the account we learn that she rejected it as a 'failure':

[The whole of the above was scored through – cancelled out and scribbled underneath: No, it didn't come off. A failure as usual. Underneath was written, in different handwriting, more neat and orderly than the long entry, which was flowing and untidy:]
   15th September, 1954
   A normal day. During the course of a discussion with John Butte and Jack I decided to leave the Party. I must now be careful not to start hating the Party in the way we do hate stages of our life we have outgrown. Noted signs of it already: moments of disliking Jack which were quite irrational. Janet as usual, no problems. Molly worried, I think with reason, over Tommy. She has a hunch he will marry his new girl. Well, her hunches usually come off. I realized that Michael has finally decided to break it off. I must pull myself together. (326)

The short entry is offered as a correction, just as Lessing seems to offer her preface as a correction to *The Golden Notebook* as a whole.[61] We read Anna's compelling, detailed account of 15 September before we know that it was crossed out. We are, therefore, confused by her rejection of it.[62] Anna's short correction to the first account leads the reader to ask, 'Were we somehow wrong to enjoy that sensual immersion in pure story?' (Danziger 58). The reader's position in relation to his/her own initially positive encounter with Anna's account of her day is indeed an uncomfortable one, as Marie Danziger explains:

   Anna/Lessing transfers her embarrassment [over wanting to make up stories] to her audience, making us question the ontological and aesthetic value of realistic fiction just as we experience our enjoyment. She entices us with her siren-like powers, and then throws cold water on our enthusiastic response. The effect, though, is hardly playful. It resembles the 'joy in spite' attitude that Anna recognizes *in others* at various points throughout the novel. (58)

The line crossing out the account of 15 September suddenly adds a parodic 'frame' to the account, suggesting that we should have read it with critical distance rather than with the pleasurable empathy it encouraged. The reader does not know whether to disown his/her previous enjoyment of Anna's account of 15 September or to assert that Anna's reading of her own account is the wrong one. Similarly, with the preface – should the reader replace his/her own reading of *The Golden Notebook* with Lessing's 'correct' one? Should the feminist reader's response to Lessing's claim that she is not a feminist writer be to assert, 'But I am a feminist reader?'

The encounter between Tommy and Anna, when he reads her notebooks without her permission, suggests that the relationship between reader and writer may well be antagonistic, a suggestion implicit in Roland Barthes's famous declaration that the birth of the reader is at the expense of the death of the author. Tommy reads *against* Anna's intentions when he reads her notebooks, refusing to ignore what she brackets off as unimportant:[63]

> Sometime later, perhaps as long as an hour, he asked: 'Why do you write things in different kinds of handwriting? And you bracket bits off? You give importance to one kind of feeling and not to others? How do you decide what's important and what isn't?'
> 'I don't know'.
> 'That isn't good enough. You know it isn't. Here you've got an entry, it was when you were still living in our house. "I stood looking down out of the window. The street seemed miles down. Suddenly I felt as if I'd flung myself out of the window. I could see myself lying on the pavement. Then I seemed to be standing by the body on the pavement. I was two people. Blood and brains were scattered everywhere. I knelt down and began licking up the blood and the brains'".
> He looked at her, accusing, and Anna was silent. 'When you had written that, you put heavy brackets around it. And then you wrote: "I went to the shop and bought a pound and a half of tomatoes, half a pound of cheese, a pot of cherry jam, and a quarter of tea. Then I made a tomato salad and took Janet to the park for a walk'".
> 'Well?'
> 'That was the same day. Why did you put brackets around the first bit, about licking up the blood and the brains?'
> 'We all have mad flashes about being dead on the pavement, or cannibalism, or committing suicide or something'.
> 'They aren't important?'
> 'No'.
> 'The tomatoes and the quarter of tea is what is important?'
> 'Yes'.
> 'What makes you decide that the madness and the cruelty isn't just as strong as the – getting on with living?' (246)

Lessing's preface seems to be a similar attempt to 'bracket bits off' and 'decide what's important and what isn't'. Like Tommy's reading of Anna's diaries, it can be fruitful to question why and how these decisions are made. Tommy's enactment of the role of the 'resisting reader' (to borrow Judith Fetterley's description of the feminist reader) can function as a model for the reader of *The Golden Notebook*.

Indeed, Lessing's preface seems to contradict her own anti-authoritarian philosophy of reading and education. She tells the student who writes to her requesting a list of articles or books about her work, 'why don't you read what I have written and make up your own mind about what you think, testing it against your own life, your own experience. Never mind about Professors

White and Black' (17). Yet in this same piece Lessing tells her feminist readers who did read her novel in this way and found her comments on gender relations to be the most significant to them, that they are wrong. She dictates to her readers *how* her novel should be read.[64] Even the positioning of the preface as a preface as opposed to an afterword such as Morrison appended to *The Bluest Eye*, places Lessing's comments in a position of authority over readings of her novel. All post-1972 readers are told first how to read *The Golden Notebook* before they encounter the text itself. Lessing discourages readers from being able to 'read what I have written and make up your own mind about what you think' in the very same preface in which she upholds this reading strategy. Margaret Atwood instructs readers,

> Pay no attention to the facsimiles of the writer that appear on talkshows, in newspaper interviews, and the like – they ought not to have anything to do with what goes on between you, the reader, and the page you are reading, where an invisible hand has previously left some marks for you to decipher. (*Negotiating with the Dead* 125–6)

This is difficult to do when the writer inserts herself between you and her text in the authoritative manner in which Lessing does in this preface.

The reading experience of being informed that Anna's account of 15 September has been crossed out parallels that of realizing the full parodic intent of 'Free Women'. Repetition and critique, what is said and what is implied, coexist in a parody. Which should the reader privilege – Anna's account or the line crossing it out? The reader has to recognize both. He/she cannot *un*read the account just read. Similarly, it is important to recognize that 'Free Women' generates meaning and coherence, even as it critiques and rejects that meaning and coherence. Certainly, the reader's own position will be an important factor in his/her decision over which aspect of 'Free Women's parody to value more – its complicit use of realism or its rejection of realism's claims to mimesis. Lessing finishes her preface with an acceptance of this:

> ...it is not only childish of a writer to want readers to see what he sees, to understand the shape and aim of a novel as he sees it – his wanting this means that he has not understood a most fundamental point. Which is that the book is alive and potent and fructifying and able to promote thought and discussion *only* when its plan and shape and intention are not understood, because the moment of seeing the shape and plan and intention is also the moment when there isn't anything more to be got out of it. (20–1)

This comment seems to cross out Lessing's commentary concerning the novel's meaning and themes as resolutely as Anna's scoring through her account of 15 September. Thus the preface mirrors Lessing's use of parody in 'Free Women': both texts express meaning in the same contradictory way as Anna's account of 15 September. Lessing simultaneously writes and crosses it out, installs and subverts, refusing to privilege one impulse over the other. In this way her novel demonstrates the 'particular autonomy and integrity' of parody which Kiremidjian insisted upon. *The Golden Notebook* upholds Kiremidjian's claim that parody does show 'itself very capable of expressing fundamental modes of experience' (231).

The Golden Notebook is a threshold or liminal novel, but not because it marks a transitional phase in the development of Lessing's style from realism to space fiction. Rather, as Nick Bentley argues, 'it stands on its own, as a more radically experimental novel than what came before or after it' (44). Its liminality is derived from its genre – parody – which is inherently liminal, always 'within and without, simultaneously enchanted and repelled' (Fitzgerald 37). As a metafictional novel it also occupies the threshold between fiction and criticism as Mark Curie's definition of metafiction makes clear and Bentley's designation of it as a 'critical fiction' confirms. Furthermore, all post-1972 readers of the novel will encounter it via the paratext of the preface. As Gérard Genette's title makes clear – *Paratexts: Thresholds of Interpretation* – this genre is also a liminal one. In addition to these threshold genres this novel also has an author and a figure of a woman author who both write but then cross out, write only for themselves but then share their work, live as feminists but then do 'matrimonial welfare work' (Lessing, *The Golden Notebook* 576) or repeatedly declare 'I have nothing in common with feminists' (Ellen 1).[65] Hence, it becomes clearer why this Nobel Laureate's 'masterpiece' has also been called a 'failure'.

Chapter 3

Parodic Self-Narratives: Margaret Atwood's *Lady Oracle* and *The Blind Assassin*

In her essay entitled 'On Being a "Woman Writer": Paradoxes and Dilemmas,' Margaret Atwood describes how women of her generation 'had to defy other women's as well as men's ideas of what was proper' in order to write:

> Most writers old enough to have a career of any length behind them grew up when it was still assumed that a woman's place was in the home and nowhere else, and that anyone who took time off for an individual selfish activity like writing was either neurotic or wicked or both, derelict in her duties to a man, child, aged relatives or whoever else was supposed to justify her existence on earth. I've heard stories of writers so consumed by guilt over what they had been taught to feel was their abnormality that they did their writing at night, secretly, so no one would accuse them of failing as housewives, as 'women'. These writers accomplished what they did by themselves, often at great personal expense; in order to write at all, they had to defy other women's as well as men's ideas of what was proper.... (*Second Words* 191)

In *Lady Oracle* and *The Blind Assassin*, Atwood tells the stories of two such writers. It may be because Atwood felt that the life story of becoming a writer was not available to women that she has been so concerned to present women writers in her novels, or at least to present women as the narrators of their own experiences. As Ellen McWilliams notes, 'From an early stage in her writing career, Margaret Atwood shows a striking interest in the fate of the female artist and author in Canada' (114). This chapter will focus on *Lady Oracle* and *The Blind Assassin*, two novels in which the female protagonists are writers. Both Joan Foster and Iris Chase-Griffen are the authors of previously published works just like Anna in Lessing's *The Golden Notebook*. Joan's list of publications is substantial. It includes a series of Gothic Romance novels published under a pseudonym and a poem constructed out of her automatic writing experiments which lends its title to the novel as a whole and to which she (disastrously) attached her own name. Iris Chase Griffen is the author of the scandalous 'The Blind Assassin'[66] which she published under her sister Laura's name. The whole of Iris's previously published novel 'The Blind Assassin' is reproduced within Atwood's novel, and parts of Joan's previous publications are included in *Lady Oracle*. Atwood presents these two authors' attempts to go back over their lives and write their most difficult narratives to date – their life stories. Both women cross the thresholds of their domestic houses in order to enter the house of fiction.

The history of women's increasing power over their own life stories and, most particularly, their recent interactions with the genre of autobiography is very usefully summarized in the chapter entitled 'Turning the Century on the Subject' in Sidonie Smith's *Subjectivity, Identity and the Body*. Smith identifies the twentieth century as a turning point in the genre of autobiography. The twentieth century was marked by a growing concern with human consciousness and subjectivity, which led to more autobiographies being written by a wider variety of authors. Partly due to developments in the distribution of books, these autobiographies are finally finding large audiences of understanding readers:[67]

> Surely, traditional autobiographical forms have been complicit with the reification of a certain kind of western subject. Configured as white, middling, and male, the old self overrode white middle-class women, working-class men and women, and men and women of color, who, if they wrote autobiography at all, spoke mutedly, circumspectly, and still could not be sure that their 'lives' would be read or readable.... Nor could diverse peoples always maneuver their stories inside the lines of the provided subjectivities and the provided narratives culturally available to them.... When newly articulate autobiographical subjects come to write, they not only enter a generic engagement through which they recapitulate the contours of subjectivity promoted in dominant discourses; they also speak as 'unauthorized subjects' who are pulled and tugged into complex and contradictory subject positions. Moreover, they fashion and refashion, then fine tune various identities through which they make meaning out of their experiences. Their maneuverings within their unauthorized positions and their engagement in fluid entanglements with subjectivity, identity, and narratives have often resulted in unconscious or conscious interrogations of traditional autobiography and its autonomous, free, coherent self, interrogations that position them to take advantage of this time [i.e., the late twentieth century] of generic instability. (61–2; my ellipses)

I have quoted at length because this theoretical and historical account of how marginalized groups have interacted with the genre of autobiography is a fruitful one to place alongside *Lady Oracle* and *The Blind Assassin*. While these texts are not actual autobiographies, they dramatize the moment when their central characters become 'newly articulate autobiographical subjects.' Atwood explores the theory, practice and politics of female autobiography through her female characters' encounters with this genre. These novels simultaneously repeat and critique 'traditional autobiographical forms.' Indeed, the relation between these novels and traditional autobiography can be defined as parodic. Georges Gusdorf defined the task of autobiography thus: 'Autobiography... requires a man to take a distance with regard to himself in order to reconstitute himself in the focus of his special unity and identity across time' (35). Iris and Joan seem purposely to disrupt this 'special unity.' They offer their readers fragments of texts, they describe multiple versions of themselves, and they jump between the past and the present moment, never achieving a consistent 'distance with regard to' themselves. Their 'maneuverings' certainly do result in 'interrogations of traditional autobiography and its autonomous, free, coherent self' which have implications and applications beyond the limits of these novels.

Roxanne Fand in her study *The Dialogic Self,* reads Margaret Atwood's short prose piece entitled 'The Page' (1983) as a key to the model of subjectivity evident in Atwood's novels.[68] 'This piece,' Fand argues, 'not only reveals the hazards of a writer facing the uncreated selves of her fiction on the blank page, but the human being facing the blank self upon which experience is inscribed' (165–6). Fand's emphasis here is on the blankness of the page and, by implication, of the self. She goes on to interpret *Lady Oracle* as a novel in which she says, 'the heroine is something of a blank page to herself, but by going through a redefining experience... manages to inscribe something meaningful that at least gives her enough direction not to become totally lost' (168). While I would agree with Fand that Joan's textual strategies save her from annihilation and return us to the issues of writing and survival that I discussed in relation to African American writers in the first chapter, I would question whether it really is the 'blankness' of her self which is most threatening. Atwood says in the opening line of 'The Page': 'The page waits, *pretending* to be blank' (*Murder in the Dark* 55, my emphasis). She suggests that 'The question about the page is: what is beneath it?' Her answer identifies a discourse which always already fills the blankness of any page: '*Beneath the page* is another story. Beneath the page is a story. Beneath the page is everything that has ever happened, most of which you would rather not hear about' (56). Thus, Atwood indicates that what is already inscribed on the page is more threatening than its blankness, an idea she echoes in her piece entitled 'If You Can't Say Something Nice, Don't Say Anything at All.' This piece was written in response to Carol Shields and Marjorie Anderson's invitation to write something that would fill in, or at least identify, the 'gaps between female experience and expression' (vii). Atwood's piece reveals her to be far more disconcerted by limiting things she *was* told, than by 'things that were not openly discussed' (136). I am certainly not attempting to argue that Atwood's novels are autobiographical (an assumption Atwood hates her readers making). However, it does seem that she shares with her heroines, Iris and Joan, a desire to contest what is 'beneath the page.' In *Surfacing* this desire emerges as nostalgia for a blank page. The protagonist wants to regress to a prelinguistic condition. In *The Blind Assassin* and *Lady*

Oracle, the attempt to contest what has already been inscribed upon the page is evident in the multiplicity of the texts. These novels acknowledge the influence of what is 'beneath the page.' Their protagonists install those narratives into their own life stories, and then contest them by subverting, parodying and contradicting them.

One important source for narratives of the socially sanctioned '"right", "normal" ways to be women,' is, of course, popular fiction. Atwood's insistence on the negative impact on women writers of 'other women's as well as men's ideas of what was proper' is pertinent here. As Daphne Watson points out in her aptly titled *Their Own Worst Enemies*, women writers of popular fiction have 'described women in terms of stereotypical behaviour patterns' (1) as much, if not more, than men have. Watson calls on women writers to replace those popular fictions which 'confirm the reader in her view of herself as society would like her to be' (13) with fictions that reassure female readers 'that they have rights, to individuation, to the realisation of self apart from societal demands and especially male expectation' (130). Watson's assumptions here about popular fiction and feminism have been widely disputed and discussed, as we shall see in Chapter 5 when we look at Imelda Whelehan's work on *The Feminist Bestseller* and Diana Wallace's study of *The Woman's Historical Novel*.

The dream of realizing the self 'apart from societal demands' is one that Atwood explores in *Surfacing*, but finally rejects as untenable. Atwood has learnt a lesson taught by postmodernism:

> Wilfully contradictory, then, postmodern culture uses and abuses the conventions of discourse. It knows it cannot escape implication in the economic (late capitalism) and ideological (liberal humanist) dominants of its time. There is no outside. All it can do is question from within. (Hutcheon, *A Poetics of Postmodernism* xiii)

As Eleanora Rao argues more specifically of *Lady Oracle* it 'revisits the past ironically, rewriting it, quoting and parodying different kinds of genre and literature, using popular fiction to produce a non-escapist text' (*Strategies for Identity* 28):

> Atwood's ironising of women's Gothic Romance fiction makes *Lady Oracle* a compelling and unsettling novel. Writing within and against the limits of the genre, exploiting and challenging its norms, she interrogates its stereotypes of womanhood as she explores the compensatory function of so-called escapist literature. ('Margaret Atwood's *Lady Oracle*' 133)[69]

While this chapter is indebted to studies like that by Rao,[70] which relate Joan's parody of popular fiction to her invention of a subversive and multiplicitous identity, it is also concerned with the real problem of agency for the decentred self. I will show how parody offers the main female characters – Joan and Iris – a strategy for negotiating their decentred sense of self while maintaining an effective degree of agency. Atwood uses parody in these novels to express the multiplicity of these characters' subjectivities, while simultaneously inscribing the very real threat the discourses of others pose to those subjects.

The Blind Assassin takes up this project where *Lady Oracle* concludes. (Joan's statement at the end of *Lady Oracle* that she will 'try some science fiction' [345] amusingly suggests this progression to the exploration of science fiction in *The Blind Assassin*.) By the end of *Lady Oracle*, Joan is finally able, through critical parody, to resist being seduced by the 'compensatory function of so-called escapist literature' as Rao calls it, and she contests her husband Arthur's version of her by 'refunctioning' his value system. Atwood depicts Joan privately narrating her life story to the reporter in hospital at the end of *Lady Oracle* but she does not show how or whether Joan's narrative reaches the public stage. Joan is clearly alienated from her public image as the suicidal authoress of the poem 'Lady Oracle.' The novel does not tell us whether the private narrative she offers to the reporter does anything to alter or contest that public image. In *The Blind Assassin* this relation between private narrative and public image is brought centre stage. Through writing their life narratives, both Joan and Iris question their relation to pre-existing discourses of femininity and the social roles they are expected to play. They wonder about themselves just as Atwood did when she set out on her writing career, and come to similar conclusions to those expressed in her piece for Shield and Anderson's anthology: 'We spent a lot of time wondering if we were "normal". Some of us decided we weren't. Ready-to-wear did not quite fit us. Neither did language' (Atwood 'If You Can't Say Something Nice, Don't Say Anything at All' 136).[71]

'Make a mess': Joan Foster's Excessive Self-Narrative

In the opening paragraph of *Lady Oracle* Joan Foster describes how her 'carefully' planned death contrasts with her meandering life, and she expresses the desire to tidy up her life after this 'death' (3). Immediately after her arrival in Terremoto, signalling the success of this 'death,' Joan attempts several rebellious acts against her husband, Arthur. She cuts her hair in the hope that one day she would be able to pass Arthur in the street and 'he wouldn't even recognize [her]' (20), she buys a picture from her landlord which she knows Arthur would dislike and she drinks too much Cinzano. All these acts result in a mess – her hair gets 'shorter and shorter, though no less uneven' (10), the picture is 'blood-red,' 'vulgar,' and full of 'noise and tumult' (15) and the Cinzano results in not quite a hangover but a feeling of not wanting to get up 'too suddenly' (17). These failed rebellions leave Joan in tears, but Joan does go on to make a resolution: 'I couldn't let Arthur go on controlling my life, especially at such a distance. I was someone else now, I was almost someone else' (20). However, the process of 'becoming someone else' is not a simple one for Joan, as the correction 'I was *almost* someone else' implies. It is not only a case of escaping from Arthur to find her own 'authentic voice.' As Molly Hite points out, although the 'confessional' narrative mode of this novel suggests that Joan will tell her story from her own view point, in telling that story 'she is immediately implicated in describing her own situation under the gaze of others; of the people who variously constitute her according to their own requirements' (127). Like Anna in *Surfacing*, Joan appears to lack an original core but, instead, is

> a seamed and folded imitation of a magazine picture that is itself an imitation of a woman who is also an imitation, the original nowhere, hairless lobed angel in the same heaven where God is a circle, captive princess in someone's head. (*Surfacing* 159)

With the 'original' lost, how can Joan reconstruct herself?

I will focus on how Joan is 'constitute[d]' to conform to her husband Arthur's 'requirements,' but it is important to acknowledge that he is not the only one to exert this type of pressure on Joan.[72] As I suggest in my reading of 'The Blank Page' above, rather than being an account of how Joan fills the 'blank page' of her self, *Lady Oracle* describes what is 'beneath the page' by showing how Joan's identity has been written and formed by the expectations of others. Joan looks into her life and sees what the heroine of *Surfacing* sees when she looks into David:

> The power flowed into my eyes, I could see into him, he was an imposter, a pastiche, layers of political handbills, pages from magazines, *affiches*, verbs and nouns glued on to him and shredding away, the original surface littered with fragments and tatters. (*Surfacing* 146)

Atwood does not suggest that Joan can ever escape from the 'pastiche,' from what lies 'beneath the page.' The dream of a 'blank page,' which seems to drive the heroine of *Surfacing* into her animal-like state, is an impossible one for Joan. However, through self-parody and the construction of a self-narrative (no matter how disjointed that narrative may appear), it becomes possible for Joan to alter her relationship to those layers, pages, verbs and nouns, and even to select which she will value and retain. In her reading of *Lady Oracle*, Fand suggests a solution to Joan's dilemma over her selfhood. She argues that 'If Joan were capable of writing herself out of this endless maze, she might develop a polyphony of voices, *including* the satirical and the romantic, but not be limited to them' (196). This reading does not view the novel itself as part of Joan's journey 'out of this endless maze.' My reading puts great emphasis on Joan's position as author of this narrative. Polyphony and excess are crucial characteristics of this text. Through her reconstructive mental journey back over her life, Joan succeeds in changing her initial desire for 'Arthur to know how clever [she]'d been' (23) in arranging her own death into the defiant sentiment in the last sentence of the novel that she does not expect she will 'ever be a very tidy person' (345). She may not write herself completely out of the maze,[73] but she does replace Arthur's negative judgement of the maze with her own more positive one through her 'refunctioning'[74] of the value system implied by the word 'mess.' This refunctioning parallels the African American refunctioning of 'funk' which I examined in Chapter 1 in relation to Toni Morrison's *The Bluest Eye*.

Joan views her own life as marked by excess and mess. 'My life,' she tells us in the opening paragraph, 'had a tendency to spread, to get flabby, to scroll and festoon like the frame of a baroque mirror' (3). As Mary Eagleton notes, '"excess of signification" is there in everything Joan writes, thinks does or is' (128). Her overweight childhood is a mark of this excess which, as many critics have noted, follows her as a ghost throughout her life.[75] 'Excessive' also seems to be an appropriate description of this novel which is constructed out of all types of genres, such as the murder mystery, the popular Gothic and the confessional, as well as several different texts, including excerpts from Joan's Gothic novels, parts of her poem 'Lady Oracle,' and film synopses.[76] As Susanne Becker usefully describes, 'excess' is a mark of the Gothic genre, and the manifestations of this 'excess' have been theorised as signs of the Gothic's parodic relationship to realism:

> 'Excess' is one of the terms most frequently, and most pejoratively, used in established gothic criticism: 'excess' in moral, but also in formal, terms....Mockery, irony, reconciliation: the terminology strongly evokes the workings of parody. Contemporary gothic criticism has emphasised the parodic implications of gothic excess, and reformulated the established, mostly New Critical, view of the gothic as allegorical form. For example, William Patrick Day writes: 'The relationship of the Gothic to the conventional world, and to the literary forms from which it derives, can best be described as parodic...' (Becker 25–6)

Joan's Gothic Romances are particularly excessive and parodic. For example, consider her descriptions of her character Felicia:

> By her red hair [Charlotte] recognized Felicia, who was wearing a very costly morning costume of blue velvet, trimmed with white ostrich feathers at the throat and cuffs, with a dashing hat to match. Her hands were concealed in an ermine muff, and as she threw back her head to laugh once more, the sunlight glimmered on her milky throat and her small teeth. (127–8)

> She was wearing a dark cloak, thrown loosely over a sumptuous costume of flaming orange silk, with blue velvet trim. (193)

The words describing Felicia's excess – 'dashing,' 'threw back,' 'sumptuous,' 'flaming' – are in themselves excessive. Furthermore, the attention to what these costumes is 'trimmed' with reminds us of Joan's description of how she learnt to write Gothic novels. The derivative[77] structure of parody is closely allied with Joan's method for writing her first novel, in that it was highly indebted to other Costume Gothics and descriptions of Victorian clothes:

> I asked Paul to get me some samples of historical romances from Columbine Books, his publisher, and I set to work. I joined the local library and took out a book on costume design through the ages. I made lists of words like 'fichu' and 'paletot' and 'pelisse';[78] I spent whole afternoons in the costume room of the Victoria and Albert Museum, breathing in the smell of age and polished wood and the dry, sardonic odor of custodians, studying the glass cases and the collections of drawings. I thought if I could only get the clothes right, everything else would fall into line. And it did.... (156)

Exaggeration is a frequent marker of both parody and the Gothic and Joan's parodic Gothics overflow with it. Thus the very form of *Lady Oracle* can be seen as a celebration of excess.

As Joan makes clear early on in the novel, her excess and messiness are things for which Arthur criticised her. Therefore, her creation of an excessive self-narrative, which parodies Arthur's attempts to contain her, is an important strategic move in her attempt to gain independence and agency. In the opening line of the novel, Joan contrasts her 'careful' death with her 'flabby' life.[79] Her planned death emerges as something she is proud of and she believes Arthur would have been surprised and admiring of its tidiness:

> It was a good plan, I thought; I was pleased with myself for having arranged it. And suddenly I wanted Arthur to know how clever I'd been. He always thought I was too disorganized to plot my way across the floor and out of the door, much less out of the country. I was the one who would charge off to do the shopping with a carefully drawn-up list, many of the items suggested by him, and forget my handbag, come back for it, forget the car keys, drive away, forget the list; or return with two tins of caviar and a box of fancy crackers and a half bottle of champagne, then try to justify these treasures by telling him they were on sale, a lie every time but the first. I would love him to know I'd done something complicated and dangerous without making a single mistake. I'd always wanted to do something he would admire.[80] (23)

The sentence describing her failed shopping trip overflows. Its seven commas and one semicolon alert us to its excessive subclauses. Any attempt to read the sentence out loud makes this amply clear. However, because many of these subclauses add humour to our reading experience, we actually enjoy those aspects of herself that she is criticizing. Her hyperbolic use of the word 'charge' to describe her leaving the house, the repetition of 'forget,' her detailed specifics of the luxury items she returns with ('*two* tins of caviar' and 'a *half bottle* of champagne') and the final subclause admitting that her claim that these items were in the sale was 'a lie every time but the first,' all add to the pleasure of our reading experience, which encourages us to sympathise with Joan. Far from censoring her for her messiness, we delight in her accounts of it. As Becker argues in relation to the excess of Gothic literature, Atwood forces us to acknowledge the pleasurable aspect of excess:

> I hope to show 'excess' as a pleasurable but also subversive gothic strategy, the emotionalising centre of the gothic's provocation as well as of its ongoing intertextualisation. *Lady Oracle*'s self-conscious postmodern play with gothicism especially highlights these possibilities of excess. (25)

The sentence I was just exploring from *Lady Oracle* demonstrates exactly 'these possibilities of excess.' The sentence's excesses not only increase the pleasure of the text but also alert the reader to the possible presence of parody. Joan's description of her shopping escapades is a self-parody, and, as Kim Worthington notes, self-parody is a step towards revising the self:

> ...self-parody is a potentially revisionary stance, one which, if possible, invalidates claims that we are merely passive victims embedded in the false 'reality' we inhabit, without the capacity to evaluate or change the prescriptive illusions it foists on us. If we are able to laugh *at* ourselves and our purported existential dilemma of ideological entrapment, then we are already some way out of it. (288)

Joan's self-parody implies that she is no longer prepared to accept the role of the incompetent wife. Throughout the novel, Joan increasingly reveals how much she acted out a part written for her by Arthur. For example, Joan describes how she started to cook because Arthur expected it. To start with her meals were not wholly successful but she came to realise that Arthur 'enjoyed [her] defeats':

> My frustration and anger were real, but I wasn't that bad a cook. My failure was a performance and Arthur was the audience. His applause kept me going.
> That was all right with me. Being a bad cook was much easier than learning to be a good one, and the extra noise and flourishes didn't strain my powers of invention. My mistake was in thinking that these expectations of Arthur's were confined to cooking. It only looked that way at first, because as far as he could tell I attempted nothing else. (211–12)

When the publication of her poem 'Lady Oracle' reveals to Arthur her considerable 'powers of invention' and (in his interpretation) her negative attitude to their marriage, he censors her. Although Joan denies Arthur's interpretation that her poem is a feminist critique of her marriage, the descriptions of her married life do not seem happy. They show Joan acquiring a set of deficiencies which Arthur and his friends expected her to have: 'I got a reputation for being absentminded, which Arthur's friends found endearing. Soon it was expected of me, and I added it to my repertoire of deficiencies' (218). This habit of developing a 'repertoire of deficiencies' and of limiting herself in order to conform to Arthur's notion of who she is clearly demonstrates the potential dangers of her multiple and fluid subjectivity. However, even in assuming these deficiencies we come to suspect that Joan did exert subtle power. For example, in the description of her chaotic shopping trips, the forgotten shopping list contained many items suggested by Arthur. Her construction of a messy, absent-minded, irresponsible identity allows her to bring home the 'two tins of caviar and a box of fancy crackers and a half bottle of champagne' instead of the items Arthur requested. Her lie about the sale echoes her other secret linguistic constructions – her Gothic novels – the income from which ironically paid for the champagne and caviar! Her ability to do 'something complicated and dangerous without making a single mistake' indicates that her inabilities were strategic rather than real. However, her repeated desire for 'Arthur to know how clever I'd been' indicates that at this stage in the novel she has not escaped from his control over her identity; nor has she started to question his value system.

A comparison between the self which Joan constructs in *Lady Oracle* and that which the unnamed protagonist in *Surfacing* discovers may help to clarify the strategic importance of parody in Joan's self-construction. In *Surfacing*, Atwood seems to present an essentialist model of the self. The protagonist experiences an epiphany, which reveals to her aspects of her past that she has suppressed and forgotten. When diving in the lake trying to find the Indian rock drawings that her father has marked on a map, the protagonist sees something 'blurred' with open eyes. It is 'something [she] knew about, a dead thing, it was dead' (136). This unclear 'something' brings memories flooding back:

> It formed again in my head: at first I thought it was my drowned brother, hair floating around the face, image I'd kept from before I was born; but it couldn't be him, he had not drowned after all, he was elsewhere. Then I recognized it: it wasn't ever my brother I'd been remembering, that had been a disguise.
>
> I knew when it was, it was in a bottle curled up, staring out at me like a cat pickled; it had huge jelly eyes and fins instead of hands, fish gills, I couldn't let it out, it was dead already, it had drowned in air. It was there when I woke up, suspended in the air above me like a chalice, an evil grail and I thought, Whatever it is, part of myself or a separate creature, I killed it. It wasn't a child but it could have been one, I didn't allow it. (137)

Following her indirect description of going on her own to a 'shabby' house for an abortion, the surfacer admits:

It was all real enough, it was enough reality for ever, I couldn't accept it, that mutilation, ruin I'd made, I needed a different version. I pieced it together the best way I could, flattening it, scrapbook, collage, pasting over the wrong parts. A faked album, the memories fraudulent as passports; but a paper house was better than none and I could almost live in it, I'd lived in it until now. (137–8)

Her rejection of her previous narratives of herself is evident in her images of fake and fraudulent paper images. She withdraws from what Worthington terms the 'communicative matrix' (304). The protagonist of *Surfacing* rejects language, symbolized here by the images of paper, claiming that 'language divides us into fragments, I wanted to be whole' (140).[81] She refuses to be represented by Joe and David in the same way as they represented Anna, so she feeds their film into the lake, destroying it. Withdrawing from society, she leaves the cabin, destroys her clothes, and does not respond to her friends' calls for her. This experience allows her to communicate with 'them,' whom we assume to be her dead parents: 'They were here though, I trust that. I saw them and they spoke to me, in the other language' (182). This 'other language' suggests communication beyond everyday language and echoes the French feminist theory of *l'écriture féminine*. Feminist theorists who developed this theory[82] described it as writing from female sexuality. The surfacer's nakedness and belief that she is pregnant[83] indicate that she does see her own body as a source of resistance to the 'American' condition of the contemporary world. As Ann Rosalind Jones suggests in her useful essay, 'Writing the Body: Toward an Understanding of *l'Écriture féminine*,' 'to the extent that the female body is seen as a direct source of female writing, a powerful alternative discourse seems possible: to write from the body is to re-create the world' (366). However, Jones goes on to ask an important question: 'Can the body be a source of self-knowledge?' (367). Her further questions and ensuing answer warn us that 'the other language' may be limited as a solution to the surfacer's condition:

> Does female sexuality exist prior to or in spite of social experience? Do women in fact experience their bodies purely or essentially, outside the damaging acculturation so sharply analyzed by women in France and elsewhere? The answer is no, even in terms of the psychoanalytic theory on which many elements in the concept *fémininité* depend. Feminists rereading Freud and Jacques Lacan and feminists doing new research on the construction of sexuality all agree that sexuality is not an innate quality in women or in men; it is developed through the individual's encounters with the nuclear family and with the symbolic systems set into motion by the mother-father pair as the parents themselves carry out socially imposed roles toward the child. (367)

The surfacer is revisiting her 'encounters with the nuclear family' and coming to terms with her own failure to achieve that social unit. She also realises that she cannot survive with the child on the island: 'if I die it dies, if I starve it starves with me. It might be the first one, the first true human; it must be born, allowed' (185). To stay will be to repeat the earlier forgotten narrative of the abortion because it will kill her child. Her child needs a 'mother-father pair.'

Atwood demonstrates her awareness of the limitations of this model of female subjectivity when she returns her heroine to the cabin. The 'escape into a "wilderness" beyond the repressive prescriptions of familial and social communities and the constraints of patriarchal language' (Worthington 278) may appear to fulfil Watson's call for women's rights to 'the realisation of self apart from societal demands' (130), which I quoted earlier in this chapter. However, Atwood 'hesitates to accept the seductive appeal of the radical self-erasure, the "loss of personal identity", which must accompany her protagonist's wholesale rejection of language and the self-definition it makes possible' (Worthington 279). As Atwood's heroine herself realises, such an enterprise would literally mean death.[84]

When the protagonist returns to the cabin following the messages from her parents, she looks in the mirror, thereby accepting her need to be represented. Through Anna's obsessive concern with being made-up, the mirror earlier came to symbolise conformity with society's expectations, especially gender expectations. Therefore, the protagonist refused to look in the mirror at the beginning of her transformation: 'I reverse the mirror so it's toward the wall, it no longer traps me, Anna's soul closed in the gold compact, that and not the camera is what I should have broken' (169). Looking in the mirror after her experience merging with nature and speaking the 'other language' marks her return to 'the communicative matrix':

> I turn the mirror around: in it there's a creature neither animal nor human, furless, only a dirty blanket, shoulders huddled over into a crouch, eyes staring blue as ice from the deep sockets; the lips move by themselves. This was the stereotype, straws in the hair, talking nonsense or not talking at all. To have someone to speak to and words that can be understood: their definition of sanity.
>
> That is the real danger now, the hospital or the zoo, where we are put, species and individual, when we can no longer cope. They would never believe it's only a natural woman, state of nature, they think of that as a tanned body on a beach with washed hair waving like scarves; not this, face dirt-caked and streaked, skin grimed and scabby, hair like a frayed bathmat stuck with leaves and twigs. A new kind of centrefold. (184)

Her reversal of the values implied by 'centrefold' shows how the protagonist appreciates her discovery of her 'state of nature.' However, the protagonist is also clearly aware that she will not be accepted back into society in her present state. The end of *Surfacing* is particularly ambiguous. Does Joe offer 'captivity' or 'a new freedom?' The protagonist 'tense[s] forward' to go and meet Joe but her 'feet do not move yet.' Joe 'won't wait much longer. But right now he waits' (186). Despite these ambiguities, the implication is that the protagonist does choose to return to Joe. She has already dressed herself in her cut-up clothes, and recognises both the importance of survival and also its impossibility alone on the island. She has even imagined the consequences of returning to Joe which, significantly, involve a return to language:

> If I go with him we will have to talk, wooden houses are obsolete, we can no longer live in spurious peace by avoiding each other, the way it was before, we will have to begin. For us it's necessary, the intercession of words; and we will probably fail, sooner or later, more or less painfully. That's normal, it's the way it happens now and I don't know whether it's worth it or even if I can depend on him, he may have been sent as a trick. But he isn't an American, I can see that now; he isn't anything, he is only half-formed, and for that reason I can trust him. (186)

Despite the difficulties which would lie ahead for them, the suggestion is that although an animal-like state does not represent a viable long-term solution to the protagonist's traumatised selfhood, the experience did allow the protagonist to discover her 'true self.' She has also identified something authentic in Joe – 'he isn't an American.'[85]

For a novel in which the central character displays so much suspicion of language, the narrative form implies a surprisingly mimetic model of language's relationship to reality.[86] Words seem to function like the Indian rock paintings. They are simultaneously highly symbolic and directly representational. In the surfacer's description of the fish jumping we can perceive the blurring of the object – the actual fish – with its idea and its representation. All are captured in the single image of the jumping fish:

> From the lake a fish jumps
>   An idea of a fish jumps
>   A fish jumps, carved wooden fish with dots painted on the sides, no, antlered fish thing drawn in red on cliffstone, protecting spirit. It hangs in the air suspended, flesh turned to icon, he has changed again, returned to the water. How many shapes can he take.
>   I watch it for an hour or so; then it drops and softens, the circles widen, it becomes an ordinary fish again. (181)

The language in *Surfacing* seems to signify in the same way. The signified, its conceptualization, and the signifier we use to represent it all turn into one another. The language does not draw attention to its own literariness but instead forms itself into increasingly simple sentences which are both directly mimetic and clearly symbolic. The stream-of-consciousness evident during the protagonist's 'experience' implies a direct link between signifier and signified, between language and consciousness: 'The animals have no need for speech, why talk when you are a word / I lean against a tree, I am a tree leaning' (*Surfacing* 175). There seems to be a certain tension between the surfacer's rejection of language – 'The animals have no need for speech' – and the poetic images with which Atwood so successfully expresses this experience. As Fand notes:

> Atwood's secular debunking voice, the one that zooms in on the banal and ugly details that mar the landscape of our society is suspended at this climatic scene in the novel, and a visionary voice takes over, in keeping with the protagonist's trance. (170)

However, the very fact that Atwood finds a language 'in keeping with the protagonist's trance' is not in keeping with the protagonist's rejection of language. Ironically, language achieves what the surfacer claims it cannot.

The similarities and contrasts to *Lady Oracle* are fascinating and illuminating. One of the clearest and most important differences is the way in which *Lady Oracle* draws attention to itself as a narrative construct, one with a tenuous relationship to truth.[87] Unlike the visionary quality of the language the protagonist uses at the end of *Surfacing*, *Lady Oracle* frequently describes Joan struggling with the popular language and formulas of Gothic Romances. Even Joan's attempts at Automatic Writing, which is supposed to eliminate the conscious mind and allow direct access to the unconscious in language, leave her alienated from her words: 'I blew out the candle and turned on the overhead light. *Bow*. What the hell was that supposed to mean?...What a dumb word, I thought' (222). Whereas *Surfacing* presents itself as an account revealing the protagonist's suppressed previous experiences, *Lady Oracle* is Joan's retrospective construction of herself in narrative; hence, my earlier distinction between the protagonist of *Surfacing discovering* herself, and Joan's self-*construction*.

In *Surfacing*, the protagonist enjoys, even requires, silence to undergo her transformation. The exiled Joan, on the other hand, hates her lack of communication:

> What price safety, I asked myself. I was sitting on the balcony in my underwear, covered with towels, taking a steamy sunbath in the middle of nowhere. The Other Side was no paradise, it was only a limbo. Now I knew why the dead came back to watch over the living: the Other Side was boring. There was no one to talk to and nothing to do. (311)[88]

Despite the fact that Joan disliked having to conform to others' versions of her, she misses the community. The protagonist of *Surfacing* chooses silence and invisibility over being misrepresented in her relationship with Joe or in their movie. Joan admits that her early weight gain was partly motivated by her fear of being invisible:

I ate to defy [my mother], but I also ate from panic. Sometimes I was afraid I wasn't really there, I was an accident; I'd heard her call me an accident. Did I want to become solid, solid as a stone so she wouldn't be able to get rid of me? (76)

To some extent, therefore, her fictional suicide was an enactment of her own worst nightmare. She does become invisible.

The reason for this difference in the heroines' attitudes to language and solitude relates to the different models of subjectivity evident in each novel. As I have indicated, in *Surfacing* the heroine seems to have an essential core, which her experiences outside of society put her in touch with. Her negative descriptions of Anna as 'an imitation of a woman who is also an imitation' (159) and of David as a 'pastiche' (146) are set up in opposition to her own authentic self. Significantly, these negative descriptions suit Joan perfectly. Susan Rosowski describes Joan's construction of selfhood in a similarly negative manner as a circular trap of creating fictional identities and then destroying them:

> The narrator begins to perceive her own creation, Lady Oracle, as 'taller than I was, more beautiful, more threatening. She wanted to kill me and take my place, and by the time she did this no one would notice the difference because the media were in on the plot, they were helping her'. (*Lady Oracle* 252) Finally, the self must destroy its own creation to save itself from being consumed. But in destroying its creation, the self must return to its own lack of identity and, finally, to the knowledge that the created character is a desperate attempt of the self to affirm its own reality. (203)

This 'taller,' 'more beautiful, more threatening' Lady Oracle is *not* Joan's own creation, however. It is the media portrayal of her as 'authoress' of the poem 'Lady Oracle.' This description of her 'dark twin' is preceded by her frustrated description of how misinterpreted and misrepresented she is. It is followed by her fear that her past, secret self will be revealed: 'Now that I was a public figure I was terrified that sooner or later someone would find out about me, trace down my former self, unearth me. My old daydreams about the Fat Lady returned...' (252). What is at stake here is not the difference between a fictional self and an authentic one (Joan dislikes her real 'fat self' even more than she dislikes the media's portrayal of her as 'Lady Oracle') but authorial power. It is to escape misrepresentation that Joan exiles herself. Of course, this results in even further misrepresentation, which is partly what drives Joan to tell the reporter her story so that she will have authorial control over it. Hospitalized by Joan's attack on him with the Cinzano bottle, he is hardly a figure of male authority as some critics have argued. Indeed, Atwood seems careful to indicate that it is Joan who is in control. Joan expresses surprise at her ability to 'knock him out like that; I suppose it's a case of not knowing your own strength' (344). She clearly takes control of the discourse: 'I said I thought the man was trying to break into the house. Luckily he was out cold, so he couldn't contradict me.' Just as he is unable to contradict this lie, he has no way of policing whether she is telling the truth in her life narrative. Joan claims she 'didn't tell any lies,' but then corrects this with 'Well, not very many,' thereby drawing attention to the reporter's powerlessness to know the difference between the 'truth' and Joan's version of it. Finally, by describing Joan as the one taking him flowers, Atwood places her in the position of seductress rather than victim of the male seducer (344).

In destroying the camera and film, the protagonist of *Surfacing* also rejects others' representations of her, but in so doing she destroys the possibility of representing herself. Her animal-like state is one that can exist only outside society. She realises that an attempt to return to society in that state would result in her being sent to hospital or the zoo. The surfacer knows she will be misrepresented ('They'll mistake me for a human being, a naked woman wrapped in a blanket' [177]) but chooses not to contest that representation.

The conclusions of both these novels are ambiguous, but the implications are that both women will return to their communities and relationships. Despite *Lady Oracle*'s greater comic content, to some extent *Surfacing* has the more positive ending in this respect. The protagonist predicts that she and Joe 'will have to talk' and that this will produce a beginning. Admittedly, she says that they 'will probably fail, sooner or later' (186), but this is certainly more hopeful than their earlier attempts to communicate:

> 'Do you love me, that's all,' he said. 'That's the only thing that matters.'
> It was the language again, I couldn't use it because it wasn't mine. He must have known what it meant but it was an imprecise word; the Eskimoes had fifty-two names for snow because it was important to them, there ought to be as many for love. (*Surfacing* 100)

The source of the surfacer's newfound hope in the possibility of language is unclear. How she will translate her communications in the 'other language' into her discussions with Joe is not at all certain. The only positive sign of a new way to communicate is the condensed, poetic language that Atwood uses to describe the protagonist's experience. However, despite these uncertainties, the future of the protagonist's relationship with Joe seems positive when compared with what Joan says of Arthur:

> And I'll have to see Arthur, though I'm not looking forward to it, all those explanations and his expression of silent outrage. After the story comes out he'll know the truth anyway. He loved me under false pretenses, so I shouldn't feel too rejected when he stops. I don't think he's even gotten my postcard yet, I forgot to send it air mail. (344–5)

Taking Joan's tendency to make a mess into account, it is difficult to see how her 'explanations' will help Arthur to better understand the 'truth.' The failure of the postcard to reach Arthur and Arthur's '*silent* outrage' (my emphasis) are examples of Arthur and Joan failing to talk and suggest that they will not even attempt a new beginning. Indeed, it is not clear what Joan is referring to when she says he will know 'the truth.' Is she referring to the fact that she is still alive, that she was fat, that she wrote Gothic Romances, that she had an extramarital affair, or that she was not really absent-minded and incompetent? Mary Eagleton also draws attention to ambiguity at the end of this novel pointing out that although Joan '*does* decide to give up Costume Gothics' she also thinks about taking up 'another fantasy form, science fiction' and, even though Joan states that she '*is* going to go back to Canada' (132) she decides that for the time being, in her own words, it would be 'easier just to stay here in Rome' (Atwood 345).

In his study of these two novels, Frank Davey groups them together with *The Edible Woman* and *Bodily Harm* as recast comedies. Unlike Shakespearean comedies where society is disrupted, in Atwood's fiction the heroines' task 'is more to heal themselves than to heal society' (57). Throughout his analysis, however, he struggles with *Lady Oracle* as it always appears to be the exception to his pattern. He reads these novels as accounts of the heroines' Freudian journeys of self-analysis. These journeys result in a reversal of the patriarchal values implicit in the comic pattern:

> The individual is restored (with the exception of Joan in *Lady Oracle*) not to order but to growth. The traditional comic pattern is in a sense overturned; order becomes equated with dehumanizing systematics, with ill-health, 'disorder'; traditional disorder becomes organic process. (72)

Joan's renewal, however, is described as 'suspect' (75) because her recognition of her own neurosis does not result in it losing its power and making 'way for long-stifled elements of the authentic self to grow' (74). Davey is looking for the authentic core of self that the protagonist of *Surfacing* discovers, but he does not see it in Joan. The protagonist of *Surfacing*, as I have suggested, achieves this new selfhood by paring herself down to a 'state of nature.' To my mind, Davey does not allow enough for the fact that Atwood presents very different notions of subjectivity in *Surfacing* and *Lady Oracle*. Joan takes the opposite approach from that taken by the protagonist in *Surfacing*. Her use of parody enables her to make a similar critique of society and its pressures on her identity as the protagonist of *Surfacing* makes, but without ever wholly withdrawing from that society.[89] Through her use of parody, Joan always manages to be in excess of any given version of herself, from being literally in excess of her mother's desires for her, to learning to perform excessive incompetence in the kitchen for her husband's satisfaction. Parody offers her a way of saying 'I am and am not this.' It allows her to narrate multiple versions of herself, all of which she simultaneously is and is not. Instead of trying to silence other versions of herself as the protagonist of *Surfacing* does, Joan's parodic treatment of others' narratives of her offers her a way of overflowing and escaping those narratives, while simultaneously acknowledging that she is partly complicit with them. By viewing *Surfacing* and *Lady Oracle* as attempts at the same thing, Davey sees *Surfacing* succeeding where *Lady Oracle* fails. He applauds the rejection of language I have identified in *Surfacing* and sees Joan's struggle with language as futile: 'She is drowning in language, wastes her energies against it in repetitive struggle' (76). In my reading, this 'repetitive struggle' is exactly what marks Joan's success.

Just as the protagonist of *Surfacing* seems isolated and distant from her friends, always trying to hide her emotions from them, so, too, does Joan. The people around her are nearly always referred to as 'Arthur's friends' rather than hers and her early self-parodies imply that she lives with a certain critical distance from her own actions. Early on in the novel this critical distance works as a survival strategy and, as we have seen in the self-parody of her shopping escapades, it enables her to negotiate some freedom from Arthur's version of her. However, as Joan's self-narrative progresses, her use of parody becomes markedly more transformative. It starts to change the value systems foisted upon her, rather than simply allowing her to coexist with those value systems. Instead of excluding Joan from the pattern of overturning the comic order, as Davey does, I would view Joan as perhaps the most successful of Atwood's heroines in her attempt to equate order 'with dehumanizing systematics, with ill-health, "disorder"' and of viewing 'traditional disorder' as 'organic process.' The difference is that for Joan it is not an 'organic process' but rather a 'narrative process.' Indeed, there is a parallel between how she rebels against the narratives others have of her, and the way her fictional character, Felicia, acts in relation to the stereotypical Gothic romance.

Joan demonstrates an ironic distance from her Gothic Romances throughout *Lady Oracle*, but towards the end of the novel that ironic distance turns into a more cutting critical distance which results in social satire.[90] Although the early sections of 'Stalked by Love' are clearly parodic, the parody does not result in a questioning of the values inherent in the Gothic Romance genre Joan is using. Her parody does laugh at the formulaic quality of her work and at any critical attempt to interpret it. Charlotte's clothes are slashed because 'Bad things always happened to the clothes of my heroines' (132). Joan candidly admits, 'I myself didn't have the least idea who'd slashed up her clothes' (132), but she sees how the incident will help propel the Gothic plot forward: 'Redmond, of course, would buy her a new wardrobe, which would fit perfectly, unlike the shabby discards she'd been wearing. She'd hesitate to accept, but what could she do?' (132). The only way in which the incident makes sense is that it leads Charlotte into a closer relationship with the Gothic hero. It is not until the character Felicia rebels against her own author that this Gothic parody becomes critical of its own values.[91] This critical distance is evident in Joan's inability to continue writing according to the rules of the genre. Her language becomes inappropriately excessive, even obscene, such as in the descriptions of Redmond's attitude towards Felicia: 'She smelled, these days, of wilted hyacinths, a smell of spring decay, not mellow like the decay of autumn but a smell like the edges of swamps. He preferred Charlotte's odor of faintly stale lavender' (320). More significantly, the plot refuses to resolve itself into the conventional happy ending:

> Felicia was still alive, and I couldn't seem to get rid of her. She was losing more and more of her radiant beauty; circles were appearing beneath her eyes, lines between her brows, she had a pimple on her neck, and her complexion was becoming sallow. (318)

Meanwhile, Charlotte was acting as if she knew that 'she would be awarded the prize' if she could 'stick it out until the murderer's hands were actually around her throat' (318). Joan starts to question why Felicia should be sacrificed for the tidy Charlotte:

> Sympathy for Felicia was out of the question, it was against the rules, it would foul up the plot completely. I was experienced enough to know that. If she'd only been a mistress instead of a wife, her life could have been spared; as it was, she had to die. In my books all wives were eventually either mad or dead, or both. But what had she ever done to deserve it? How could I sacrifice her for the sake of Charlotte? I was getting tired of Charlotte, with her intact virtue and her tidy ways. (321)

The name Charlotte, of course, reminds us that the novels of Charlotte Brontë inform Joan's sense of what 'the rules' of the Gothic genre are.[92] Joan's sympathy for Felicia can actually be situated within a tradition of feminist readings or rewritings that focus on the sacrifice of the existing wife or the 'madwoman in the attic' as a way to disrupt and subvert the 'rules' of the Gothic novel and to question the ideal femininity implied by the Gothic genre's conforming heroine.[93] 'Sympathy for Felicia' is precisely the strategy that Jean Rhys uses in her attempt to write back to Charlotte Brontë in *Wide Sargasso Sea*. Rhys purposely wrote 'against the rules' by giving a sympathetic account of the first wife's life-story, thereby answering Joan's questions, 'But what had [the existing wife] ever done to deserve it? How could I sacrifice her for the sake of [the careful, conforming Gothic heroine]?' The effect of Rhys's strategic rewriting is to give voice to those that Brontë's Gothic novel silenced. Rhys's politics in *Wide Sargasso Sea* echo Jane Flax's description of postmodernism's politics:

> Rather, power operates as innumerable instances of constraints; its effects can be seen whenever a population [or, in this case, a text] appears to be homogeneous, unconflicted, orderly, and unified. Such order always depends upon the subjection of localized, fragmented knowledges, which is a necessary condition for appearance of the 'totalizing' discourses of authority.

> By interrogating and disrupting these totalizing logics, postmodernists hope to open up spaces in which suppressed heterogeneity, discontinuity, and differences will reappear. The inherent instability of power relations can once again be set in motion if the artificial unity imposed by the fictive narrative of the human sciences is dissolved. (41)[94]

Through our (and Joan's) sympathy with Felicia we are forced to become aware of the 'heterogeneity, discontinuity, and differences' within and between women. The 'homogeneous, unconflicted, orderly, and unified' notion of femininity that the Gothic heroine upholds 'depends upon the subjection of' women such as Felicia and the younger, overweight Joan. These sacrifices are demanded by what Hite terms 'the rigorous requirements of femininity' (148). One of those requirements she describes as the paradox of 'excess as deficiency' (147–8).

It is Felicia's excess that her husband comes to hate:

> He'd become tired of the extravagance of Felicia: of her figure that spread like crabgrass, her hair that spread like fire, her mind that spread like cancer or pubic lice.[95] 'Contain yourself,' he'd said to her, more than once, but she couldn't contain herself. (320)

Felicia's excessive desire and sexuality are figured in her transformation into 'an enormously fat woman' (323), reversing Joan's own transformation. Felicia exceeds even Joan's control ('I couldn't seem to get rid of her' [318]) as their worlds collide. Arthur's name repeatedly replaces 'Redmond,' as Joan realises the real danger Arthur poses to her. The four female ghosts whom Felicia/Joan finds in the maze indicate that Joan has died more than just the one fictional death with which this novel starts. The fat child she killed through her construction of a new more 'convincing' (150) self-narrative returns to haunt her. Indeed, Joan's encounter with her past selves in the heart of her fictional world parallels the surfacer's underwater encounter with her lost child and the visitations of the ghosts of her parents. The Gothic narrative world at the end of *Lady Oracle* certainly seems to function like the organic one in *Surfacing*. Just as the protagonist returns from the wilderness in *Surfacing*, Joan will not be stuck in the maze forever. As she admits to herself, she is 'an escape artist':

> Why did every one of my fantasies turn into a trap? In this one I saw myself climbing out a window, in my bibbed apron and bun, oblivious to the cries of the children and grandchildren behind me. I might as well face it, I thought, I was an artist, an escape artist. I'd sometimes talked about love and commitment, but the real romance of my life was that between Houdini and his ropes and locked trunk; entering the embrace of bondage, slithering out again. What else had I ever done?

This thought did not depress me. In fact, although I was frightened, I was feeling curiously light-hearted. (335)

Even if Joan does embark on a 'nurse fantasy' romance with the journalist, the implication is that she will always be able to exceed and escape his narrative. The formal excess of this novel and its comic pleasure suggest that, like Houdini's, Joan's escapes will always deserve an audience. As the audience of this account of Joan's escape attempts, we join her in her reversal of Arthur's definition of 'mess.' The 'mess' which Joan made has amused and entertained us. We are positioned by the novel as a whole, just as we were in relation to the sentence describing the shopping escapades. Our laughter makes us accomplices.[96] The reader of this novel is like the reporter who was 'out cold' and was therefore unable to 'contradict' Joan's claim that she 'thought this man was trying to break into the house' (344). Her narrative so excessively fills the page and includes within it her own self-criticism that we have no blank space in which to inscribe a contradictory story.

'Without Memory, There Can Be No Revenge': Iris Chase Griffen's Textual Revenge in Margaret Atwood's *The Blind Assassin*

Prompted by the large picture of her grandfather, Benjamin Chase, in the converted Button Factory, Iris describes him as a man who 'prided himself on the conditions in his factories' (54). She presents him in a series of authoritative sentences that start repeatedly with a capitalized 'He.' After repeating her grandfather's promise that 'conditions for the females in his employ were as safe as those in their own parlours,' Iris makes the parenthetical comment that 'He assumed they had parlours. He assumed these parlours were safe' (54).[97] This irony prepares us for the next paragraph, in which Iris acknowledges the source for her information concerning her grandfather:

> Or this is what is said of him in *The Chase Industries: A History*, a book my grandfather commissioned in 1903 and had privately printed, in green leather covers, with not only the title but his own candid, heavy signature embossed on the front in gold. He used to present copies of this otiose chronicle to his business associates, who must have been surprised, though perhaps not. It must have been considered the done thing, because if it hadn't been, my Grandmother Adelia wouldn't have allowed him to do it. (54)

Although this text presents itself as a history of the industries, her grandfather's 'own candid, heavy signature embossed on the front in gold' points to the fact that this history is, to a great extent, his own life-story, his autobiography.[98] Not only does he have the freedom, power and money to authorize his own version of himself, but it is a practice that the culture encourages – 'It must have been considered the done thing' (54). Despite Iris's attempts to question its authority and treat it with ironic contempt, evident in her parenthetical comment about women's parlours, it remains the only version of events.[99]

The contrasts between *The Chase Industries: A History* with its green leather covers and the first edition of 'The Blind Assassin'[100] are significant, and point to that work's parodic relationship with *The Chase Industries*. Iris describes the five copies of the first edition of 'The Blind Assassin' which she has stored in her steamer trunk:

> Also five copies of the first edition, with the dust jackets still in mint condition – tawdry, but dust jackets were then, in the years just after the war. The colours are a garish orange, a flat purple, a lime green, printed on flimsy paper, with an awful drawing – a faux Cleopatra type with bulbous green breasts and kohl-rimmed eyes…Acid is eating into the pages, the virulent cover fading like the feathers of a stuffed tropical bird. (285, my ellipsis)

The materials are of bad quality compared to those used for *The Chase Industries: A History*. The paper is 'flimsy,' the drawing is 'awful,' the colours are 'fading,' and 'acid is eating into the pages.'[101] The 'lime green' echoes the green leather of *The Chase Industries* just enough to install the parodic relationship between the two texts. Instead of a gold embossed signature across the front, the author of 'The Blind Assassin' is presented thus:

> On the inside jacket flap was a touching biographical note:
> Laura Chase wrote The Blind Assassin before the age of twenty-five. It was her first novel; sadly, it will also be her last, as she died in a tragic automobile accident in 1945. We are proud to present the work of this young and gifted writer in its first astonishing flowering.
> Above this was Laura's photo, a bad reproduction: it made her look flyspecked. Nevertheless, it was something. (509)

The lack of authority implied by this publication which the dead author is unable to sign is even more extreme when we consider that Iris, not Laura, was its author. Instead of having her 'own candid, heavy signature embossed on the front in gold,' Iris was unable to put her own name to this first version of her 'autobiography' at all, but, instead, inserts a false author inside the jacket flap.

A further difference between these two autobiographies lies not in their physical presentations but in their relations to their readers. Grandfather Chase's practice of giving his book as a present to his business associates guarantees it an audience. There is no fear here of whether he will be read, because even if his text goes unread, the green leather cover and gold embossed signature

Lady Oracle *and* The Blind Assassin

will have fulfilled the book's function – to impress on others his authority. In contrast, 'The Blind Assassin' is at first ignored and then viewed as transgressive of authority: 'When the book came out, there was at first a silence. It was quite a small book, after all...Then the moralists grabbed hold of it, and the pulpit-thumpers and local biddies got into the act, and the uproar began' (509, my ellipsis).

Indeed, at the presentation of the Laura Chase Memorial Prize, Iris describes 'The Blind Assassin' as

> unmentionable – pushed back out of sight, as if it were some shoddy, disgraceful relative. Such a thin book, so helpless. The uninvited guest at this odd feast,[102] it fluttered at the edges of the stage like an ineffectual moth. (40)

The fear of not being read becomes more urgent in the second attempt at autobiography that Iris writes as an old lady. In this second autobiography she repeatedly questions whom she is addressing:

> For whom am I writing this? For myself? I think not. I have no picture of myself reading it over at a later time, *later time* having become problematic. For some stranger, in the future, after I'm dead? I have no such ambition, or no such hope.
>
> Perhaps I write for no one. Perhaps for the same person children are writing for, when they scrawl their names in the snow. (43)

This parallel between Iris's autobiography and children's graffiti in the snow is one we can also observe in Iris's enjoyment of the 'scribblings' on the washroom wall in the doughnut shop. These are her favourite washrooms because the inscriptions 'remain on view much longer.' The effect of this is that 'you have not only the text, but the commentary on it as well' (84), just as Iris offers her reader her previously published novel and a 'commentary on it as well.' Even Iris's notions concerning the authorship of these 'washroom scribblings' echo the complicated authorship of 'The Blind Assassin':

> Sometimes I think – no, sometimes I play with the idea – that these washroom scribblings are in reality the work of Laura, acting as if by long distance through the arms and hands of the girls who write them. A stupid notion, but a pleasing one, until I take the further logical step of deducing that in this case they must all be intended for me, because who else would Laura still know in this town? But if they are intended for me, what does Laura mean by them? Not what she says. (419)

This playful notion frightens Iris with its ensuing responsibility of interpreting Laura's message. In the next sentence, she admits 'a strong urge to join in, to contribute; to link my own tremulous voice to the anonymous chorus of truncated serenades, scrawled love letters, lewd advertisements, hymns and curses' (420). Iris is attracted to this space in which there are no limits on self-expression; however, this space also points to problems of readership and reception. In creating or 'playing with' the idea that Laura wrote these scribblings, Iris expresses her anxiety over 'anonymous' writing and undefined audiences. Identifying a specific reader in her grand-daughter, Sabrina is a celebratory and empowering moment at the end of Iris's life because it allows Iris to 'join in, to contribute' without risking exposure to 'the anonymous chorus.' Finally, she comes to believe that she will be read.

These differences between *The Chase Industries: A History* and 'A Blind Assassin' point to important differences between the positions of their authors and the strategies available, or necessary, to each of them in order to tell their own stories. *The Blind Assassin* is not only Iris's account of her life, but also an explanation of why she was unable to author her own life previously. Her later narrative is an attempt to emboss her own signature on 'The Blind Assassin.' In *The Blind Assassin*, Atwood charts the history of the entry into autobiography of previously unauthorized subjects – namely, women. As Ellen McWilliams argues of Atwood's contribution in this novel and *Cat's Eye* (1988) to the genre of the *bildungsroman*, these two novels

> share an interest in the challenges and paradoxes of 'writing a life' and draw attention to the processes of evasion, subversion, and illusion that are at work in all narratives of selfhood, but are perhaps, necessarily, most dramatically manifested in narratives that are self-consciously committed to writing women's lives. (113)

Keeping in mind Mark Curie's comments about metafiction's relationship to criticism, I argue that Atwood's metafictional novel, *The Blind Assassin*, plays out feminist theories of autobiography.

Grandmother Adelia's power in 1903 is limited to editing her husband's version of his public life so that it fits into a socially acceptable narrative form. She is able only to define herself within the limits of what is 'proper.' She has to give up things like travel and art, in order to conform to her position as Benjamin Chase's wife in the industrial town of Port Ticonderoga. Benjamin Chase experienced fulfilment, success and self-expression through the Chase Industries. Adelia's relationship to the Chase Industries resulted in self-sacrifice, and the adherence to 'proper' limits of self-expression and experience. However, in 1999, Iris passes considerable freedom onto Sabrina to define herself as she wishes:

> Your real grandfather was Alex Thomas, and as to who his own father was, well, the sky's the limit. Rich man, poor man, beggar-man, saint, a score of countries of origin, a dozen cancelled maps, a hundred levelled villages – take

your pick. Your legacy from him is the realm of infinite speculation. You are free to reinvent yourself at will. (513)

Given that Sabrina has no idea who her father was, we might question Iris's assumption that having no idea who her great-grandfather was would give Sabrina the freedom to 'reinvent herself at will.' Surely, Sabrina would always have had a great deal of freedom to 'reinvent herself' due to her unclear paternity and the early death of her mother: 'Who, for instance, was Sabrina's father? Hard to say, and Aimee never did. Spin the wheel, she'd say, and take your pick' (434). In this situation, it might well be more appropriate to view the invention of identity as a necessary task for Sabrina, rather than a newly acquired freedom. The fact that Sabrina is already travelling, a pleasure Grandmother Adelia feels it is not 'proper' to allow herself, is another indication of Sabrina's homelessness and need to define herself.

As the contrast between her grandfather's publication and her own makes clear, Iris cannot 'maneuver [her story] inside the lines of the provided subjectivities and the provided narratives culturally available to [her]' (Smith 62). Indeed, it is unclear whether any narratives are 'culturally available to [her]' at all, a possibility evident in her initial inability to claim 'The Blind Assassin' as her own. By informing us that 'nobody knows I am an author,' Iris's later narrative functions rather like the t-shirt logo Leigh Gilmore analyses in the conclusion of *Autobiographics*:

> The t-shirt logo that reads 'NOBODY KNOWS I'M A LESBIAN' simultaneously conceals ('nobody knows') and discloses ('I'm a lesbian'). An ironic play on confession, this declaration asks how knowledge of sexual identity is constituted, even as it suggests the presence of that identity. (226)

Iris's inability to publish 'The Blind Assassin' under her own name was intimately tied to her sexual identity: as she wrote of her female protagonist in that novel, 'Her body as usual would get in the way of free speech' (464). Iris's later narrative, however, focuses more on issues of authorship than sexuality.

Iris's rejection of what Smith terms traditional autobiography's 'autonomous, free, coherent self' (62) and her addressing a particular audience (particularly a private, female audience) have been identified by many feminist critics as two distinctive marks of female autobiography. These critics established a body of critical work on autobiography which critiqued earlier work by men on this genre. Susan Stanford Friedman's widely cited essay 'Women's Autobiographical Selves: Theory and Practice' is an example of this criticism. She argues that, far from illuminating women's autobiography, much early work on autobiography (such as that carried out by 'Gusdorf, Olney, Mehlman, and many others') developed 'related individualistic paradigms for the self' which have actually 'obscured the presence and significance of women's autobiography in literary tradition' (37–8). Friedman identifies a specifically female model of identity, one that is neither purely individualistic nor wholly collective. Women's autobiography is often written against a silence which has been historically imposed upon them:

> the self constructed in women's autobiographical writing is often based in, but not limited to, a group consciousness – an awareness of the meaning of the cultural category WOMAN for the patterns of women's individual destiny. Alienation is not the result of creating a self in language, as it is for Lacanian and Barthesian critics of autobiography. Instead, alienation from the historically imposed image of the self is what motivates the writing, the creation of an alternate self in the autobiographical act. Writing the self shatters the cultural hall of mirrors and breaks the silence imposed by male speech. (40–1)

Nancy Walker uses Friedman's theory of women's more collective model of selfhood to demonstrate how 'group consciousness' influences the way women writers conceive of their audiences. In her consideration of Emily Dickinson, Alice James and Virginia Woolf, Walker argues: 'Each of these women whose personal, autobiographical writing is considered here makes it clear in one way or another that she feels some ultimate public eye upon her as she writes' (275). As we have seen above, Iris repeatedly expresses a similar sense of having an audience.

Iris's identification of Sabrina as her addressee is a parodic inversion of Grandfather Chase's traditional public male autobiography. It helps to ease her anxiety over her audience and is an important move in her negotiation between her private self and her public representation. Iris states that what she desires from Sabrina is 'Only a listener, perhaps; only someone who will see me' (521). Just as Iris constructs an understanding of her Grandmother Adelia by recognizing the compromising limitations Adelia's position as a woman imposed upon her, so too does Iris hope that Sabrina's position as her grand-daughter will enable her to 'see' Iris. J. Brooks Bouson emphasizes this generation gap suggesting that the older generation's feminine ideals haunt the twenty-first century:

> That Laura is a kind of missing person in the text, existing somewhere between the realms of social realism and cultural myth, suggests that the utterly 'good' sacrificial woman is both a kind of textual illusion and a lingering female and cultural fantasy in the postfeminist world of the late-twentieth and early-twenty-first century. (1)

The sort of 'group consciousness' that Friedman identifies as characteristic of feminist autobiography is also evident in Iris's belief that 'The Blind Assassin' was co-authored. After stating of 'The Blind Assassin' that 'Laura didn't write a word of it' (512), Iris goes on to dismiss this as only 'technically' accurate. In a more important sense, 'what Laura would have called the spiritual sense,' Iris describes Laura as her 'collaborator.' 'The real author,' Iris argues, 'was neither one of us; a fist is more than the sum of its fingers' (513). Iris's model of a communal author for her autobiography is a parodic critique of her grandfather's autobiography which erased the contributions Iris's grandmother made to the Chase Industries and to her grandfather's life story. The image of the fist is significant because it echoes Friedman's notion that for many women the act of 'writing the self' is one that 'shatters' and 'breaks' both images and silences. In the closing pages of her later autobiography, Iris consciously identifies the collective aspects of her text as positive, empowering and self-constructing. She describes her writing as an 'account of Laura's life – of my own life,' as if the two are inseparable: 'Laura was my left hand, and I was hers. We wrote the book together. It's a left-handed book. That's why one of us is always out of sight, whichever way you look at it' (513). This image expresses Iris's important rejection of traditional autobiography's unified, single subject, and points to her ironic doubt about whether her autobiographical attempts reveal or conceal her life story. The left hand or the 'bodiless hand' haunts this text. Karen Stein takes this image as the title of her article on *The Blind Assassin* and relates it to the themes of concealment and revelation that are so central to the novel: 'In the process of writing her memoir of Laura, Iris first conceals and then reveals her own story' (138). The 'bodiless hand' gathers significance through Iris's many references to it. For example, there is the anecdote of Laura as a child expressing concern over who sits at God's left hand (513); Iris describes her own experience of writing as one of dissociation from her hand, which takes on 'a life of its own, and will keep on going even if severed from the rest of me' (373). Of course, the most poignant and significant instance of this image of the hand is the severed hand in the photograph of Laura, Iris and Alex at the picnic. Laura reproduces two copies of this photograph, one for each of them, and cuts out the other sister leaving only a 'bodiless hand.' Allan Hepburn offers a concise but extremely suggestive analysis of the hand image in his review of *The Blind Assassin*. He argues that Iris 'figures the agony of writing in tropes of hands severed from bodies' (133). Exploring Iris's role as 'the hand that passed [Laura] on,' Hepburn states that 'the hand also becomes a synecdoche for service: the handmaid's hand, the hired hand. Iris feels her secondhandedness acutely' (133). Indeed, this is one respect in which Iris's position as author of 'The Blind Assassin' actually parallels that of the 'commissioned' author of *The Chase Industries: A History*.[103] Its final manifestation is in the image of Iris handing these texts onto her granddaughter, Sabrina.

Although feminists such as Friedman and Walker would applaud this handing on of a subversive autobiography to her granddaughter, Atwood includes three further sections that function to contradict this 'happy ending' somewhat and remind the reader that the 'subversive' elements of Iris's autobiography also mark her need to speak 'mutedly' due to her 'unauthorized' position (Smith 61). The epilogue to 'The Blind Assassin' reiterates Alex's point that narrative is by definition composed of 'loss and regret and misery and yearning' (518). As he tells Iris earlier in 'The Blind Assassin,' 'taken to its logical conclusion, every story is sad, because at the end everyone dies' (349). Unlike Joan Foster's fictional and reversible death in *Lady Oracle*, the deaths in *The Blind Assassin* are final. Death in fact motivates much of the writing in *The Blind Assassin*. Iris writes 'The Blind Assassin' as a 'memorial' to Alex, publishes it under Laura's name so that she is not forgotten and rushes to finish her later life story because her own death is imminent. Indeed, this epilogue is followed by Iris's obituary, which describes all her identity positions – sister, daughter, granddaughter, wife, sister-in-law, grandmother – in which she was unable to speak. These are the identities from which her narrative has struggled to escape. As Iris packs her steamer trunk for Sabrina in the face of her impending death, she recognizes the possible dangers of handing on her text to the reading process: 'But I leave myself in your hands. What choice do I have? By the time you read this last page, that – if anywhere – is the only place I will be' (521). The literal death of the identity we have watched creating itself through these pages means that Iris will never be able to enact her daydream of telling Sabrina this life story at the kitchen table. Iris's parody of her grandfather Chase's autobiography positioned Sabrina as a private audience in contrast to her grandfather's public one. Here Iris realizes that handing herself over to a single private reader can be just as dangerous an act as publication.

This image of two women at the kitchen table echoes the earlier encounter between Iris and her daughter, Aimee, during which Iris did attempt to share her story over the kitchen table. To echo this earlier encounter at the end of *The Blind Assassin* is to warn us not to read Iris's autobiography too positively. The earlier encounter between Aimee and Iris confirms Iris in her belief that 'Her body as usual would get in the way of free speech' (464). When Iris makes this comment, she is referring to the fact that her female body will prevent her from speaking freely with men. In the encounter with Aimee, Aimee's rejection of Iris's maternal body prevents free speech. Aimee accused Iris of not being her real mother, of hiding the fact that Laura was her mother and of killing Laura. When Iris denies this Aimee reacts violently:

> She used a number of words I won't repeat here, then picked up the smile-button coffee mug and threw it at me. Then she came at me, unsteadily; she was howling, great heart-rending sobs. Her arms were outstretched, in a threatening manner, I believed. I was upset, shaken. I retreated backwards, clutching the banister, dodging other items – a shoe, a saucer. When I got to the front door I fled.
>
> Perhaps I should have stretched out my own arms. I should have hugged her. I should have cried. Then I should have sat down with her and told her

the story I'm now telling you. But I didn't do that. I missed the chance, and I regret it bitterly. (436–7)

This earlier failure of language, evident in Aimee's use of swear words ('She used a number of words I won't repeat here'), in her non-linguistic expression of grief and anger ('she was howling'), and in Iris's realization that she was silent when she should have spoken ('I *should* have sat down with her and told her the story' [my emphasis]), is partly corrected by Iris's later writing. However, the text also makes us very aware of the costs of Iris's earlier silence and the final sections warn us not to be too celebratory, despite Iris's hope that her autobiography is now readable by Sabrina.

The trunk of texts left to Sabrina certainly does not make 'an easy read.'[104] Perhaps the most striking characteristic of the text created by Iris's struggle with autobiography is how fragmented it is, with its rapid jumps in time, place, voice and genre. To what extent do these fragments enable Iris or her reader to make 'meaning out of [her] experiences' as Smith suggests life writing should? The novel does not give any indication how Sabrina reacts to the narrative. Furthermore, we might question more generally whether Smith, Friedman and Walker's obvious optimism over the feminist appropriate of autobiography is entirely justified. Rosalind Coward suggests in an essay entitled 'The True Story of How I Became My Own Person' that the confessional novel has become itself a formulaic genre, replacing the formulas of nineteenth-century realist romances, but without questioning that a woman's most valuable experiences are her sexual ones. Coward recognizes that 'Women-centred novels represent a fictionalized version of our culture's contemporary obsession with autobiography' (43), and that we have come to expect certain 'intimate revelations' from these novels:

> it has become a standing joke that we are to expect the first period, first kiss, first (fumbled) intercourse, first (disastrous) marriage, lesbian affair and usually lonely resolution. The end product is normally that the protagonist feels she has 'become her own person'. (42)

What concerns Coward is that in this type of literature, women's development and knowledge are 'focused exclusively on sexual experience' (44):

> Women again defined through their sexuality, are the sex to be interrogated and understood. Becoming my own person or woman is in the grain of the sexual; it is how a woman deals with her sexuality.... There's a danger that such structures reproduce the Victorian ideology that sexuality is somehow outside social relations. (45; my ellipses)

What is so striking about the descriptions of Iris's affair with Alex Thomas is that they are far more textual than sexual. Their sexual activities are usually described in a few short sentences. It is Alex's telling of his science fiction stories that dominate their meetings. During one of the most memorable encounters between them in a small park just outside Iris's house, they hardly even touch each other:

> He doesn't put his arm around her. He knows she wants him to. She expects it; she feels the touch in advance, as birds feel shadow. (21)
>
> He hasn't kissed her; he won't, not tonight. She senses it as a reprieve. (23)

Indeed, the sexual is noticeably marginal to this woman-centred novel. For example, Iris's account of her wedding night is marked by ignorance and restraint. 'About my bridal night, or rather my bridal afternoon,' she writes, 'I will tell very little' (241). Thus, *The Blind Assassin* avoids defining its heroine 'in the grain of the sexual.' Furthermore, Iris parodies this separation of the sexual and domestic from the political and public which Coward is concerned that women-centred novels replicate.

Iris's obituary describes her in exactly the false, silent social positions that she has attempted to resist in both trying to become her own person and writing about it. She is described as 'the sister of noted local authoress Laura Chase,' 'daughter of Captain Norval Chase,' 'grand-daughter of Benjamin Chase,' 'wife of the late Richard E. Griffen,' and 'sister-in-law of Winifred Griffen Prior' (519). The only hint that this account might be invalidated is that Sabrina's visit 'to see to her grandmother's affairs' could result in her reading Iris's 'true story.' Smith's point that when 'newly articulate autobiographical subjects come to write' they 'speak as "unauthorized subjects"' and are, therefore, 'pulled and tugged into complex and contradictory subject positions' through the writing process (61–2) is helpful here. In her story of 'how she became her own person,' Iris never reaches her destination, as her description of herself in terms of the characters from 'Little Red Riding Hood' makes clear:

> off I set, step by step, sideways down the stairs, like Little Red Riding Hood on her way to Granny's house via the underworld. Except that I myself am Granny, and I contain my own bad wolf. Gnawing away, gnawing away. (366)

The sense of continuous action ('gnaw*ing*') and of a journey ('step by step,' 'via the underworld') emphasizes the fact that 'my own person' is a process not a final destination. In the ordering of the final sections of *The Blind Assassin*, the final chapter of Iris's autobiography entitled 'The threshold' comes to us *after* her death. Even death does not fix Iris's identity – Sabrina's reading process will continue to contribute to her narrative.

Although Iris's wish for a private funeral is respected, a public memorial service is also held. It is almost as if the death of Iris as a public persona and the death of Iris, the private person, are two separate deaths and cannot, therefore, be mourned at a single event. The complicated relationship between the private and public in autobiographical writing, and especially autobiographical writing by women, is self-consciously explored throughout this novel as Bouson has already suggested. Iris blurs this separation between private and public, revealing it to be an irrelevant romantic ideal. She experiences the very intimate connections between the private and public to her cost. Iris's marriage, for example, clearly subverts the Victorian ideology that Coward fears is reproduced in the 'intimate revelations' of 'women-centred novels.' Far from being 'above the economy,' and thereby able to validate the social structure which separates the 'public, economic realm from the domestic,' as Coward suggests the sentimental marriage of the Victorian heroine tends to, Iris is clearly aware that she is part of the economic exchange between Richard Griffen and Norval Chase. The traditional notion that women are possessions in their positions as daughters and wives is too clearly at work here for this to be a 'feminist' moment in the text, but it certainly deconstructs the binary opposition between the domestic and social which Coward fears 'women-centred novels' tend to reproduce. Iris's lack of choice or economic agency in regards to her marriage parallels the sacrificial virgins of Sakiel-Norn. However, what leads me finally to view the conclusion of this narrative as positive and subversive, despite that final obituary, is Iris's refusal to continue being victimized and alienated by her public representation, and her attempt to insert the private into the public arena. Through her parody of traditional autobiography, Iris simultaneously reveals that women have experienced the private/public dichotomy differently from men, and she shows how this dichotomy has served patriarchal ends. In *The Blind Assassin* as a whole, Atwood demonstrates how this dichotomy can be reconfigured for feminist ends. She teaches her readers to read against this division between the private and public. Indeed, Iris's previous demonstrations of the dissonance between her portrayal in the local press and her own experiences have trained her reader to view that final obituary with a certain degree of ironic detachment. In Grandfather Benjamin Chase's autobiographical text, his public and personal identities do not contradict each other. The name of his business is also his name. In contrast, Atwood dramatizes the feelings of alienation and misrecognition that Iris experiences in relation to public representations of herself by metafictionally drawing attention to Iris as author.[105]

Iris's resistance to the dissonance between her private and public selves finally starts with the letter she leaves for Richard:

I left a letter for Richard. I said that in view of what he'd done – what I now knew he'd done – I never wanted to see him again. In consideration of his political ambitions I would not request a divorce, although I had ample proof of his scurrilous behaviour in the form of Laura's notebooks, which – I said untruthfully – were locked away in a safe-deposit box. If he had any ideas about getting his filthy hands on Aimee, I added, he should discard them, because I would then create a very, very large scandal, as I would also do should he fail to meet my financial requests...

I signed this letter *Yours sincerely*, and, while licking the envelope flap, wondered whether I'd spelled *scurrilous* correctly. (502)

Although not a public document, it demonstrates Iris's willingness to enter the public domain if necessary – 'I would then create a very, very large scandal.' She lies competently about Laura's notebooks, which, in fact, neither would provide 'ample proof' nor are 'locked away in a safe-deposit box.' These lies suggest that Iris is parodying official legal public discourse. She knows her entry into the public domain would need to be authorized by documentation that would stand up in a court of law. Her use of the word 'proof' is important as it implies that Iris has the necessary authorizing texts to be listened to in the public sphere which has hitherto silenced and distorted her, rather than voiced and represented her. This public legal discourse is clearly not Iris's own voice. She parodies this language in order to make strategic use of it. Her publication of 'The Blind Assassin' under Laura's name reveals her reluctance to enter the public realm, just as her anxiety over her spelling of the word 'scurrilous' reveals her discomfort with the official public discourse she must learn to manipulate in order to get what she needs from Richard.

Richard's desire for fame contrasts with Iris's desire throughout most of the novel not to be seen. When meeting Alex, it is imperative that she not be seen. She publishes 'The Blind Assassin' under Laura's name mainly because of her fear of the spotlight.[106] This fear can be traced back to her honeymoon, during which Iris was fascinated and horrified by her first experience of watching a cabaret dancer:

> People sat at their tables watching her and listening to her, and having opinions about her – free to like or dislike her, to be seduced by her or not, to approve or disapprove of her performance, of her dress, of her bottom. She however was not free. She had to go through with it – to sing, to wiggle. I wondered what she was paid for doing this, and whether it was worth it. Only if you were poor, I decided. The phrase *in the spotlight* has seemed to me ever since to denote a precise form of humiliation. The *spotlight* was something you should evidently stay out of, if you could. (244–5)

To be represented in this way is also to be trapped, commodified, objectified, and consumed. After Laura's death, however, Iris learns that 'unshed tears can turn you rancid. So can memory. So can biting your tongue' (508). Although the spotlight certainly has its perils, silence as its alternative offers no possibility whatsoever for representation. Iris realizes that she should not have remained silent about her sister's life because '[w]ithout memory, there can be no revenge' (508):

Officially, Laura had been papered over. A few more years and it would be almost as if she'd never existed. I shouldn't have taken a vow of silence, I told myself. What did I want? Nothing much. Just a memorial of some kind. But what is a memorial, when you come right down to it, but a commemoration of wounds endured? Endured, and resented. Without memory, there can be no revenge. (508)

This confrontational model of 'The Blind Assassin' as 'revenge' is echoed in the violence suggested by Iris's claim that neither Laura nor Iris is the 'real author' of that text because 'a fist is more than the sum of its fingers' (513). Although Iris wants the reader to view her decision to publish 'The Blind Assassin' under Laura's name as 'a failure of nerve' or 'simple prudence,' or even as a conscious act of collective authorship which 'was merely doing justice, because I can't say Laura didn't write a word' (512), the more confrontational motives for writing are more convincing. Despite Iris's initial willingness to leave Richard's public political image undamaged, she does come to wish for revenge on Richard through the very instruments he used to silence herself and Laura – the competent use of public discourse and an insistence on sexual fulfilment. The autobiographical novel offered Iris the perfect genre for inserting the personal into the public because the confessional novel is a genre through which it has been acceptable for women to enter the public arena. To borrow J. Brooks Bouson's argument: 'Iris's memoir, which serves as the narrative anchor of Atwood's novel, reinforces the idea that the memoir is a feminist genre' (1). Its conventions very much emphasize the personal and private, but the act of publication introduces that personal narrative to a public readership. The genre itself, therefore, seems to express the complex and contradictory relationship between personal experience and public image that Iris is struggling to negotiate.[107] By naming Laura as the author, Iris is able to enact this textual revenge without risking the dangers she associates with the spotlight.

It is the dead Laura who is commodified and consumed. Iris does attempt to resist this consumption of Laura. 'Laura Chase is not your "project". She was my sister,' she writes to 'Professor Z,' 'She would not have wished to be pawed over after her death, whatever that pawing over might euphemistically be termed. Things written down can cause a great deal of harm. All too often, people don't consider that' (287). This novel clearly demonstrates how 'things written down can cause a great deal of harm.' To some extent, the harm brought to Iris and Laura by Iris's marriage to Richard is caused by 'things written down' – the illustrious *The Chase Industries: A History* – the legacy of which their father is so keen to preserve. As Iris's father says to her just before Richard proposes, a 'certain amount depends on' her acceptance:

'I have to consider the business. It might still be saved, but the bankers are after me'.... 'I don't want it all to have been for nothing. Your grandfather, and then... Fifty, sixty years of hard work, down the drain.' (226)

The Chase Industries: A History was based on a parallel silenced history of female sacrifice, a history which Iris finally steps into the spotlight to tell. For, despite its extensive portrayal of the harm caused by 'things written down,' above all, *The Blind Assassin* warns of the dangers of silence. As Allan Hepburn succinctly puts it in his review of *The Blind Assassin*: 'Words both condemn and rescue. Words both praise and damn' (136).

Chapter 4

Inheritances: Zadie Smith's *On Beauty*

Indebtedness, Inheritance, and Theft

Margaret Atwood's *Payback: Debt and the Shadow Side of Wealth* opens with an anecdote about Ernest Thompson Seton which inverts the usual economic relationship between father and son:

> Canadian nature writer Ernest Thompson Seton had an odd bill presented to him on his twenty-first birthday. It was a record kept by his father of all the expenses connected with young Ernest's childhood and youth, including the fee charged by the doctor for delivering him. Even more oddly, Ernest is said to have paid it. I used to think that Mr. Seton Senior was a jerk, but now I'm wondering, What if he was – in principle – right? Are we in debt to anyone or anything for the bare fact of our existence? If so, what do owe, and to whom or to what? And how should we pay? (1)

Instead of inheriting wealth from his father, Seton pays his father for all the expenses of his upbringing. The conclusion of Atwood's book, however, makes it clear that indebtedness is not in conflict with inheritance but is closely related to it. Her concluding argument that 'Maybe we need to calculate the real costs of how we've been living, and of the natural resources we've been taking out of the biosphere' (203) is clearly concerned with what kind of biosphere we leave for our children to inherit. Her implication is that we are stealing from the future. We 'owe' both previous and future generations.

The complex relationships between indebtedness, inheritance and stealing are played out in the events surrounding the Haitian portrait of Maîtresse Erzulie by Hector Hyppolite in Zadie Smith's *On Beauty* (2005). Kiki Belsey's son, Levi, steals this painting from Monty Kipps, with the help of his Haitian friend Choo, as a politically motivated direct action to '*redistribute*' the wealth of the painting because 'that money belongs to the Haitian people' (429). Just as Kiki comes on '"all Florida", which was the same thing, in Kiki terms, as "going postal"' (427) on her son for his theft, yelling at him that 'I *know* no son of mine steals ANYTHING – no child I ever raised took it into his head to steal ANYTHING FROM ANYBODY' (427), Jerome ironically discovers that, indeed, it is not only Levi who is guilty of theft in relation to this painting. He finds a note slipped into the back of the painting that reveals that Carlene Kipps had bequeathed it to Kiki. At this shocking news, Kiki and the painting are appropriately prevented from falling to the floor by Levi's 'intervention' (431). Kiki proceeds to sue Monty Kipps for her right to inherit this painting from his dead wife, Carlene.

At the end of the novel, Levi indicates that Kiki plans to sell the painting and donate the profits to the Haitian Support Group (437). This suggests that Levi's argument that all of Kiki's children and even she, herself, do in fact 'steal' had an impact on her. Levi explains his clear vision of how the people of Wellington 'steal' from Haiti:

> People in Haiti, they got NOTHING, RIGHT? We living off these people, man! We – we – living off them! We sucking their blood – we're like vampires! *You* OK, married to your white man in the land of plenty – *you* OK. *You* doing fine. You're living off these people, man! (428)

He stuns his mother when he accuses her of being directly written into this exploitation by paying their maid, Monique, only four dollars an hour. 'If she was American you wouldn't be paying her no four dollars an hour. Would you?' (429) he accusingly asks her. Smith earlier describes Monique as 'a squat Haitian woman, about Kiki's age, darker still than Kiki' (10) and has informed the reader that Kiki is 'nervous of what this black woman thought of another black woman paying her to clean' (11). What does Kiki owe this woman of her own race and age? In deciding to sell the painting and donate the money to Haitian Support Group, Kiki can be seen to be turning her inheritance into a debt payment as, according to Levi, this is what is owed to the Haitian people. This decision simultaneously asserts and resists Kiki's inheritance from Carlene. Carlene has instructed Kiki to '*enjoy this painting*' because it '*needs to be loved by someone like you*' (430). In an earlier conversation about the picture, Carlene dismisses its economic value commenting that '[i]t's worth a great deal, I believe, but that's not why I love it' (175). She then goes on to assert her ownership of it, remarking on the fact that she 'got it in Haiti itself on my very first visit, before I met my husband' (175). Michael and Amelia – Carlene's son and his wife – parallel the reaction of Ruth Wilcox's children in *Howards End* when they discover the note she had written leaving her house to Margaret Schlegel. Both sets of children insist on the fact that these notes from their mothers are not legally binding and accuse Kiki and Margaret of manipulating their mothers during the last days of their lives. Michael directly contrasts his mother's attitude to the painting by immediately drawing attention to the painting's economic worth – '"Look that painting is worth, what? About three hundred grand? Sterling?"' – and insists that Carlene wouldn't let it '"fall out of the family"' (278). Just as Forster in *Howards End* explains Ruth Wilcox's family's inability to understand her note about leaving Howards End to Margaret

Schlegel – 'To them Howards End was a house: they could not know that to her it had been a spirit, for which she sought a spiritual heir' (107) – so, too, does Smith reveal Carlene's family to be concerned with issues of financial worth that were not of consequence to Carlene herself with regards to bequeathing the painting. In suing Monty Kipps for her right to inherit this painting, Kiki perpetuates Carlene's positioning of it as her own possession outside of her marriage and family. Carlene's comment about acquiring the painting before her marriage to Monty and the subject matter itself – the Voodoo goddess Erzulie – which, as Nicole King has explicated, can be read as a symbol of 'feminist creolisation' in the novel, suggest that this painting is something that is most appropriately inherited by one woman from another. However, in selling the painting for the Haitian Support Group, Kiki recognizes the importance of its financial value to the Haitian community and so resists Carlene's instruction to 'enjoy it'. Like the house her great-grandmother inherited from her white master, it 'is ennobled by the work' it does to correct social and historical inequalities (17).[108]

Levi's recognition of his own and his family's privilege within a system that secures that privilege at the expense of others echoes Margaret Schlegel's growing recognition in E. M. Forster's *Howards End* (1910) that 'all our thoughts are the thoughts of six-hundred-pounders':

> [Mrs Munt] and I and the Wilcoxes stand upon money as upon islands. It is so firm beneath our feet that we forget its very existence. It's only when we see someone near us tottering that we realize all that an independent income means. Last night, when we were talking up here round the fire, I began to think that the very soul of the world is economic, and that the lowest abyss is not the absence of love, but the absence of coin. (72)[109]

The developing awareness of Margaret Schlegel and Levi Belsey of the ways in which the 'very soul of the world is economic' reflects Forster and Smith's shared concern with the relationship between economic and cultural capital. These types of capital are intricately tied up with issues of both indebtedness and inheritance.

Most of the early reviewers of *On Beauty* and several critics have explored Smith's indebtedness to or inheritance of E. M. Forster's *Howards End*. Susan Alice Fischer, for example, starts her essay by parodying Forster and Smith's opening sentences: 'One may as well begin with Zadie Smith's literary debt to E. M. Forster' (285). However, Fischer goes on to explore Smith's debt to Zora Neale Hurston in more detail than her debt to Forster. Maeve Tynan explores Smith's use of Forster in her essay '"Only Connect": Intertextuality and Identity in Zadie Smith's *On Beauty*', posing the 'the delicate question of literary debt'. Tynan suggests that 'the connection between books' 'raises the contentious dilemma in ascertaining when does homage end and plagiarism begin?' (81) and references Julie Sanders's helpful exploration of 'the complex ethics of indebtedness' in *Adaptation and Appropriation*. However, even Tynan does not explore in sustained detail how Smith's inheritance of Forster's plot performs formally the thematic exploration of inheritance and indebtedness present in both *Howards End* and *On Beauty*.[110] I want to suggest that, in rewriting *Howards End*, Smith enacts 'the complex ethics' and problematic politics of inheritance and indebtedness that both Forster and Smith explore in detail in the content of their novels. Smith's literary inheritance of plot elements from *Howards End* is closely linked with her cultural inheritance of liberalism from Forster. *On Beauty* not only replays Forster's plots but also his ideological discussions about capitalism and liberalism, and the role of inheritance in both. For both of these authors, nostalgia and being 'old-fashioned' function politically and ethically as a means to critique their contemporary worlds.

'A Practice of the Untimely'

In 'Are Parody and Deconstruction Secretly the Same Thing?' Robert Phiddian takes the view that 'parody *is* a form of deconstruction', that it is not simply '*like* deconstruction' but rather parody and deconstruction are 'secretly the same thing' (681). However, in one respect he argues that parody differs from deconstruction and that is in its ability to turn into satire:

> ...I propose that parody, as a genre, has already seen its way out of the deconstructive impasse that treats language as an endless and odorless play of differences. For it is true that parody, generically in its forms and linguistically in its textuality, works on fundamental assumptions about the nonreferentiality of language and form very like these, but it normally does so cannily, knowing that language *does* connect with the world, mimesis, and intention, however messily. This is where and why parody nearly always turns into satire. This is not a *necessary* event – pure parody which bombinates endlessly in the void of textuality is at least imaginable – but parody nearly always admits referential impurity. Its first lesson is always to defamiliarize, to show that language forms, distorts, and masks the world, that it is an impure medium, and that pure referentiality is a crazy and often dangerous dream. However, there is almost always a supplementary movement in parody (that seldom accompanies deconstruction) which returns the reader to something resembling the world. (691)

This is a similar point to that which Smith makes about Forster in 'Love, Actually'. Here she argues for a direct relationship between narrative and ethics, between the experience of reading novels and reading real lives:

> It seems that if you put people on paper and move them through time, you cannot help but talk about ethics, because the ethical realm exists

nowhere if not here: in the consequences of human actions as they unfold in time, and the multiple interpretive possibility of those actions. Narrative itself is the performance of that very procedure. This is something we know as readers of novels and readers of our own lives; it is this deep, experiential understanding of the bond between the ethical realm and the narrative act that we find crystallized in that too familiar homily 'Two sides to every story', a version of which truism one will find in every culture in the world. This is the good that novels do, and the good that they are. (6)

Smith, therefore, shares Phiddian's rejection of deconstructive understandings of text and language as 'purely' nonreferential. Her comments clearly suggest that she is not making intertextual use of *Howards End* in order to 'bombinate endlessly in the void of textuality', but rather because she wants to continue the ethical work of Forster's novel. This raises questions about the relation of *On Beauty* to *Howards End*; for it is not at all clear that *On Beauty* is, in fact, a parody of *Howards End* at all, despite the comic parodic tone of her rewriting of its famous opening line: 'One may as well begin with Jerome's e-mails to his father' (3).

David James has suggested in his 2007 essay 'The New Purism' that 'the commonplace tenets of postmodern self-referentiality fall short of explaining how writers choose to advance by adhering to what seems past, contemplating their originality through the lens of inheritance' (687). Indeed, Smith herself views her own rewriting of *Howards End* as 'old-fashioned', explaining in 'On the Beginning' that

> With a brazen ahistoricism I can't intellectually defend, around February 2003 I indulged myself and sat down to write the big, 'realist' (better to say in the style of Realism), slightly Edwardian novel that I had dreamt of writing as a child. It was a book I couldn't quite manage when I was 20, sitting down to write *White Teeth*. (web)[111]

In '"Only Connect": Intertextuality and Identity' Maeve Tynan juxtaposes Smith's *On Beauty* helpfully with other postcolonial texts such as Jean Rhys' *Wide Sargasso Sea* to demonstrate how 'while being a novel dealing with hallmark postcolonial concerns, and a rewriting of a canonical Western novel, Smith's *On Beauty* veers from the traditional format of a typical postcolonial rewriting' (78) and is 'not in the business of putting Forster on trial' (76). It is pertinent to note that in her introduction to Zora Neale Hurston's *Their Eyes Were Watching God*, Smith mentions being introduced to *Wide Sargasso Sea* by her mother and not liking it or, as she puts it more accurately in parentheses, having 'not *allowed* myself to like' it (vii). In contrast to Rhys, we can see that Smith is *inheriting* Forster, carrying forward his cultural capital, rather than using parody and irony to critique his text.

Jane Elliott has argued that one of the key disagreements between second and third wave feminists has been about the issue of timeliness which Smith resists in the 'brazen ahistoricism' she embraces by retelling *Howards End*:

> Often underlying such debates was the question of which version of feminism was more appropriately situated in time: third-wave feminists often accused second-wave feminist analysis of being out of date, and second-wave feminists accused third-wave feminists of anachronistically reinventing the wheel. This insistence on fidelity to one's moment inheres in even the most thoroughgoing critiques of progress narratives in feminist theory. (Elliott 1700)

Returning to Forster offers Smith a chance to 'interrupt the contemporary moment with a practice of the untimely' as Elliott puts it. Elliott is keen to point out that 'such interruptions need not appear historically new' because if 'we assume that familiar approaches can no longer serve as tools to dislodge the present, we demonstrate a continued affinity for the modern logic that equates the new, the interesting, and the valuable' (1701). Interestingly, Forster also perceived himself, and was widely perceived, as 'old-fashioned'. As Brian May argues in 'Neoliberalism in Rorty and Forster': 'Most critics regard the Edwardian and modern novelist E. M. Forster as a latter-day Victorian liberal, but one who is no less committed than belated' (185). As we shall see in my analysis of Smith's inheritance of Forster's liberalism below, another key figure to voice this idea is Brian Barry in his attempt to demonstrate how liberalism can accommodate multiculturalism in *Culture and Equality*. His argument echoes Elliott's directly:

> Especially among the pop academics and their journalistic hangers-on, it is now a commonplace that something they call the 'Enlightenment project' has become outmoded. But ideas are not like designer dresses. There, the latest fashion is the most desirable simply in virtue of being the latest. There is only one parallel to ideas: new fashions in ideas help to sell books as new fashions in *haute couture* help to sell clothes. But in the case of ideas we can ask a question that does not make sense in the case of clothes: is the latest fashion right or wrong? It is my contention that the anti-Enlightenment bandwagon is misdirected. (9)

Nostalgia is a key issue in *Howards End* itself. Henry S. Turner has argued that the 'novel articulates an ambivalent fascination with material substances of all types, as Margaret nostalgically embraces objects for their promise of cultural permanence and stability even as the narrative voice regards them with detached irony, mistrust, or even disgust' (330) and Elizabeth Outka explores 'commodified nostalgia' in the novel in her article 'Buying Time: *Howards End* and Commodified Nostalgia'. Indeed, one of Margaret's criticisms of Henry

Wilcox in her conversation with Helen about his proposal to her is that 'He cares too much about success, too little about the past' (177). In contrast, an early description of Ruth Wilcox coming to the scene of the row between Mrs. Munt and Charles speaks of her as possessing 'that wisdom to which we give the clumsy name aristocracy. High-born she might not be. But assuredly she cared about her ancestors, and let them help her' (36). In appropriating Forster's novel, Smith seems to be allowing 'her ancestors' to 'help her' in just such 'a practice of the untimely' as Elliott advocates.

Tynan sees Smith's gesture as a positive act of identity politics that makes visible the fact that 'novelists such as Zadie Smith, who are frequently housed under the banner of black British writers, *are* British' (78). Acknowledging the problematics of the phrase 'black British' which can suggest that these writers exist in a 'semi-detached relationship with Britain', Tynan also sees the phrase as 'conceptually worthwhile to the extent that the very Britishness it espouses underlines the entitlement of its writers to claim the culture of the colonizer as part of *their own* literary tradition' (78). Thus, as a 'black British' writer reusing Forster's *Howards End*, Smith 'highlights continuity and prerogative – the passing on of traditions' (78) by positioning herself within the tradition of the 'English comic novel', as Smith herself terms it in 'Love, Actually'. Given the context of Forster's contemporary, Joseph Conrad's infamous suggestion in *Heart of Darkness* (1902) that all Congolese natives are cannibals, Peter Kemp's choice of language to criticize Smith's use of Forster takes on interesting racial overtones:

> Smith's preface speaks of offering 'homage' to Forster. But *cannibalising* one of his novels, giving its components a gaudy respray and recycling them into what turns out to be a ramshackle vehicle for an ill-sorted heap of concerns seems a curious way of going about this. (my emphasis)

Kemp seems to read critically and negatively the same racial politics as Tynan views positively in her essay.

Tynan's positive reading and Kemp's negative criticism of Smith's use of *Howards End* replay the debate about colonial and postcolonial subjects' relation to white English and American literary canons that I examined in the earlier chapter on Toni Morrison's *The Bluest Eye*. As Morrison makes clear through Pecola Breedlove's desire for 'bluest' eyes, Merle Hodge demonstrates through Tee's creation of Helen in *Crick Crack, Monkey* and Ngugi wa Thiong'o theorizes in *Decolonizing the Mind*, the postcolonial subject's encounter with the English language and literary traditions is often highly problematic and can threaten to dislocate the black self from itself. The black, postcolonial subject cannot recognize him or herself in the narratives he/she reads, resulting in the fragmentation of and dislocation from the self evident in Tee's creation of 'Helen', a 'double' who 'loved to visit her Granny for then they sat by the fireside and had tea with delicious scones' (67) and who becomes Tee's 'Proper

Me. And me, I was her shadow hovering about in incompleteness' (68). In the case of Pecola Breedlove this dislocation from her own self proves maddening and life-threatening. Smith demonstrates her consciousness of these black writing traditions by pointing towards her own black British ancestor – Sam Selvon. Several critics have pointed to the relationship between Selvon and Smith in her earlier work.[112] Smith makes the link clear in *On Beauty* by including in the list of items that would appear in Carlene Kipps obituary in *The Times* that she had been a '*Windrush* passenger' (280). This is a significant and surprising aspect of Carlene's life as there is believed to have been only two women aboard the *Windrush* when it docked at Tilbury in June 1948 with its 492 passengers. The event places Carlene as a fellow passenger of Sam Selvon who arrived in England aboard the famous ship.

The optimistic multiculturalism of Carlene's funeral reads rather like a parody of Smith's own earlier novel *White Teeth* which many critics read as an optimistic celebration of London's multiculturalism and some commentators also critiqued for being idealistic. As Claire Squires explains in her summary of the reception of *White Teeth*, 'More open to debate...was the question of whether Smith was portraying an actual or an ideal situation' (75). In the description of Carlene's funeral, Smith seems to be parodying those reviewers and critics who Corinne Fowler suggests contributed to the commercial success of *White Teeth* by reading the novel as serving 'a celebratory cosmopolitan agenda' and 'subjugated' its more 'radical elements' and 'critique of UK multiculturalism' (Fowler 83) in order to position it as a naïve 'celebration of intercultural exchange' (84). The multiculturalism of Carlene's funeral is first noticed by Jerome: '"Every kind of person", whispered Jerome, because everybody was whispering. "You can tell she knew every type of person. Can you imagine a funeral – *any* event – this mixed, back home?' (282). His observation is confirmed by his family:

> The Belseys looked around themselves and saw the truth of this. Every age, every colour and several faiths; people dressed very finely – hats and handbags, pearls and rings – and people who were clearly of a different world again, in jeans and baseball caps, saris and duffle coats. (282)

The exaggerated optimism and multiculturalism of this event juxtaposed against the unlikelihood of Carlene having been one of only two women in 492 passengers suggests that Smith is playing here with the intertextual relationships between this novel, *White Teeth*, reviews of *White Teeth*, and Sam Selvon's far from idealized depiction of 'multicultural' London in *The Lonely Londoners*. These additional intertextual references play interestingly into *On Beauty*'s relationship to *Howards End* because they suggest alternative parallels.

As a fellow passenger of Selvon's on the *Windrush*, Carlene can be seen to be aligned with Selvon's dispossessed characters in *The Lonely Londoners* who struggle via a number of both legal and illegal strategies (including pigeon killing and eating! (117–22)) to avoid the 'abyss' as Forster terms it in *Howards End*. These characters are positioned in relation to London and inheritance much as the dispossessed Leonard Bast who has to 'degrade himself to a professional beggar' and use 'blackmail' to get his family, who disowned him at the time of marriage to Jacky, to send him money (309).[113] This, therefore, suggests that Leonard Bast finds a parallel not only in the rapper Carl in *On Beauty* but also in Carlene Kipps herself. Daniel Born argues that 'when Forster comments on Bast's attempts at self-education, he shows not only Leonard's inadequate grasp of Ruskin, but also, and just as pointedly, social critic Ruskin's inability to understand men like Leonard' (149–50). Carlene enacts a similar critique of her and Kiki's husbands' intellectual discourse when she and Kiki discuss the painting of Maîtresse Erzulie, as Fiona Tolan notes:

> Showing her friend a beautiful Haitian portrait of a goddess, Carlene dismisses its economic aspect, explaining, 'It's worth a great deal, I believe, but that not why I love it'. When Kiki attempts to appropriate Howard's language in compensation for what she fears to be her critical incompetence, her friend sweeps away her pretensions: 'That's a very clever way to put it. I like the parrots' (175). For Carlene, in absolute contrast to Howard, and even in opposition to her husband, for whom art is informed by religious principles, the value of the painting rests solely in its beauty, which transcends all other aspects of its power, and it is the beauty of art that makes it transcendent. (133)

This passage works in juxtaposition to the student shorthand description of Howard's class which Victoria informs him is 'all about never *ever* saying *I like the tomato*' (312). It also connects with Bast's description of his experience of walking all night in which he similarly debunks the Schlegel's intellectual and Romantic discourse. 'But was the dawn wonderful?' asks Helen Schlegel; to which Bast replies with what the narrative voice informs us is 'unforgettable sincerity', 'No'. He goes on to explain to the Schlegels that 'The dawn was only gray, it was nothing to mention–' (126). This is a character surely capable of saying 'I like the parrots' in a moment of 'unforgettable sincerity', too. I would suggest, therefore, that the criticism of Ruskin's inability to understand men like Leonard implied by Forster's treatment of Leonard's encounter with Ruskin is also evident in Smith's implied criticism of Monty Kipps via the juxtaposition of his discourse and politics with those of his *Windrush* passenger wife. Like Ruskin, he too, is unable to imagine men like Leonard or Carl Thomas.

When Kipps realizes that the Hyppolite painting has been stolen from his university office, ironically it is Zora who is called to assist the faculty to find Carl who Kipps has already labelled 'a thief', 'from the "wrong side of the tracks,"' and 'likely' to have a 'criminal record' (422). This scene is ironic in multiple ways. First, Zora is in love with Carl and has battled hard to ensure he is allowed to continue to attend Wellington. Secondly, it is Kipps's own daughter, Vee, who is having a sexual relationship with Carl. Thirdly, Zora is one of the few who know of Kipps's sexual relationship with the student, Chantelle, who is also 'illegally attending' (in Kipps's words (365)) Wellington and is presumably also, therefore, 'from the "wrong side of the tracks"'. Finally, Zora will return home to find her own brother is the thief they are looking for and that incident will reveal Kipps himself to be the thief of the *Maîtresse Erzulie*.

The Blues Aesthetic

The character who most obviously parallels Leonard Bast is, of course, Carl Thomas. His name suggests a parallel to Carlene and they share a similar anti-intellectual stance towards aesthetics. Carl is a crucial character in working out Smith's position in relation to the aesthetics theories her novel presents. The battle over the painting draws particular attention to the battles between the different characters' senses of the aesthetic in the text. Carl represents yet another aesthetic – the blues aesthetic. The reader first meets Carl at the free outdoor performance of Mozart's *Requiem* in one of the scenes that most closely parallels Forster's *Howards End*. Carl is positioned as Bast because he has his Discman (rather than umbrella) stolen from him by Zora. As the concert ends, the Belseys all react very differently to the piece. Jerome is moved to tears by what his father dismissively and sneeringly refers to as 'the Christian sublime' (71). Kiki tries to protect her son from his father's deconstructive critique by describing the *Requiem* as 'the work of a genius' (71), only to goad her husband further so that he groans and demands a definition of 'genius'. Meanwhile Zora emerges from her CD recording of Professor Gould's commentary which 'carefully guided her through each movement' as her mother observes that she 'lived through footnotes' (70). It is Carl who seems to react most productively to the concert. He describes himself to Levi as someone who gets his 'culture where [he] can' (76), an autodidact who is very much in the tradition of Leonard Bast. He attends 'Anything happening that's free in this city and might teach me something' (76), which is exactly how he finally ends up in Zora's creative writing class with Claire Malcolm.

Aware of the collective composition of Mozart's *Requiem*, Carl describes the history of the piece to Zora when they bump into each other at the campus swimming pool:

Obviously [Mozart] passed away halfway through, and then other people had to be brought in to finish it off. And it turns out that the main business of the *Lacrimosa* was by this guy Süssmayr – which is the *shit*, man, 'cos it's like the *best thing* in the Requiem, and it made me think *damn*, you can be so close to genius that it like lifts you up – it's like Süssmayr, this guy, stepped up to the bat, right, like a rookie, and then he went and hit it out of the park and all these people be trying to prove that it's Mozart 'cos that fits in with their idea of who can who can't make music like this, but the *deal* is that this amazing sound was just by this guy Süssmayr, this average Joe Shmo guy. I was tripping when I read that shit. (136–7)

While Carl is as keen to question the myth of 'genius' as Howard, he is less quick to wholeheartedly dismiss beauty and artistic perfection. Instead, he is excited by the possibility that unexpected and unlikely people can artistically 'hit the ball out of the park'. This phrase echoes his own enthusiastic description of his creative process when writing poetry: 'When I be rhyming I'm like BAM. I hit it on the *nail*, through wood and out the other side' (138). The next time Zora sees Carl he is demonstrating that he is, indeed, 'like BAM' because he '*killed* at the Bus Stop' (233) where Zora is on a 'kind of *field trip*' (199). This idea of a 'field trip' emphasizes the sense of it being off campus, 'outside' the academy, thereby drawing attention to the boundary that Zora rather rudely alluded to during her first encounter with Carl when she described Claire Malcolm as 'a *poet* poet' (77). This comment promptly wiped the smile off Carl's face. Carl 'kills' with a piece which is clearly in the blues tradition with its pleasurable and energetic enjoyment of loss and pain. It 'calls' on the audience in a way that even the MC, Doc Brown cannot resist responding to. Thus, Carl can be seen to represent a non-academic, non-canonical, vernacular aesthetic.

When Monty Kipps's objections to non-paying members of the community joining in university classes threaten Carl's position in Claire Malcolm's class, she goes to Erskine for help saying significantly, 'I just don't want to kick him back out on to the street. I really don't' (370–1). This reference to 'street' is pertinent. Of all the Belsey family it is initially Levi who seems to have most in common with Carl and invites him along to the family party. Levi's 'street' aesthetic and ethics are problematic in this novel. On the one hand, his 'street' credentials are 'faked'. The description of Levi's 'faux Brooklyn accent which belonged to neither Howard nor Kiki and had only arrived in Levi's mouth three years earlier, as he turned twelve' is satirically described as 'inexplicable' (11) early on in the novel. Similarly, the encounter with Bailey is very difficult to read:

> 'I *know* where you're from. Those kids don't know shit, but I know. They nice suburban kids. They think anyone in a pair of baggy jeans is a gangsta. But you can't fool me. I know where you *pretend to be from*', [Bailey] said, his anger newly virulent, still holding the door but leaning in towards Levi. 'Because that's where *I'm from* – but you don't see me acting like a nigger. You better watch yourself, boy'. (191–2)

On one hand, the reader is shocked by this adult supervisor's treatment of his teenage employee. On the other hand, however, we know that Levi is 'faking' and has no real experience of material deprivation or the 'street'. Given his own 'inauthenticity', the reader is primed to be suspicious of Levi's judgement of Carl once Carl has taken on the job of '*Hip-Hop Archivist*' (372), a job Erskine invents for him in order to solve Claire's problem of not wanting to throw Carl 'back out onto the street' (370–1). Levi calls Carl a 'feckless brother' (389) and 'just the kind of rapper white folk get excited about' (238). Levi has a simplistic and essential notion of racial identity. Felix who is 'blacker than any black man Levi ever met in his life' seems to be to Levi 'the *essence* of blackness in some way' (242). Levi sees Felix's skin colour and anger as the epitome of the blackness he yearns for. When Carl explains that he's not performed at the Bus Stop recently because 'Rap should be about *proportion*, for me, as I see it' but 'you go to the Bus Stop these days, it's all these really angry brothers kinda...*ranting*...and I'm not really feeling that' (388), Levi decides that 'Carl just didn't impress him any more' (389) and defensively suggests to Levi that 'Maybe they got shit they angry about' (388).

What redeems Levi from being a 'fake' is his genuine openness. Smith describes him as having 'a liberal susceptibility to the pain of others' that all the Belseys share. What marks Levi as different, more 'soft and open' than the other Belseys, is that he 'had no hard ideological shell to protect him' (355). Levi demonstrates the sort of openness to beauty that Elaine Scarry celebrates in *On Beauty*. In Chapter 1, I explored Anne Anlin Cheng's argument that in perceiving beauty 'the observer's own subject position' is compromised 'more than the viewer would like or can afford to acknowledge' (203) and noted Cheng's emphasis on Toni Morrison's own pain in the encounter with her friend's internalized racial self-hatred and distorted sense of beauty. It is this kind of self-disrupting pain that Levi is capable of when viewing his 'street' 'brothers'. As Smith says of him, 'The experience of reading both books [about Haiti and Tupac] had wounded him' (355).

These two characters, Levi and Carl, can be seen to correct each other's position over the course of the novel. Levi's pain at reading the book about who killed Tupac is mirrored in Carl's work in the university. Carl loves his job at the university because he is perfectly qualified for it:

> Never in his life had Carl had a job like this one. The pay was basic admin wage...That wasn't the point. He was being hired because he knew about *this* subject, *this* thing called hip-hop, and knew much more about it than the average Joe – more maybe than anyone else in this university. He had a skill, and this job required his particular skill. He was an *archivist*. (372)

This skill is evident when he sits down to write a 'context card on Tupac Shakur' at ten o'clock and 'By lunchtime he'd written five thousand words' (375). Carl's research into hip-hop leads him to the image of the crossroads which, of course, links him directly to the blues aesthetic. As Houston Baker, amongst other theorists of the blues aesthetic, has argued, the blues is an aesthetic of *motion*. This motion is linked directly to the image of the crossroads that Carl comes to understand in his research:

> To suggest a trope for the blues as a forceful matrix in cultural understanding is to summon an image of the black blues singer at the railway junction lustily transforming experiences of a durative (unceasingly oppressive) landscape into the energies of rhythmic song. The railway juncture is marked by transcience. Its inhabitants are always travellers – a multifarious assembly in transit. The 'X' of crossing roadbeds signals the multidirectionality of the juncture and is simply a single instance in a boundless network that redoubles and circles, makes sidings and ladders, forms Y's and branches over the vastness of hundreds of thousands of American miles. Polymorphous and multidirectional, scene of arrivals and departures, place betwixt and between (ever *entre les deux*), the juncture is the way-station of the blues. (7)

This is Houston Baker in *Blues, Ideology, and Afro-American Literature: A Vernacular Theory*, but it might just as well be Carl in his context card on the crossroad (378). The university with its system of tenure for life is not a 'scene of arrivals and departures' in the way that the railway station is. When Carl does come finally to experience the rage that Levi feels is missing from his attitude to the world, Carl decides to move on. Cat Moses argues that:

> The catharsis and the transmission of cultural knowledge and values that have always been central to the blues form the thematic and rhetorical underpinnings of *The Bluest Eye*. The narrative's structure follows a pattern common to traditional blues lyrics: a movement from an initial emphasis on loss to a concluding suggestion of resolution of grief through motion. (623)

This is also the structure of Carl's development in *On Beauty*, but also, just as importantly, the structure of Kiki Belsey's growth.

In borrowing her title from Elaine Scarry, Smith seems to propose a very different attitude to beauty from that expounded by Morrison in *The Bluest Eye*. In that novel, Morrison describes 'romantic love' and 'physical beauty' to be '[p]robably the most destructive ideas in the history of human thought' (122). As I demonstrated in Chapter 1, *The Bluest Eye* retells a white reading primer in order to critique the damaging way in which black children are 'taught' their own ugliness. In response to the question 'Do you think that young black females are still dealing with the same self-acceptance issues as your character Pecola Breedlove was in *The Bluest Eye*?' in an interview for *Time* magazine, Toni Morrison responds by saying 'No, not at all' adding that 'they don't even know what I'm talking about'. She says that she finds 'young African American women much more complete. They seem to have a confidence and almost a feeling of superiority in some ways that I recognize that they take for granted' (web). However, in the figure of Kiki Belsey, Smith seems to inherit Morrison's blues aesthetics from *The Bluest Eye* as much as other aspects of *On Beauty* critique Morrison's rejection of beauty. In her introduction to Zora Neale Hurston's *Their Eyes Were Watching God*, Smith lists *The Bluest Eye* as one of the novels her mother prescribed for her as a child and she admits she 'resented the interference'. This resentment lead her to not enjoy *The Bluest Eye* (vii) and, in many ways, Smith could be viewed as one of those young black women who 'take for granted' their 'feeling of superiority' so that they 'don't even know what [Morrison was] talking about' in *The Bluest Eye*. However, it is clear from Kiki's character that Smith does. Kiki emerges like a grown up Claudia.

To Claire she was 'proof that a new kind of woman had come into the world as promised, as advertised' (227). However, Kiki repeatedly expresses concern about the dominant ideology's pressure towards self-hatred that directly echo Morrison's concerns in *The Bluest Eye*:

> This was why Kiki had dreaded having girls; she knew she wouldn't be able to protect them from self-disgust. To that end she had tried banning television in the early years, and never had a lipstick or a woman's magazine crossed the threshold of the Belsey home to Kiki's knowledge, but these and other precautionary measures had made no difference. It was in the *air*, or so it seems to Kiki, this hatred of women and their bodies – it seeped in with every draught in the house; people brought it home on their shoes , they breathed it in off their newspapers. There was no way to control it. (197–8)

In her depiction of Zora's weight worries and experiments with her clothing, Smith certainly does seem to suggest that young women today do indeed know what Morrison was talking about. Kiki also expresses similar worries with regards to racial self-hatred when she debates affirmative action with Monty Kipps. She counters Kipps's criticism that 'These children are being encouraged to claim reparation *for history itself*' (365) with the argument that 'isn't the whole point that here, in America – I mean I accept the situation is different in Europe – but here, in this country, that our opportunities have been severely retarded, *backed up* or however you want to put it, by a legacy of stolen rights – and to put *that* right, some allowances, concessions, and support are what's needed?' (367–8). This argument returns us to the opening quotation of this chapter from Atwood as Kiki counters Kipps's argument that 'Rights are earned' (367) with the vocabulary of previous theft and a debt that is owed. What concerns her deeply about Kipps's argument is that 'it stinks of a kind of, well, a kind of *self-hatred* when we've got black folks arguing against opportunities for black folks' (368).

Kiki makes her argument, of course, from a position of having had her debt paid. She inherited her grandmother's house who was bequeathed it by the white master she nursed and, as Kiki realizes, 'if it were not for the bedside charm of my grandmother...there would have been no inherited house'. This leads her to wondering whether she would have met Howard or '*know* people like this' (54) without having had the inheritance of that house. Although she recognizes gratefully that, 'An inheritance of that scale changes everything for a poor family in America: it makes them middle class' (17), she is also aware of how it has isolated her from other black people. Levi is often treated with suspicion when he is walking home and Kiki's own husband, Howard, is clearly uncomfortable with the racial identity of his children. At one point this is described in quite a sympathetic way when he is musing over the wonder of his independent children and thinks, 'They weren't even the same colour as him. They were a kind of miracle' (386). However, when Smith reveals earlier that, 'He disliked and feared conversations with his children that concerned race' (85), her tone is more critical. Thus, when Kiki launches an angry attack on Howard about his blindness to her race, we are primed to be sympathetic:

> You don't even notice it – you never notice. You think it's normal. Everywhere we go, I'm alone in this...this *sea* of white. I barely *know* any black folk any more, Howie. My whole life is white. I don't see any black folk unless they be cleaning under my feet in the fucking café in your *fucking* college. (206)

As Tracey Walters states, 'Kiki is definitely disconnected from her cultural heritage' (131). What Kiki is yearning for is the very blues aesthetic that Carl and the Hyppolite painting represent. What Kiki's inheritance has taught her is that the blues aesthetic does have a very close connection to one's material living conditions, as Amiri Baraka argues:

> Culture is the result of a 'common psychological development'. But the common psychological development is based on experiencing common material conditions which are defined, ultimately, politically and economically. (101)

In the case of the blues, those common material conditions are street corners and railways. The blues does not require 'a room of one's own'. In her blues development from 'an initial emphasis on loss to a concluding suggestion of resolution of grief through motion', to quote Cat Moses again, Kiki goes from the realization that there is an 'antechamber of misery' 'in the mansion of their marriage' (15) to a realization that her inherited house has cost her the experience of sharing 'common material conditions' with other 'black folk' and a decision to move on. As Zora says of her inheritance of Carlene's painting, she could 'buy a goddamn island' (436). Instead, Kiki realizes her nostalgia for the black vernacular, for the 'street', and for the blues aesthetic and informs Levi of her decision to sell the painting for the Haitian Support Group. What Kiki inherits from Carlene is an example of black vernacular art not a house like Margaret inherits from Ruth Wilcox in *Howards End*. Kiki has learnt Claudia's lessons. I would agree with Tracey Walter's argument that, 'At first it is hard to see Kiki beyond the mammy stereotype, but toward the end of the text Kiki's character evolves, and the traits that associate her with the stereotype are abandoned' (132). Christopher Douglas's work demonstrates that the opposition between Kiki as 'stereotype' and Kiki as a person with a particular 'cultural heritage' are both 'ideal forms that are created by the elimination of a certain amount of alterity' (161). Smith's *On Beauty* demonstrates this is clearly as Morrison's *The Bluest Eye* does.

In trying to understand the competing aesthetic systems Smith puts into play in this novel, one enormous and problematic challenge is that of Victoria Kipps. Susan Alice Fischer performs critical acrobatics to try to show how '[a]ssociating Victoria with Erzulie and with Hurston's use of the voodoo loa adds a much-needed dimension to understanding Victoria's sexuality and its transformative power in the novel' (115). Although Fischer does an excellent job of tracing this parallel through the novel as a whole, I find it difficult to be convinced by a positive reading of Vee as a transformative force in the novel. Other critics have suggested that Howard objectifies Vee rather than responds to her beauty, despite his own claims that 'It's true that men – they respond to beauty... it doesn't end for them, this... this *concern* with beauty as a physical actuality in the world – and that's clearly imprisoning and infantilizes...' (207). Although Elaine Scarry is concerned with human beauty she makes no comments about the relationship between the pleasures of beauty and those of pornography. The implication of her silence seems to be that pornography is a different category of experience from that of beauty which Scarry argues 'seems to place requirements on us for attending to the aliveness or (in the case of objects) quasi-aliveness of our world, and for entering into its protection' (90). This notion of the impact of beauty on the viewer seems very different from the impact of pornography on the viewer, as Smith's description of Howard's 'lusty week of intense hard-ons at his desk' opening Victoria's pornographic email attachments suggests (379). Smith does not seem to resolve this issue of how pornography inflects Scarry's arguments about beauty and the character of Victoria remains a disruptive and problematic one throughout the novel.

Liberalism and Multiculturalism

In *Harvest of the Sixties* (1995), Patricia Waugh suggests that the *Lady Chatterley* Trial and the Salman Rushdie affair are 'convenient literary frames through which we might gain a purview of the continuing cultural preoccupations of the period, but also of the cultural distance separating 1960 from 1990' (49). Whereas the first trial was held in a national court with common assumptions about the values under which the trial would be decided, the Rushdie affair was played out in the international media with no clear frame of reference according to which to judge the case. As Waugh explains in more detail:

The Obscene Publications Act of 1959, pioneered by Roy Jenkins, had effectively ratified the liberal Romantic view that art is ultimately beyond good and evil. Each side in the *Chatterley* trial thereby concurred that the sexual scenes in the novel were justifiable, providing their aesthetic presentation honoured the moral requirement that sex be portrayed as a form of spiritual symbolic communion.... The trial revealed that the axiomatic values of English culture in 1960 were still those of traditional liberal individualism: honesty, conscience, choice, fulfilment, commitment, dignity, and freedom.... Turning to the Rushdie affair, however, one is confronted with a global media event, fought not within the privacy of a courtroom or even the national press, but staged internationally before millions of newspaper readers and television viewers and involving a confrontation of the incommensurable values of Western secular liberalism with an Islamic fundamentalism still medieval in its canons of blasphemy and heresy. If a liberal consensus could prevail over the trial of *Lady Chatterley's Lover*, it was powerless to reconcile the multicultural contradictions in the case of *The Satanic Verses*. (49–50; my ellipses)

Another striking difference between the two trials that Waugh notes is that 'If most of the members of the prosecution in 1960 were willing to accept lessons in literary appreciation, most of those of 1989 had not even read the book' (50). Waugh goes on to identify a crucial irony in the Rushdie affair:

Throughout the twentieth century Western writers have struggled with the desire to protect the freedom of the artist by arguing for the autonomy and transcendence of art, but have recognized that the price for such freedom may be its social and political marginalization. These were the issues at the heart of the *Lady Chatterley* trial. In placing the death sentence upon Western art, the Ayatollah conferred upon it a cultural significance which even its own practitioners had come to doubt in the thirty years since that trial. (53–4)

Robert Phiddian makes a similar point in his article 'Are Parody and Deconstruction Secretly the Same Thing?' when he says that

the *fatwa* shows how the verbal play of the *Satanic Verses* attaches to textual and material reality. The argument that the novel 'is just fiction' has never been an honest or a good defense for Rushdie, because he was clearly writing about India, Britain, and Islam. The text operates in a way liable to offend a fundamentalist because it relativizes sacred narratives (and not just Islamic sacred narratives – it works over several of the cherished narratives of Englishness, empire, and liberalism), and it does not treat them with anything like the respect they think they deserve. (692)

As the trial of *Lady Chatterley* was Forster's last public speaking appearance, and Zadie Smith has been widely compared to Salman Rushdie,[114] Waugh's positioning of these two trials is highly pertinent to Smith's use of Forster across the even greater 'cultural distance separating' 1910 from 2005.

Waugh's argument that the encounter with multiculturalism created a crisis in the liberal consensus which was 'powerless to reconcile the multicultural contradictions in the case of *The Satanic Verses*' has been widely debated. Brian Barry's reading of the affair, for example, is very different. In his analysis, although 'Liberalism is, indeed, culturally "thinner" than other normative systems', 'a liberal cannot coherently believe that liberal principles should themselves be compromised to accommodate the demands of anti-liberals' (283). Discussing Charles Taylor's 'genuine regret that the case of Rushdie does not lend itself to compromise', Barry points out that compromise could have been attempted but would have been completely undesirable from the liberal perspective:

> There would have been nothing to prevent the British government from proposing to the Iranian authorities some compromise solution. For example, it might have been possible to reach a deal according to which the British government would undertake to transport Rushdie to some neutral venue and an expert Iranian limb-severer would be flown in to remove some agreed portion of his anatomy – say the right arm. The problem is not that it is hard to think of compromises, as Taylor suggests. The problem is, rather, that it would be utterly revolting, from a liberal point of view, to compromise on the proposition that Rushdie should not suffer a legal penalty for writing *The Satanic Verses*. Compromise over liberal principles is not, and cannot be, a liberal value. (283)

In Barry's opinion,

> the correct analysis of the British government's not punishing Rushdie or handing him over to others for punishment (whether within some legal process or outside it) is not 'This is the way we do things here'. It is, rather, that this is the way things ought to be done everywhere: we do things that way here not because it is part of our culture but because it is the right thing to do. (284)

Despite liberalism being 'culturally "thinner" than other normative systems', Barry here suggests that liberalism should be assertive enough to resist the kind of self-contradiction and internal crisis that Waugh argues its encounter with the contradictory multicultural claims of the Rushdie affair provoked.

As Waugh's positioning of these trials indicates, this crisis in liberalism is directly related to its position in time. It is perceived as unable to address the *new* challenges of a globalized and multicultural world. Similarly, Forster's

Victorian liberalism was perceived to be incompatible with the challenges of modernity. His famous statement that, 'If I had to choose between betraying my country and betraying my friend, I hope I should have the guts to betray my country' (*Two Cheers* 76) which appears in his 1939 essay 'What I Believe', for example, is motivated precisely by contemporary pressures to do exactly the opposite in the face of the approaching Second World War. Thus, in both Forster and Smith's novels, their considerations of liberal thought are dismissed largely for being 'untimely', to borrow Elliott's word.

Smith's use of Forster can be read as part of a philosophical and political project to resist this positioning of liberalism as 'out-of-date'. Barry's insistence that 'ideas are not like designer dresses' (9) is part of this attempt to resist the notion that ideas can simply become inappropriate because of their age rather than whether they are 'right' or not. Daniel Born is engaged in a similar attempt in 'Private Gardens and Public Swamps: *Howards End* and the Revaluation of Liberal Guilt' when he argues that

> Forster's novel need not be rescued; is has steadily endured. Yet the tone of much criticism does treat the book, in the spirit of Forster's own wry self-appraisal, as if it were a fossil, an elegiac swansong for an ailing liberal creed. (144)

He goes on to note just how many critics have 'perceived the novel as a touching but nonetheless terminal account of flawed liberalism'. 'It seems now', however, 'that liberalism is not as doddering as either Forster or his critics believed' (144) and that 'given the current atmosphere, much of the criticism of Forster, in its tacit assumptions about liberalism's decay and death, sounds premature' (145). Richard Rorty is the philosopher Born points to in particular as creating the 'current atmosphere' of re-evaluating liberalism that he identifies in this 1992 article. Rorty's influential *Contingency, Irony, and Solidarity* appeared in 1989 and Brian Barry's *Culture and Equality* was published in 2001. Thus, Zadie Smith's return to Forsterian liberalism in 2005, which she perceives as an act of 'brazen ahistoricism', actually demonstrates a notable timeliness.

For Daniel Born one of the central ways in which Forster points towards Rorty's work is via Margaret's reaction to the burden of guilt they all share with regards to Leonard Bast's death. Born suggests that 'Rorty, like Margaret, acknowledges the financial order upon which the life of the mind and culture rests' but that 'he does not want to admit that the sources of one's private pleasures are quite possibly the sources of others' pain' (158). When Margaret tells her sister Helen that she 'can't have you worrying about Leonard. Don't drag in the personal when it will not come. Forget him' (328), Born argues that she is actively deciding to detach their 'private pleasures' from their systematic connections to 'others' pain'. 'Rorty's position', Born explains, 'like Margaret's, is finally meant to relieve us of the burden of guilt – the guilt engendered by seeing systematic connections' (158). It is in this creative response to guilt that we can see a continuity between Smith's *On Beauty* and Forster's *Howards End*. Unlike Margaret and Rorty in Born's reading of their positions, Kiki does decide to see the 'systematic connections' that her son Levi so passionately expresses to her. However, she is able to see them because she is also enabled to do something to deal with the guilt 'seeing systematic connections' engenders in her. She is able to sell the 'private pleasures' of the Hyppolite picture and donate the money to the Haitian Support Group. Born concludes his reading of how Forster's *Howards End* 'engages present debates about the future of liberalism itself' by functioning 'as a criticism of Rorty's influential brand of neoliberal thought' (143) by drawing attention to the fact that Howards End is haunted by the end of the novel by both Mrs. Wilcox and Leonard Bast:

> That Forster interrupts his final scene with awareness of the encroaching London mass suggests he is not entirely happy with this one-sided vision of serene, private, poeticized culture. The conclusion of the book, which remains stubbornly unsettling, indicates crucial truths about Forster's conception of the liberal imagination: that it cannot relax if it is to remain functional; that any attempt to waft away the odors of the abyss is not only intellectually dishonest but also damaging to one's liberal ideals; and that the spirit of Bast competes with Mrs. Wilcox for the privilege of hovering over the final scene in the meadow. The suggestion in this novel – a suggestion more timely than ever given the giddy and unreflective currents of liberal triumphalism that swirl about – is a simple one. For Forster, the liberal imagination retains its vitality only so long as we are able to revalue, and not dispense with, liberal guilt. (159)

I quote at length because this seems to be the central understanding of liberalism that Smith inherits from Forster. Her novel is particularly fascinated by the workings of liberal guilt. The inheritances she explores – Kiki's inheritance of the painting from Carlene and her grandmother's inheritance of the house from her master – are intimately connected to debts that history and society owe.

The debate I have already discussed above between Kiki and Kipps about reparations is not resolved between those two characters but instead is extended into a legal battle over the painting. The blues movement of Kiki out of grief and towards 'black folk' indicates her creative attitude to both of her inheritances – her house and her painting – and towards her guilt over those inheritances. Zadie Smith's retelling of E. M. Forster's *Howards End* is similarly creative. As David James suggests, Smith chooses 'to advance by adhering to what seems past, contemplate[es] [her] originality through the lens of inheritance' (687). This is not retelling as parody but retelling as inheritance.

Chapter 5

The Politics of Nostalgia: Jane Austen Recycled

Rewritings, sequels and adaptations of Jane Austen have proliferated over the past two decades. Even after reducing the scope of this field by focusing only on retellings, sequels, and adaptations of Austen's *Pride and Prejudice* (1813), the range of texts is still remarkable including Helen Fielding's loose adaptation of Austen's plot to contemporary times in *Bridget Jones's Diary* (1996), Emma Tennant's careful recreation of Austen's voice and historical context in *Pemberley* (1993), Hugo Petrus and Nancy Butler's graphic novel (2009), the BBC's hugely popular televised costume drama (1995), examples of 'the American-influenced "bodice-ripper" or "erotic historical"' (as Diana Wallace calls it) such as 'self-described "Texas farm wife"' Linda Berdoll's *Mr Darcy Takes a Wife: a Novel* (2004), and attempts to tell the story from Mr Darcy's perspective such as Amanda Grange's *Mr. Darcy's Diary* (2007). Indeed, the range of *Pride and Prejudice* branded products is so great that Suzanne R. Pucci and James Thompson have termed it 'The Jane Austen Phenomenon' and the media coined the word 'Austenmania.'

In her article 'A Tale of Two Novels: Developing a Devolved Approach to Black British Writing' Corinne Fowler contrasts the fate of hugely successful and highly marketed Zadie Smith with that of Joe Pemberton, a much less commercially successful black British author whose novel, *Forever and Ever Amen*, is set in Manchester's Moss Side. Her comparison examines 'the commercial and cultural logic by which novels are coded as worthy of national and international readerships by corporate publishers and high street retail outlets' and she argues that 'academic studies of contemporary British writing should not mirror too closely the critical and commercial decisions of mainstream publishers' (76). 'The Jane Austen Phenomenon' brings these market forces to the forefront of our attention. It also raises questions about bestsellers, popular fiction, female readers, and feminism.

These are, of course, questions relevant to the authors this book has examined already. The focus of the last chapter – Zadie Smith – is the example of commercial success that Fowler explores in her article. Margaret Atwood examines this issue of the bestseller in *Negotiating with the Dead* and offers a wonderful anecdote from her own experiences as a 'bestseller':

> I can still hear the sneer in the tone of the Parisian intellectual who asked me, 'Is it true you write the *bestsellers?*' 'Not on purpose', I replied somewhat coyly. (68)

Atwood explores in some detail the position of the writer (and particularly the Canadian writer[115]) in relation to money and recognizes the long-standing prejudice that 'to write *for* money, or even to be thought to have done so, put you in the prostitute category' (68). She explains this 'mythology' further: 'Either poor and real, or rich and sell-out with a price-tag on your soul. So goes the mythology' (69). Imelda Whelehan points out that this 'mythology' is apparent in feminist scepticism about the 'bestseller', too, as 'the fact that individual women could make a great deal of money out of their feminist convictions caused great controversy within the Women's Movement at the time' (2). She explores the tension and contradiction inherent in the phrase she takes as the title of her study, *The Feminist Bestseller*, and recognizes the validity of the scepticism of members of the Women's Movement regarding these novels. The feminist bestseller was 'written and marketed in such a way as to suggest naked commercialism and feminists were inclined to remain suspicious of texts which might understandably be viewed as selling out to the capitalist "malestream"' (13). However, Whelehan insists that '[t]he question of whether these books and their writers are "selling out" is a difficult one to answer. Commercial success clearly brings with it celebrity and wealth and in any case well-known authors become fetishized individuals' (14). This process of turning the individual woman author into fetish contrasts uncomfortably with the high value the Women's Movement placed on collectivity and sisterhood.

However, these histories of suspicion towards the bestseller – due to both the traditional cultural assumptions about the writer that Atwood explores and the feminist politics Whelehan examines – do exist alongside a counter-history of celebrating women authors' commercial success. We are reminded of Virginia Woolf's insistence on the need for £500 per year and a 'room of one's own' to be able to write at all. If writing itself made these material conditions possible, the relationship between money and writing could be seen as harmonious. As we shall see in this chapter, the importance of the commercial success of women's writing goes back at least as far as Jane Austen. Jan Fergus's chapter in *The Cambridge Companion to Jane Austen* makes a persuasive case for the fact that 'being a professional writer was, apart from her family, more important to her than anything else in her life' (13).

This final chapter, therefore, examines retellings that are more explicitly commercially motivated and 'popular' than the novels I have examined so far. One of the questions this chapter poses relates to the commercial success of these retellings. I am interested in why there is such a large audience for Austen retellings. As Pucci and Thompson explain,

Even though the world that Austen's novels represent is ostensibly located in the time, space, and conventions of early-nineteenth-century England, the story of Austen's recently exploding popularity across a proliferating variety of media and technologies (film, Internet, tourism, television) is an event, or rather a constellation of events – in other words, a phenomenon that has crystallized at a particular moment in our own contemporary culture. (1)

This chapter will examine what is so attractive about Austen's 'time, space, and conventions' to the late twentieth- and early twenty-first-century reader. Due to the sheer volume of these adaptations, rewritings and serials, I will examine these issues by focusing on one particular retelling: the ITV television series *Lost in Austen* (2008) directed by Dan Zeff.

Lost in Austen: An Adaptation about Adaptation

The opening credits of the ITV television series *Lost in Austen* feature a series of 'cut out' characters from Jane Austen's *Pride and Prejudice* 'popping' into the screen like figures from a children's pop-up book or images from a graphic novel.[116] Among these period costumed figures are images of Jemima Rooper in the character of Amanda Price. She is first portrayed engrossed by *Pride and Prejudice* at a bus stop in London, where she is surprised by Elizabeth Bennet (played by Gemma Arterton) appearing suddenly in front of her. Amanda Price then 'pops' into a stylized Regency setting alongside the central characters from *Pride and Prejudice* in her contemporary dress, now looking totally shocked. Finally, she is portrayed, still in contemporary costume, looking smilingly at the camera from in front of a period garden fountain with Darcy (played by Elliot Cowan) standing in the background and Pemberley (Harewood House) behind him. The effect of portraying the characters like they were 'cut out' and pasted onto the background is to highlight the series' indebtedness to other sources and to position the entire television series as if in quotation marks. Indeed, it is like the characters have been cut out from other costume dramas and pasted into *Lost in Austen*. This series is an adaptation of *Pride and Prejudice* which is as much about adaptation as it is about Austen's novel.

Lost in Austen is highly self-conscious of its status as an adaptation or 'appropriation', to borrow Julie Sanders' term for an adaptation that 'affects a more decisive journey away from the informing source into a wholly new cultural product and domain' (26). It appropriates not only Jane Austen's *Pride and Prejudice*, but also Andrew Davies's 1995 television adaptation of *Pride and Prejudice* for the BBC with Colin Firth as Darcy. Indeed, at one point, the contemporary Amanda Price requests Elliot Cowan as Darcy to re-enact a famous scene from the BBC's adaptation by submerging himself in the garden pond. In her Marxist critique of how adaptations of Austen have replaced historical reality with a partial, idealized image of Regency England in the popular mind, Moyra Haslett points out that 'Many of the visitors to Lyme Park enquired if they could see the pond where Darcy/Colin Firth swam, which might suggest that they were as interested in him as they were in the country house itself' adding that 'In the 1990's, it is sex, as much as money, which sells; and the male body, as much as *objets d'art*, which is commodified' (222).[117] Martine Voiret reads this scene in the context of Regency costume and the fact that this period 'represents an interesting moment in [the] evolution' from a time when 'men and women followed similar standards of beauty' to the 1830s, a period in which '[t]he requirements of beauty and appearance now become the sole province of womanhood' (230–1). She suggests that 'with the influence of gay esthetics' those representations have started to shift and young men are now depicted in advertisements in poses that are 'traditionally considered feminine postures: leaning back, in languid poses' (232). Discussing the male white linen shirt of this period, Voiret suggests that it playfully reverses the modesty traditionally expected of women and 'begs to be untied' (232). Voiret describes exactly the scene that Amanda requests Darcy to replay for her in a knowing re-enactment of the Darcy parties at which, Voiret informs us, 'Female viewers would repeatedly play the scene of Darcy diving and emerging in his wet clothes, his opened white shirt sexily sticking to his dripping body' (232–3). Voiret's reading of this kind of commodification of the male body in Austen adaptations is positive: 'it allows the female viewer the pleasures of agency and looking usually reserved to the male viewer' (231). I will return to this issue of sexual pleasure and Austen adaptations shortly. We can certainly agree that Amanda Price's request for a re-enactment of that scene playfully reveals *Lost in Austen*'s knowing awareness of what Pucci and Thompson call 'The Jane Austen Phenomenon' (1) or, with a greater emphasis on the commercial powers at play, what their book title calls *Jane Austen and Co.*[118]

At another point in *Lost in Austen*, Amanda also makes the comment that 'even Colin Firth isn't Colin Firth – they had to change the shape of his head with make-up.' This comment has comic effect but also self-consciously draws our attention to the series' anxiety about 'authenticity', 'fidelity', and indebtedness. In his 'Afterword: On Fidelity', John Wiltshire makes exactly this point about Jane Austen adaptations: 'The later films derive as much from the earlier films as they do from the novels: they are hybrid, or even miscengenated works, which derive only in part from the cinematic Jane Austen' (170).

As well as playing self-consciously with these layers of adaptation and the pleasures of the historically costumed male body, the series also borrows its title from another adaptation or appropriation of Jane Austen – Emma Campbell Webster's *Lost in Austen: Create Your Own Jane Austen Adventure* (2007). This interactive book requires the reader to turn to different pages depending on their answers to certain questions. The reader collects Confidence, Intelligence and Fortune points on their journey through the book attempting to reach the successful conclusion of marriage with Mr. Darcy. The ITV television series adapts the central idea of Webster's book – that the reader becomes Elizabeth Bennet. Indeed, another intertext for the opening series of *Lost in Austen* in which the contemporary character finds herself confronted with Elizabeth Bennet as she waits at a contemporary London bus stop and then suddenly appears in the costume world of Regency England is that of gaming. Like Webster's book, the ITV series turns *Pride and Prejudice* into a virtual world or game for Amanda Price. This is the same strategy as Laurie Viera Rigler uses in *Confessions of a Jane Austen Addict* (2008) in which Californian Courtney Stone wakes up as 'Jane Mansfield', a composite Austen character. As a result of 'being such a Jane Austen addict' (2), Courtney, like Amanda Price, wakes up to find herself in 'Austen-land.'

Lost in Austen also self-consciously adapts 'chick lit' by installing several key characteristics of that genre in its opening scenes – the urban single girl with a female flat-mate, divorced mother and disappointing boyfriend. This reference to the genre of 'chick lit' appropriates the argument of those who claim that Jane Austen wrote 'the original chick-lit masterpiece' (Swendson 63). Shanna Swendson ends her essay of that title by suggesting that 'A smart publisher would put a cartoon cover on *Pride and Prejudice* and reissue it in a trade paperback edition, where it would fit in perfectly with all those other chick-lit novels on the 'new in paperback' table at the bookstore' (69); and, indeed, 'smart publishers' have! For example, see the stylized images of women on the front cover of the 2007 Vintage Classics edition; the hand-written title on the cover of the 2009 Penguin Classics edition; the handwritten title and pencil drawing of a bird cage on the Signet Classic of 2009; and the pink, handwritten title and stylized images used on the cover of the 2006 edition from Headline Book Publishing along with the added subtitle, 'A Classic Romance.'[119] Swendson's argument gains a great deal of credence from the importance of Austen to what is widely acknowledged to be the first classic of 'chick lit' – *Bridget Jones's Diary*.

Helen Fielding has been widely quoted in newspaper articles and interviews admitting to having 'stolen' Jane Austen's plot from *Pride and Prejudice* and says that she was as obsessed by the BBC miniseries starring Colin Firth as the rest of Britain was at the time she was writing the original newspaper columns that built up to the novel, *Bridget Jones's Diary* (1996). There were two particularly important overlaps between the BBC television series of *Pride and Prejudice* and the film adaptation of *Bridget Jones's Diary* (2001) – the use of Colin Firth to play the contemporary Mark Darcy after his having played Darcy in the BBC series and Andrew Davies's input into the script for *Bridget Jones's Diary* after his authorship of the screenplay for the BBC's *Pride and Prejudice*. As Suzanne Ferriss carefully documents in her book chapter, 'the movie version strengthens the allusions to Austen's novel' (73).[120] *Bridget Jones's Diary* was so popular and successful that it can be seen to have spawned a phenomenon of its own that 'stole' (to use Fielding's vocabulary) audiences and appeal from 'The Austen Phenomenon' even as it added to it. For despite Fielding's transgressive vocabulary ('stole'), she took from Austen because she thought her plots were 'very good' (qtd in Ferriss 71). Thus, there is homage and respect in her intertextual allusions to Austen.

As I have already suggested, *Lost in Austen*'s multiple intertexts and the series' opening credits function rather like putting inverted commas around the 'Austen' of the series' title – Amanda is *Lost in 'Austen.'* '[O]ne of the curious properties of these typographical signifiers', as Marjorie Garber points out in *Quotation Marks*, is that 'in their present condition of use, they may indicate either authenticity or doubt'(8). Furthermore, as Garber goes on to argue, 'In some ways quotation is a kind of cultural ventriloquism, a throwing of the voice that is also an appropriation of authority' (16) and 'we might say that *every* quotation is a quotation out of context, inevitably both a duplication and a duplicity' (21). *Lost in Austen* simultaneously displays anxiety about putting 'Austen' in quotation marks, while also gleefully gaining a great deal of its cultural authority and comic effect from its 'ventriloquism' of Austen.[121] In a scene in which Caroline Bingley reveals her lesbian sexuality to Amanda, Amanda effectively puts words into Jane Austen's mouth when she comments to the audience 'Goodness, Jane Austen would be fairly surprised to find she'd written that!' The series celebrates the duplicity generated by quoting out of context here, as this reference to lesbian sexuality in Austen is yet another intertextual adaptation or appropriation – in this case, of the media storm and controversy initiated by Terry Castle's review of Jane Austen's letters. 'Jane-ites' would remember the 1995 controversy in which Castle was repeatedly misquoted as having argued that Austen was an incestuous lesbian.[122] However, *Lost in Austen* also gestures towards 'authenticity' and 'fidelity' via the meticulous recreation in costume and set of Regency England, which is documented in the 'behind the scenes extras' on the DVD and contributes greatly to the series' visual effectiveness. Dan Zeff describes his contradictory goals of wanting to capture the 'fun' of the idea of a real contemporary person entering the fictional world of the novel, while also achieving a 'sense of authenticity.' He offers the analogy of being in a museum, 'but a museum in which you can touch the exhibits.' His dual goals echo Garber's description of quotation marks as being capable of conveying 'both absolute authenticity and veracity, on the one hand, and suspected inauthenticity, irony, or doubt, on the other' (12).

One of the ways in which the series deals with its anxiety about its relationship to its Austen source text is to suggest that the new heroine, Amanda Price, is only able to go back and enter the story because of her own love, respect and repeated reading of *Pride and Prejudice*. The opening sequence of *Lost in Austen* seems to blur the three kinds of 'modes of engagement' that Linda Hutcheon identifies in *A Theory of Adaptation*: 'to tell, show or interact with stories' (22). Hutcheon roughly aligns telling with text, showing with visual media like films, plays and operas, and interacting with new media such as virtual reality, games and also theme park rides. (She does, however, admit that these alignments are approximate and that, for example, one could interact imaginatively with a novel to a greater extent than with certain video games.) The opening sequence of *Lost in Austen* purposely tries to blur these distinctions.

When reading, Amanda seems to 'see' the novel's events as the image of her reading on the sofa is replaced by scenes that we will later recognize as being from the TV series itself. This device suggests that she becomes a first-person player in the world of *Pride and Prejudice* via her reading. The device of time travel through the portal in her bathroom enables Amanda to do exactly this, but what is interesting is how this opening series links the first-person player experience of time travel to the more common experience of reading.[123]

For Amanda, reading is a refuge from a world in which twice during the early sequence depicting her journey home from work, she is physically pushed around by men – a man with a rucksack on the bus and then a man riding a bicycle on the pavement.[124] Reading is presented as a particularly female strategy for coping with the contemporary world. Or, as the (male) reviewer, Thomas Sutcliffe put it in *The Independent*, 'The reluctant time traveller in *Lost in Austen* is Amanda Price, an Austen devotee who uses the novels much as some women use Valium, to smooth out the disappointments of daily life' (website). Amanda's panicked reaction upon waking up to find herself still in the world of Austen after her first night there could lead us to add to Sutcliffe's analogy for Amanda's 'use' of Austen, 'or much as some men use pornography, to smooth out the disappointments of daily life.'

Finding that she is still stuck in what appears to her to be a Regency costume drama set of some kind, and discovering Lydia Bennet in bed alongside her, Amanda immediately assumes that she has been part of a reality TV trick and that the producer will want some kind of sexual action from the two women. 'What are you after guys?' she asks the invisible cameras she assumes are hidden in the room. This dissonant moment makes clear one aspect of the contemporary world that Amanda experiences as threateningly pervasive. Robert Jensen has identified in *Getting Off: Pornography and the End of Masculinity* what he calls the 'paradox of pornography' – 'the way sex is done in pornography is becoming more and more cruel and degrading at the same time that pornography is becoming more normalized than ever' (16). When Amanda tells her mother that she 'loves the manners, and the language, and the courtesy' of Austen's novels and that she does not 'trust' her boyfriend because he 'had it off with a waitress' 'two nights running', she is questioning the real benefits for women of the Sexual Revolution. In this respect, Amanda's nostalgia for the world of Austen actually aligns her with a feminist critique of the Sexual Revolution. As Imelda Whelehan helpfully summarizes in *The Feminist Bestseller*,

> Feminists generally saw this vision of a Sexual Revolution as a chimera where women were being sold the idea of sex as liberation but often it cast them in just as strong a thrall to men, with new pressures to perform sexually at every occasion. (109)

The clash between feminism and the Sexual Revolution is often forgotten in contemporary culture. Voiret's positive reading of the sexuality depicted in adaptations of Austen because they tend to allow 'the female viewer the pleasures of agency and looking usually reserved to the male viewer' (231) is typical of post-feminist reactions to women and sexual desire. Voiret fails to question whether this reversal of the usual gender of the viewer is really evidence of a feminist impulse in Austen adaptations, or simply a result of the commercial logic of late capitalism which looks to sell everything it possibly can, to as many different sections of the market as it can attract.[125] Certainly, it would be difficult to read the gender politics of Linda Berdoll's insertion of sexually explicit scenes between Elizabeth and Darcy in her *Mr Darcy Takes a Wife: a Novel* as 'feminist.' Her novel relishes the scandal of Darcy's previous sexual exploits without pursuing any feminist critique of the double-standard at work.

Despite her desire for 'courtesy' and preference for Jane Austen, Amanda is clearly somewhat versed in the clichés of pornography as she offers the hidden cameras 'girl on girl action', asks if she has to 'snog' Lydia to 'get out of here', and finally shows them 'her pubes', revealing a 'landing strip – standard pubic topiary' to the shocked Lydia who gasps, 'What have you done to yourself?' Amanda's strangely contradictory response to finding herself in what she believes to be a live cable reality porn show – both furious and yet complicit – demonstrates Angela McRobbie's concerns that feminism is being 'undone':

> If we turn attention to some of the participatory dynamics of leisure and everyday life which see young women endorse (or else refuse to condemn) the ironic normalisation of pornography, where they indicate their approval of and desire to be pin-up girls for the centrefolds of the soft porn so-called lads' mags, where it is not at all unusual to pass young women in the street wearing T-shirts bearing phrases such as 'Porn Queen' or 'Pay To Touch' across the breasts, where in the UK at least young women quite happily attend lap-dancing clubs (perhaps as a test of their sophistication and 'cool'), and where *Cosmopolitan* magazine considers how empowering it is for young women to 'flash' their breasts in public, we are witness to a hyper-culture of commercial sexuality, one aspect of which is the repudiation of feminism which is invoked only to be summarily dismissed...Thus the new female subject is, despite her freedom, called upon to be silent, to withhold critique in order to count as a modern sophisticated girl. Indeed this withholding of critique is a condition of her freedom. (17–18)

Amanda's reaction is that of a woman who is well aware of this social contract, believing that complicity with the pornographic cable show she fears she is now in, will get her 'out of here' most quickly. Diane Negra makes a similar point by pointing to the purely commercial benefits of complicity with patriarchy for women living in a Western world where they are endlessly fed images of luxury to aspire to while actual wealth is decreasing for all but the very rich:

> Yet in another sense there is an economic logic at work here too in terms of the new authority that working-class women are granted to 'own' their

sexual labor in the marketplace. As Imelda Whelehan reminds us, the 'only sphere in which women's pay consistently outstrips men's is in the realm of heterosexual pornography'. (100)

The juxtaposition between pornography and the world of Austen that *Lost in Austen* sets up in this scene has a precedent in critical debates over Austen's depictions of sexuality. Claudia L. Johnson critiques appeals to the self-evidence that Austen was 'proper' in 'The Divine Miss Jane':

> Pressing fantasies about the serenity of Regency England into the service of heterosexual presumption, Kimball and Rosenblatt place Austen *before* the advent of such ills as industrialization, dubiety, feminism, homosexuality, masturbation, the unconscious. In her novels, men are gentlemen, women are ladies, and the desires of gentlemen and ladies for each other are intelligible, complementary, mutually fulfilling, and, above all, *inevitable*. (144)

I've already mentioned Eve Kosofsky Sedwick's famous essay, 'Jane Austen and the Masturbating Girl', which explores Austen's awareness of 'the masturbating girl' as an emerging and possible sexual identity and, thereby, also critiques this positioning of Austen as '*before.*' Another helpful essay which questions the assumption that Austen predates feminism, homosexuality, masturbation and pornography is Jill Heydt-Stevenson's '"Slipping into the Ha-Ha": Bawdy Humor and Body Politics in Jane Austen's Novels.' Johnson and Heydt-Stevenson conclude their essays similarly. Johnson argues that

> it has been not only Austen's detractors but her admirers, too, who have suspected that the 'Passions' were (as Brontë put it[126]) 'entirely unknown' to her not because Austen was such a good girl but because in some secret, perhaps not fully definable way, she was so bad. (163)

Heydt-Stevenson ends with Auden's famous quotation:

> In her bawdy/body humor Austen frankly breaches normative ideologies, integrating these instances of immodest and risqué humor into the narratives as a whole: in other words, they are not odd moments to pass over and to titter about in private, but pleasurable and unabashed inscriptions of a sexuality that is foundational rather than incidental or anomalous. As W. H. Auden wrote of Austen: 'You could not shock her more than she shocks me; / Beside her Joyce seems innocent as grass'. (339)

Lost in Austen seems knowingly aware of these debates in this scene of Amanda Price's first morning in Austen-land. By assuming she is in a costume pornographic reality TV series, does Amanda Price move into a space already present, though repressed, in Austen's text or is she entirely dissonant in juxtaposing this fear with Austen's portrayal and awareness of sexuality?

The (Female) Pleasures of Reading

These debates about sexuality and pleasure return us to the opening scene of *Lost in Austen*, and the selfish and pleasurable nature of reading Austen for Amanda Price. Amanda's opening comments and her determination that she will spend an evening at home alone reading *Pride and Prejudice* as a preferential alternative to spending the evening with her boyfriend echo the opinion of Constance Reader in Adam Roberts's satirical piece 'Jane Austen and the Masturbating Critic.' Roberts's parody attempts to give voice to the pleasure Jane Austen fans experience in reading her novels:

> CONSTANCE READER: And let me begin by saying that I do not merely *like* Jane Austen's books. No, I *love* Jane Austen. I know all of her novels, and I reread them regularly. Indeed, reading is one of my chief pastimes. I have many favorite authors, but Jane occupies a special place in my affections.
>
> PROFESSOR ACADEMICUS: I am pleased to hear it, madam. As a salaried university professor of English Literature, I have built my reputation as a scholar of the early years of the nineteenth century, with a number of articles and monographs on Austen's novels. I share your approbation of her writing.
>
> CONSTANCE READER: And there, sir, is precisely my problem. I do not believe that you, and your kind—
>
> PROFESSOR ACADEMICUS: My *kind*? Madam! What do you mean?
>
> CONSTANCE READER: I mean the type or species of academic critics – I cannot believe that any of *you* truly understand what it is about Austen that makes her worthy of her readers' love. *I* know what I love about her writing. (51)

The gender politics here are pertinent. The academic critic is significantly male, and the adoring Austen fan is female. Roberts uses this to his advantage in order to throw these two allegorical characters together in a passionate embrace at the end of his piece with Professor Academicus exclaiming

> My love! For too long my pleasures – my reading of Austen, my writing about Austen, my dreaming of Austen's worlds – have been solitary pleasures, secretively and even furtively undertaken. But now, with you, I have someone with whom I can share my pleasure!

Constance Reader replies:

> And I too, my love! For too long Jane's novels have been, in my life, merely a lonely substitute for the love-connection they describe. I have wallowed in this solitary emotional pleasure instead of making that outward connection with another human being...but no longer! (62)

Roberts's effect here is clearly predominantly comic but he does have Professor Academicus articulate the realization that he has been 'sometimes, unregarding of the needs of the broader reading public' (61). The pleasure of reading Austen is a central theme of *Lost in Austen*, because, as I mention above, it is Amanda's love of her novel that allows her through the portal in her bathroom and into the world of Austen.

This is a crucial strategy for positioning *Lost in Austen* in relation to its market audience. Given that ITV would want to count Austen fans amongst the audience for this series, it was crucial to find a way to change the novel while retaining the audience's sympathy. Robert Stam has been one of many critics to identify that

> [t]he traditional language of criticism of filmic adaptation of novels...has often been extremely judgmental, proliferating in terms that imply the film has performed a disservice to literature. Terms such as 'infidelity', 'betrayal', 'deformation', 'violation', 'vulgarization', 'bastardization', and 'desecration' proliferate, with each word carrying its specific charge of opprobrium. (3)[127]

By introducing an entirely new, contemporary character into Austen's novel, *Lost in Austen* demonstrates significant anxiety about its failure to be 'faithful' to Austen. In the 'behind the scenes extras' on the DVD, Hugh Bonneville is quick to describe the relationship between *Lost in Austen* and *Pride and Prejudice* as loving rather than a betrayal, reassuring those who are 'appalled at the idea of Jane Austen being tampered with' that *Lost in Austen* is an 'affectionate tribute.' This anxiety about changing *Pride and Prejudice* becomes a central element of *Lost in Austen*'s plot as Amanda Price does all she can to try to pair the characters up as they should be in the novel. Ironically, her own prejudice that Darcy must end up with Elizabeth Bennet is what causes her to faithfully mirror Austen's plot by remaining blind to her own love for Darcy until well into the series. As Linda Hutcheon has argued in *A Theory of Adaptation*, 'the appeal of adaptations for audiences lies in their mixture of repetition and difference, of familiarity and novelty' (114). The appeal of repetition is deep and complex:

> Freudians too might say we repeat as a way of making up for loss, as a means of control, or of coping with privation. But adaptation as repetition is arguably not a postponement of pleasure; it is in itself a pleasure. Think of a child's delight in hearing the same nursery rhymes or reading the same books over and over. Like ritual, this kind of repetition brings comfort, a fuller understanding, and the confidence that comes with the sense of knowing what is about to happen next. (Hutcheon 114)

However, as Hutcheon goes on to explain, 'But something else happens with adaptations in particular: there is inevitably difference as well as repetition' and

'To focus on repetition alone, in other words, is to suggest only the potentially conservative element in the audience response to adaptation' (115).

This appropriation of *Pride and Prejudice* plays with these expectations. On the one hand, we share Amanda's distress that her entry into Austen's novel has changed the events of the novel and caused her to lose that 'confidence that comes with the sense of knowing what is about to happen next.' The negative events in *Lost in Austen*'s new plot – Jane's marriage to Mr. Collins and Charlotte Lucas's decision to go as a missionary to Africa – function to critique Austen's idealized version of Regency England by making much more starkly clear the limited choices and financial pressures women faced in this period. Indeed, in his interview on the DVD, Zeff expresses his aim of capturing some of the 'less comfortable' aspects of Georgian England and Amanda spends most of the first two episodes feeling most uncomfortable in Austen's world.[128] Some of these discomforts are trivial and amusing, like cleaning her teeth with chalk and twigs. However, others, like the experiences of Jane and Charlotte, are more significant. When Amanda and Darcy travel to contemporary London, the series highlights via two references – Darcy's racist comment on the bus and Amanda's roommate, Pirhana's, response to her invitation to see Austen's world for ten minutes[129] – the serious and threatening discomfort experienced by people of colour in Austen's world.

Although Zeff's series does offer up the familiar images of Regency England for easy consumption that Haslett is uncomfortable with – the country houses and dances – it does hint at a critique. For example, as they approach the ball Amanda can't help but exclaim at the extravagant sight of the lanterns – 'You could park a bloody jumbo!'[130] – thereby drawing attention to the conspicuous consumption and display of wealth. At the dinner party at Lady Catherine de Bourgh's, she criticizes Darcy for having no purpose or work in his life. In the exchange with Caroline Bingley in which Caroline admits her lesbian sexuality, Amanda is given a short speech criticizing 'you people' in which she states: 'if just one of you actually said or did something you actually meant, that had any kind of emotional integrity, the rest of you would die of fright.' All of these are examples of Zeff and Andrews offering critiques of Regency England even as we nostalgically enjoy their recreation of that world. Brandy Foster uses the word 'pimp' – meaning 'to customize' – to explain how appropriations of Austen like Zeff's attest to 'readers' need to have Austen their way' (2).[131]

The Feminist Politics of Nostalgia

In its insistence on the primacy of Austen's text and by suggesting that Amanda can only enter the story because of her love of it and familiarity with it, *Lost in Austen* is predominantly nostalgic and deferential rather than critical in its treatment of *Pride and Prejudice*. It offers a greater degree of homage than criticism of Austen's world mainly through its focus on the heterosexual plot between Amanda and Darcy. Amanda's relationship with Darcy closely follows the plot development from misunderstanding and judgment to a slowly developing love that Austen's novel so famously employs, and Amanda does choose Austen's past over her own present. We need to acknowledge that the untold story of Elizabeth Bennet's preference for London in the twenty-first century over her own role in Austen's novel acts as a corrective to Amanda's idealized nostalgia for Regency England. This story remains hidden below the surface of the film but is just visible enough to trouble Amanda's assumptions that any woman would prefer to live in Austen's world rather than contemporary England. However, the series ends with the heterosexual union of Amanda and Darcy in a world into which we must presume Amanda cannot take her enormous fortune of 'twenty-seven thousand a year.' Thus, she is no longer the financially independent single woman of her twenty-first-century incarnation, but, instead, is as poor and financially dependent on Darcy as Elizabeth Bennet is in Austen's original text. Tim Teeman comments on the implications of this ending in his review in *The Times*:

> The sexual politics of this were momentarily unsettling – the worrying prospect of one's fictional romantic hero being more fulfilling ultimately than anyone in present-day reality – but then I had another chocolate and marvelled at the sharp yet frothy, subversive-yet-utterly-respectful-of-Austen brilliance of it all.

Indeed, Teeman's comment prompts the question: what are the sexual politics of Amanda's nostalgic preference for Austen's world? To some extent, it could be argued that adaptations are always inherently nostalgic, choosing to return to a previous text rather than start afresh. Thus, Amanda's nostalgia is shared by the viewer of the adaptation and is an inevitable consequence of the adaptation genre. But what are the politics of this nostalgia? John Ellis argued in 1982 that the 'process of adaptation should thus be seen as a massive investment (financial and psychic) in the desire to repeat particular acts of consumption within a form of representation that discourages such a repetition' (4–5). He suggests that there is something contradictory between film adaptation and the logic of capitalism which calls always for the new. However, the actual history of the relationship between capitalism and adaptation since 1982 rather belies Ellis's comments, as Hutcheon points out: 'It is no surprise that economic motivation affects all stages of the adaptation process' (88). Jennifer Ladino, in her consideration of the progressive potential of nostalgia, lists 'its easy cooptation by capitalism' as one of its 'admittedly problematic traits' (88). In her feminist consideration of the uses of memory, Gayle Greene positions nostalgia as 'merely regressive' (298), arguing that

> [n]ostalgia is not only a longing to return home; it is also a longing to return to the state of things in which woman keeps the home and in which she awaits, like Penelope, the return of her wandering Odysseus. But if going

back is advantageous to those who have enjoyed power, it is dangerous to those who have not. (296)

It is interesting to note that in both *Lost in Austen* and *Kate and Leopold*, it is the woman who travels back in time.

This understanding of nostalgia as 'regressive, ahistorical, or uncritical', to borrow Ladino's list of negative synonyms for 'nostalgic', has been more recently revised. One field in which this has occurred is that of ecocriticism in which Ladino is operating to try to 'breathe new life into nostalgia, to revitalize and rearticulate its diverse narrative possibilities, and to redeploy it in the service of more progressive politics' (88). In ecopolitics, temporality is often inverted. We are haunted by our future and our children's future rather than the past, and to look nostalgically back is to engage in critique of the current moment and the trajectory we have taken. Another context in which nostalgia has received revisionist readings is that of affect theory. Nostalgia is an emotional rather than rational response to the past. It is its affective power that leads Sinead McDermott to rethink Gayle Greene's rejection of nostalgia. McDermott suggests that

> nostalgia is a necessary ingredient of such memory-work. When we long for the past, we long for what might have been as well as what was; it is only by incorporating such longings into our narratives that we can suspend the past and ultimately change its meaning in the present. (405–6)

Roberta Rubenstein's *Home Matters* offers a similar reconsideration of this negative evaluation of nostalgia.

For Martine Voiret, nostalgic adaptations of Austen allow for playing in the past, which is helpful for identity formation in the present:

> With its play on costume and disguise, the historical drama encourages multiple identifications. The genre invites the spectator to try out the different roles presented by the various characters. This process is never a simple movement of going back to outdated modes of being. Part of the attraction of costume drama, of course, is that it gives the spectator license to identify with roles or characteristics now devalued. More important, costume drama is invested with the needs and fantasies of the present. (230)

Thus, for Voiret, the Austen historical drama offers the possibility of occupying 'now devalued' subject positions and experimenting or 'playing' with opinions and possibilities. Diana Wallace makes similar arguments for popular historical fiction by women in her study of *The Woman's Historical Novel*. Just as Voiret suggests that costume drama reflects current 'needs and fantasies', Wallace argues that,

Although readers are often attracted to historical novels because they believe they will learn about the past time recreated in the novel, any historical novel always has as much, or perhaps more, to say about the time in which it is written. (4)

Furthermore, Wallace's assertion that 'As a genre, the historical novel has allowed women writers a license which they have not been allowed in other forms' (6) echoes directly Voiret's notion that costume dramas 'give the spectator license.'

In *Jane Austen and Co*, Pucci and Thompson argue that:

> The striking surge in Austen's cultural capital has been mostly commonly explained away as 'nostalgia', but such an explanation is at best a circular response, begging the question of what we are nostalgic for and why now. When academic and journalistic commentators designate the interest in Austen as an escape from modernity into some idealized past, such a response offers little explanation of what it is specifically that readers and viewers are seeking, and, moreover, what it is that they find. (2)

These are difficult questions, but the fact that they are difficult should surely not be a reason to rule out nostalgia *per se*. Furthermore, as Claudia L. Johnson's 'The Divine Miss Jane: Jane Austen, Janeites, and the Discipline of Novel Studies' reveals, there is a significant history of nostalgia for Austen, of reading her novels for escape, refuge or redemption (154–5). Thus, the question 'why now?' should really be 'why again?'

In her wonderfully written account of nostalgia, Svetlana Boym illustrates that nostalgia emerged alongside modernity. Pursuing nostalgia's 'historical rather than psychological genesis' (7) she demonstrates how nostalgia is not only a spatial desire to return to a place called 'home' but is also a temporal experience. It is a longing for the time before 'time' became 'money' (9). For Boym then, the nostalgic image of 'country mirth' as the people 'joined in circles, / Rustically solemn or in rustic laughter' dancing in the 'time of seasons', 'time of milking and time of harvest' in 'East Coker' (196–7), is as direct an expression of T. S. Eliot's reaction to modernity as the 'crowd' that flows over London Bridge 'To where Saint Mary Woolnoth kept the hours' all 'undone' by 'death' (65) in his bleak depiction of London in *The Waste Land* (1922). Boym reads nostalgia as an inevitable symptom of modernity:

> Somehow progress didn't cure nostalgia but exacerbated it. Similarly, globalization encouraged stronger local attachments. In counterpoint to our fascination with cyberspace and the virtual global village, there is a no less global epidemic of nostalgia, an affective yearning for a community with a collective memory, a longing for continuity in a fragmented world. Nostalgia

inevitably reappears as a defense mechanism in a time of accelerated rhythms of life and historical upheavals. (xiv)

Boym's historical reading of nostalgia's development alongside industrialization and the mechanization of time points us towards these retellings' relationship to 'postmodern nostalgia.' In *Confessions of a Jane Austen Addict*, Laurie Viera Rigler's protagonist, Courtney, is 'caught watching the *Pride and Prejudice* DVD in the middle of the night for the umpteenth time' by her boyfriend, Frank, who 'sneeringly referred to my fascination with Jane Austen's world as postmodern nostalgia' (88). Courtney, like Constance Reader in Adam Roberts's satirical piece 'Jane Austen and the Masturbating Critic', rejects Frank's intellectual approach to her pleasurable return to Austen by telling the reader confidentially, 'Not that I have the faintest idea of what "postmodern" means, despite Frank's having spent many hours lecturing me on the topic' (88). As Zadie Smith demonstrates in relation to both Monty Kipps and Howard Belsey in *On Beauty*, intellectual men are not necessarily ethical men, and the reader is encouraged to share Courtney's dismissal of Frank's intellectual explanation of her nostalgia because he cheated on her just before their planned marriage with their wedding cake designer. It is assumed that the reader shares Courtney's addiction to Austen and the first person narration encourages the reader to sympathize with Courtney rather than Frank. Like Professor Academicus, Frank is depicted as a man out of touch with emotion. It is ironic, therefore, that it is partly Frank's behaviour that prompts Courtney's nostalgia because one thing this recycling of Austen demonstrates is a nostalgia for the English gentleman. In contrast, to the ironic parodies I examined in the first three chapters, one thing some of these Austen retellings want to escape from is irony. Nostalgia for and romance with the English gentleman operates as a way of resisting what Negra termed the 'ironic normalization of pornography.' Given the ways in which 'the new female subject is, despite her freedom, called upon to be silent, to withhold critique in order to count as a modern sophisticated girl', it may be possible to view her nostalgic preference for the Regency gentleman as a silent critique, a coded comment about the 'ironic normalization of pornography' (Negra 17–18; qtd above).

As Christine Berberich suggests in her study of *The Image of the English Gentleman in Twentieth-Century Literature*, 'Old values, traditions and institutions are often evoked when compiling lists of Englishness, or of the prerequisites of the gentleman, and a sense of nostalgia is often inevitable' (27). In both Rigler's novel, *Confessions of a Jane Austen Addict* and in the ITV series *Lost in Austen*, the female protagonists' nostalgia for 'Austen-land' is motivated to a large degree by their disappointment in their contemporary boyfriends, particularly their boyfriends' sexual infidelity. This is one of Bridget Jones's motivations, too. It is Daniel Cleaver's failure to be a 'gentleman' that contributes to Bridget's slow realization of Mark Darcy's attractiveness. In her analysis of *Bridget Jones's Diary* in *Overloaded* (2000), Imelda Whelehan reads Bridget Jones as 'a woman who recognises the rhetoric of feminism and empowerment, but isn't always able to relate this to her fulsome desire for a hero from a Jane Austen novel' (136).[132] Interestingly, Whelehan's chapter on 'The Bridget Jones Effect' comes immediately after her chapter entitled 'Men Under Siege' in which she argues that 'modern man is in crisis' but the 'response *has* to amount to more than simply laying the blame on feminism' (134). She goes onto explain why changing 'masculinity' is such a slow process:

> All contemporary men's movements are taking part in this process of reassessment – even though one might be sceptical about their observations – in that they are forced to reflect upon what 'being a man' means. Sadly, few take up the challenge to reinvent themselves or enter the 'private sphere' in more meaningful ways, thus forcing a re-evaluation of men's relationship to work, parenting, sexuality and women in general. Unfortunately, 'men in crisis' fall into the easy trap of blaming women's growing 'advantages' as the cause of their malaise: this satisfies nobody and turns us away from a more politicised recognition that changing employment structures are gradually crippling us all and fatally skewing our relationship to ourselves and each other. (134)

Instead of viewing Bridget's failure to live up to feminist ideals as caused by the misguided belief that feminism 'is incompatible with heterosexuality because of the tough choices it might be seen to present once one "politicises" one's own relationships' (138), perhaps it would be more fruitful to relate her failure to the 'men in crisis' of the previous chapter. It is fascinating that while men regularly blame feminism for the crisis in masculinity, (heterosexual) women tend to be reluctant to blame men for the difficulties of living a feminist life despite the popular media depiction of feminists as 'men-haters' (or perhaps in an anxious correction of that popular view). As Lessing put it so clearly in a quotation I have already referred to in Chapter 1 from *The Golden Notebook*: 'What's the use of [women] being free if [men] aren't? I swear to God, that every one of them, even the best of them, have the old idea of good women and bad women' (404). Indeed, Whelehan's wish that more men would 'take up the challenge to reinvent themselves or enter the "private sphere" in more meaningful ways' finds a positive response in the final lines of Robert Jensen's *Getting Off: Pornography and the End of Masculinity*:

> If my options as a man are being part of a mob that is on the edge of violence or being cut off from myself and others, I desperately want to choose something else.
> I choose to renounce being a man.
> I choose to struggle to be a human being. (185)

Thus, the post-feminist nostalgia evident in these retellings of Austen may reflect not so much women's frustrations at or rejection of feminism, so much as a disappointment with contemporary masculinity.

I have already indicated above one way in which we can read Amanda's nostalgia as critical rather than conservative – by seeing how *Lost in Austen* juxtaposes contemporary sexual conventions with those of Georgian England. The first episode, in particular, achieves this partly via Amanda's frightened and angry assumption that she is trapped in a strange period pornographic reality TV show. Her reaction suggests Jensen's point that, 'At the moment, it's the pornographer's world. They are the ones telling the most influential stories about gender and power and sex' (184). Austen's stories of the gentleman and of romance offer alternative narratives to that of the pornographer. Contemporary Amanda's misrecognition of which story she is in offers a critique via nostalgia of the current 'influential stories about gender and power and sex.' However, the third episode in the *Lost in Austen* series disrupts Amanda's nostalgia for the sexual conventions of Georgian England by having Darcy reject Amanda for not being 'a maid.' Amanda's equally dismayed reactions to on the one hand her 'real' contemporary boyfriend's, Michael, extremely unromantic proposal and on the other to Darcy's withdrawal of his proposal when he discovers she is not a virgin demonstrate that the Sexual Revolution has involved losses as well as gains for women. Although the series does not offer any social solutions to Amanda's predicament, by historicizing her dilemmas, it does depict the changing nature of ideals of femininity. It also tells other stories about gender relations. As we saw in Morrison's *The Bluest Eye*, historicizing contemporary culture is a crucial step in undermining the assumption that the current situation is 'natural' and 'immutable.'

Alongside the conservative elements of this appropriation of Austen – such as the heterosexual union at the end for which Amanda gives up financial independence and the suppression of Elizabeth Bennet's story – there are suggestions that Amanda's nostalgia for Austen's world does imbue her with transformative agency. Crucially, she refuses the drunken proposal of her cheating boyfriend despite her mother's urging her to accept because he does not beat her up or take drugs. Indeed, in one thing the worlds of Elizabeth and Amanda are remarkably and depressingly similar. In both worlds, their mothers urge a loveless marriage as a woman's only means to be secure. In the twenty-first century, Amanda's divorced mother ironically tells her to accept her boyfriend's drunken marriage proposal as it may be her only hope to have someone to 'help her off with her coat' when she is old. This is despite the fact that her broken marriage has left her alone with no one to 'help her off with her coat', not to mention her serious addictions to decorating and smoking. Similarly, in *Lost in Austen*, Mr. Bennet removes himself from the marital bed and sleeps in his library when, after the wedding of Jane to Mr. Collins, his wife continues to insist that he should be happy for the marriage she has imposed upon their daughter. Both mothers encourage their daughters to marry despite significant reasons to think the marriages will be unhappy and their own unhappy marital situations.

It is interesting to place this repeated trope of the generational clash in the context of contemporary feminism because generational rhetoric has dominated recent feminist theory and discussions. To a great extent, *Lost in Austen* replays these negative inter-generational relationships as Amanda clashes with her own mother and with Elizabeth's. Despite Amanda's clashes with her mother and Mrs. Bennet, perhaps the anachronism of this adaptation offers a possible mode of resistance, a chance to 'interrupt the contemporary moment with a practice of the untimely' as Jane Elliott puts it. As we have seen in the previous chapter, Elliott is keen to point out that 'such interruptions need not appear historically new' because if 'we assume that familiar approaches can no longer serve as tools to dislodge the present, we demonstrate a continued affinity for the modern logic that equates the new, the interesting, and the valuable' (1701). By drawing on Austen to strengthen her resolve to resist her mother's urging that she marry the boyfriend who has already disappointed her, Amanda clearly seems to be engaged in 'a practice of the untimely.' Her decision to return to Austen-land does, indeed, 'dislodge the present.' Even though, as Ladino and Greene warn us, nostalgia and nostalgic adaptations have often been co-opted by capitalism and involve returning women to a time when they had less power, perhaps they can offer the possibility to resist the logic of capitalism that demands always the new and the timely. In its nostalgic reconstruction of Austen's world, *Lost in Austen* does offer the contemporary feminist a reminder of just how much ideals of femininity have changed and the opportunity to reflect upon the costs and benefits of what Elliott calls the 'current direction of the world.' It also offers an alternative story to the dominant contemporary one pornography so widely tells us 'about gender and power and sex.' Certainly, we must, as Berberich warns us, remember the problematic class politics behind the idea of the 'gentleman' but the desirability of that image to contemporary (female) viewers and readers of Austen and recycled Austen productions and texts suggest the contemporary need for alternative models of masculinity.

One notable aspect of the sequels to *Pride and Prejudice* in particular is that they 'write beyond the ending' (to borrow Rachel Blau DuPlessis's phrase) of traditional novels. Whereas *Pride and Prejudice* itself ends with one of the two traditional endings DuPlessis identifies – marriage or death for the female protagonist – all the sequels by their very nature start at that ending. Thus, sequels like Emma Tennant's *Pemberley*, Linda Berdoll's *Mr Darcy Takes a Wife*, Marsha Altman's *The Darcys and the Bingleys*, and Jane Dawkins's *Letters from Pemberley* must all find ways to depict marriage that are interesting and attractive to their readers. These nostalgic texts, therefore, return their readers to the house. They are narratives of happy housewives. The popularity of these texts is in interesting juxtaposition with the bestselling 'Mad Housewives' novels that Whelehan documents in her chapter of that name in *The Feminist Bestseller*. As Moyra Haslett's Marxist critique of Austen adaptations makes clear, however, the class politics of Austen's housewives in our contemporary era of celebrity wives are problematic.

In *Ludic Feminism and After* (1996), Teresa Ebert identified an on-going need for 'historical materialist critique' and she pointed out that 'ludic feminism' was failing to see the ways in which capitalism continued to place women in disadvantaged positions:

> For instance, feminism has helped bring about increased gender flexibility, allowing women to more easily take up the attributes of power and authority, while encouraging men to take up nurturing and child-care responsibilities. These gender shifts and the increasing presence of women in professional and management positions, however, are largely confined to the middle and upper classes because they serve the interests of late-capitalist, postmodern patriarchy. First of all, they maintain the middle-class (patriarchal) nuclear family that now requires two incomes, and second they fill the expanding need for a highly educated professional and managerial labor force from the pool of white, middle-class women, while most people of color, the working class, and the poor continue to be excluded from these positions. (10–11)

Given that now, even more so than in 1996 when Ebert was writing, two incomes are required to support the middle-class nuclear family, middle-class women readers' enjoyment of these sequels to *Pride and Prejudice* could well reflect a nostalgia for the role of housewife, especially when that role is being presented from the idealized point of view of an upper-class housewife with a full staff to assist her. These novels function rather like television programmes about celebrity homes by reflecting the current widespread fascination with the very rich and escapist fantasies of wealth. In her analysis of the popular historical novel, Diana Wallace identifies two 'uses of history' in these novels by and (mainly) for women – 'escape and political intervention' (2) – and she sees these two purposes as much more intimately connected than might initially appear. Both 'uses of history' are motivated by frustration with the present moment. We can conclude, therefore, that the feminist politics of getting 'lost in Austen' are complex and contradictory. It can offer a nostalgic escape from the contemporary moment but it can also be an adventure into the past that encourages critical thinking about current gender relations and constructions of gendered identities.

Afterword: Belatedness

In their retellings, the novels I have examined have ranged over varied terrain. Toni Morrison's *The Bluest Eye* teaches us the importance of understanding the history of our contemporary moment. Doris Lessing's *The Golden Notebook* raises questions about authorial intention and reading communities in relation to parody. Margaret Atwood enacts theories of autobiography in her critical metafictions, *Lady Oracle* and *The Blind Assassin*, revealing the potential of textual revision for writing women's lives. Zadie Smith inherits E M Forster's liberalism and Elaine Scarry's encouragement to examine beauty differently in *On Beauty*. Finally, I have explored the problems and pleasures of getting *Lost in Austen*.

As I mentioned in the introduction, the sense of belatedness that was identified in the postmodern period has, if anything, deepened in the twenty-first century. As we see publications exploring 'postfeminism,' 'moving beyond postcolonialism,' and 'theory after "theory,"' the need for what Jane Elliott has described as 'the practice of the untimely' (1701) has become pressing. Increasingly authors are, as David James suggests, choosing 'to advance by adhering to what seems past, contemplating their originality through the lens of inheritance' (687). This book has attempted to map some of those 're-visions,' suggesting that contemporary women writers engaged in a practice of parody during the 1960s and 70s that has been increasingly replaced by a sense of inheritance and nostalgia. In these rather uncertain times, one thing is clear: the house of fiction has far more female occupants than when Lessing, Atwood, and Morrison first started their writing careers.

Notes

Introduction

[1] Roberta Rubenstein's *Home Matters* offers an excellent account of how Lessing allows herself the comfort of nostalgia in her autobiographical writings after *The Golden Notebook* (13–33).

[2] The relationship between the novel and houses is an intimate one, as the significant number of novels with house names as titles suggests: *Mansfield Park* (1814), *Wuthering Heights* (1847), *The Tenant of Wildfell Hall* (1848), *Bleak House* (1853), and *Howards End* (1910) are just a few examples.

[3] My theory of parody is based on the work of Linda Hutcheon (see, in particular, *A Theory of Parody: The Teachings of Twentieth-Century Art Forms*. London: Routledge, 1985). Margaret Rose offers a more historical rather than theoretical account of parody in *Parody: Ancient, Modern and Post-Modern*. Despite my not offering a complete theory of parody, my study certainly contributes to parody studies by examining the implications of women's strategic use of parody.

[4] See Victoria Rosner's 'Home Fires: Doris Lessing, Colonial Architecture, and the Reproduction of Mothering' for an examination of the significance of Lessing's childhood home.

[5] See especially the chapter entitled 'Modelling the Postmodern: Parody and Politics' in Hutcheon's *A Poetics of Postmodernism* and the chapter entitled 'The Politics of Parody' in *The Politics of Postmodernism*.

Chapter 1

[6] See the discussion earlier in the introduction about Heilbrun's *Women's Lives: The View from the Threshold*.

[7] Although the word 'whitemale' is a politically useful construction for Morrison's consideration of the literary canon, its totalizing impulse should be resisted. See John N. Duvall's *The Identifying Fictions of Toni Morrison* for a discussion of how a white male *can* engage with Morrison's work (1–2; 22–4).

[8] The other three are that
   1) there is no Afro-American (or third world) art.... 3) it exists and is superior when it measures up to the 'universal' criteria of Western art. 4) it is not so much 'art' as ore – rich ore – that requires a Western or Eurocentric smith to refine it from its 'natural' state into an aesthetically complete form. (206)

[9] The other two future projects Morrison calls for are:
   Another is the examination and re-interpretation of the American canon, the founding nineteenth-century works, for the 'unspeakable things unspoken';

for the ways in which the presence of Afro-Americans has shaped the choices, the language, the structure – the meaning of so much American literature. A search, in other words, for the ghost in the machine.

A third is the examination of contemporary and/or non-canonical literature for this presence, regardless of its category as mainstream, minority, or what you will. (210)

10. In the chapter entitled 'Figures of Signification' in *The Signifying Monkey*, Gates states: 'Before attempting to demonstrate how such a theory of Signification obtains in Afro-American literary history, let us consider received definitions of parody and pastiche and compare these to Signifyin(g)' (107). However, Gates employs the terms 'parody' and 'Signifyin(g)' as if they were synonyms. He talks of using 'literary parody to Signify' as if parody is a method by which Signifying can be achieved, without actually discussing the similarities and differences between 'received definitions of parody and pastiche' and his theory of Signifyin(g). His examples do not clarify whether there is a difference either. (See my comments below concerning his example of the white racist parodying the black vernacular.)

11. This is Gates's own word, which gains particular relevance through his discussion of the speaking book. See his analysis of Hurston's *Their Eyes Were Watching God* as an example of a 'speakerly' text (*The Signifying Monkey* 170–216).

12. Barbara Christian offers an example of this tendency to identify white literary parents for successful black authors in her essay 'Layered Rhythms: Virginia Woolf and Toni Morrison.' Discussing the criticism linking Morrison to Woolf and Faulkner, Christian asks, 'Why must you be studied in relation to such writers, icons of twentieth-century European and Anglo-American literature? Is it that as an African-American woman writer, and clearly a "genius", you must have a Western white literary father and mother?' (20).

13. Reviews of Gates's work usually fall into one of three types – a descriptive account of his theory (Spikes), a celebration of the importance of his work (Fox), and criticism of his professional activities and methods which are sometimes extremely personal (Mazrui, Joyce and Kilson). Brad Bucknell's essay 'Henry Louis Gates Jr. and the Theory of "Signifyin(g)"' approaches a critical engagement with Gates's theories, but even that essay is descriptive and keen to justify Gates's critical methodology. I found Diana Fuss's chapter entitled '"Race" Under Erasure? Poststructuralist Afro-American Literary Theory' in *Essentially Speaking* very helpful. However, it is not focused on Gates, but discusses several African American critics (73–96). Joyce's consideration of Gates 20 years on does not reference any previous critiques of Gates.

14. Brad Bucknell uses Gates's own theory of Signifyin(g) to account for Gates's relationship to Western criticism: 'Gates is of course "signifying" on the Western critical tradition here, repeating and revising, if not attempting, through inverting historical precedent, to out-do Western tropological history by showing the difference between it and the black cultural matrix he is trying to explicate' (73).

15. Bucknell's earlier description of Gates's project seems much more aware of its problematic nature than the explanation quoted in the footnote above:

For Gates, 'Signifyin(g)' is an attempt to find a distinctly black method of reconciling history and form, textuality and experience, at least in part through a reappropriation of contemporary literary theory. The issues that such an endeavour raise are complex, not least because of the problems in finding a distinctive critical method that is not already inhabited by dominant Western values. (67)

16. Spikes, for example, critiques Gates for so closely reworking Harold Bloom's theory of the 'anxiety of influence':
    In all his discussions of Signifyin(g), Gates sounds very much like a prominent white theorist who was teaching at Yale when Gates was a student, Harold Bloom....Bloom argues that literature is produced through anxiety-driven revisionary strife between authors; by one text's creative swerves from another. This view is so close to Gates's that Kenneth Warren has claimed 'one can read *The Signifying Monkey* as Gates's rewriting of Bloom's oedipal drama for the black tradition in which psychology gives way, once again, to rhetoric and "Signifyin(g)" replaces "anxiety"'. Though Gates contends that the notion of Signifyin(g) is built into the black tradition, that he is identifying a practice inherent in black texts, one might legitimately ask whether or not he would have 'discovered' this practice in the first place, or at least whether or not he would have articulated it in the terms he does, if he had not already been familiar with Bloom's influential theory. (62–3)

17. One way in which he inverts Bloom is to suggest that the Signifyin(g) Monkey is the 'slave's trope' rather than Bloom's 'master trope.'

18. The monkey seems to have come centre stage as an attempt to reverse the Western image of the black man as closer to the ape than to the white man in the 'Great Chain of Beings' Gates discusses (130).

19. See, for example, his argument in *Loose Canons*:
    That, literally, every day, scores of people are killed in the name of differences ascribed to 'race' only makes even more imperative this gesture to 'deconstruct', if you will, the ideas of difference inscribed in the trope of race, to take discourse itself as our common subject to be explicated to reveal the latent relations of power and knowledge inherent in popular and academic usages of 'race'. (*Loose Canons* 50)

20. Although this is *not* what Gates is calling for, his deconstructive approach has drawn accusations from other critics that in fact he is trying to erase race.

21. See Dwight A. McBride's article entitled 'Speaking the Unspeakable: On Toni Morrison, African-American Intellectuals and the Uses of Essentialist Rhetoric' for a helpful discussion of Morrison's uses of essentialism in 'Speaking the Unspeakable.' His argument is based on Diana Fuss's notion of a 'strategic essentialism.' Fuss argues that 'Neither a pure constructionist approach nor an unalloyed essentialist one is sufficiently equipped to come to grips with a question as theoretically complex and politically urgent as the place and function of "race" in the era of poststructuralism' (92).

22. Many critics have addressed this unusual repetition and Carl Malmgren offers a useful summary of the critical consensus:
    The standard critical reading of the three versions is that the first represents the life of white families, orderly and 'readable', the second, that of the MacTeer family, confused but still readable, and the last, that of the Breedlove family, incoherent and unintelligible. (257)

There is, in fact, an interesting difference among critics who do read the primer sections as operating in this directly representative way. Phyllis Klotman, for example, reads the three versions as 'symbolic of the lifestyles that the author explores in the novel.' In her reading, the first version 'is clearly that of the alien white world' and she specifically associates this version with the Fisher family (123). Although Chikwenye Okonjo Ogunyemi agrees that the reading primer describes 'a white American ideal of the family unit,' the specific family in the novel that he associates with the first version is Geraldine's. As he argues, 'her clean house belongs to the only black family in the novel that draws near this ideal' (112).

23 Within this context, Gibson disagrees with the more common reading that the third repetition of the reader is nonsensical:

> The inference to be drawn is that the final version is incomprehensible. But that is not true. It is, arguably, perfectly comprehensible. The difference between the first and third versions is that the third forces us to participate in the reading in a more active way by demanding that we identify individual words and supply from our own past experience of reading the first version the proper punctuation. The reader is once again, in the very act of reading, taught to read. The meaning is not, as it appears, drained away from first to final draft, but simply concentrated. (161)

24 See, for example, her online interview with *Time* magazine on 15 May 2008.

25 Timothy Powell has suggested that 'Morrison is literally deconstructing the essential white text, removing capitalization, punctuation, and finally the spacing until the white text is nothing more than a fragmentation of its former self at the beginning of the chapters' (51).

26 The working-class, juvenile authors of the story 'The Tidy House,' which is the focus of Carolyn Steedman's study, similarly recognize their parents' ambivalence towards them. As Steedman explains:

> What informed the writing of 'The Tidy House' was the tension that lay at the roots of the writers' existence. They knew that their parents' situation was one of poverty and that the presence of children only increased it. 'If you never had no children', said Carla... 'you'd be well off, wouldn't you. You'd have plenty of money'... They knew that children were longed for, materially desired, but that their presence meant irritation, regret and resentment. (25)

27 Susan Willis has defined 'funk' as 'really nothing more than the intrusion of the past into the present' (325). Willis's definition is based on a nostalgic history of the black community's loss of its rural and communal roots. Morrison's emphasis on how women like Geraldine go about learning how to suppress 'funkiness' and how difficult it is for them to do so suggests to me that Morrison views 'funk' as being very much a part of the black community even today, not an 'intrusion of the past.'

28 See Emma Parker's essay '"Apple Pie" Ideology and the Politics of Appetite in the Novels of Toni Morrison' for a helpful exploration of the 'significance of sugar.'

29 Timothy Powell, for example, argues that: 'The all-too-familiar lines of the Dick-and-Jane primer also serve as an important contrast, pointing out an essential difference between the cold, clear logic of the white text and the often irrational

pain of the black text which is to follow' (48). Furthermore, Powell argues, 'it is Morrison's shattering contrasts between the "big and strong," "smiling" Father of the white text and broken-spirited Cholly, the father in the black text, which make clear the inadequacies of the white mythology for representing the black self' (51). Carl Malmgren does note the similarity of subject matter between the primer epigraphs and the sections describing Pecola's family, but he also emphasizes the ironic differences:

> Subsequent sections use as epigraphs primer lines describing Dick and Jane's family, the cat, Mother, Father, the dog, and a friend of Jane's. The section following the epigraph focuses on that figure in Pecola's life but relates tales of misery that are an ironic counterpoint to the fairy-tale world depicted in the primer itself. (257)

Dorothy Lee also describes the reading primer's relationship to the rest of the narrative as one of 'counterpoint': 'For each segment of this idealized picture of secure family life, Morrison offers in counterpoint the bleak specifics of Pecola's existence: shabby home, bitter and hostile parents, and two encounters with animals that are death-giving to her spirit and sanity' (347). Phyllis Klotman argues that Morrison uses the repetition of the reading primer 'to juxtapose the fictions of the white educational process with the realities of life for many black children' (123). While emphasizing contrasts, Klotman does identify an important instance of repetition and complicity. She aligns the first version of the reader which 'is clear, straight, rendered in "Standard English" – correct and white' (123) with the Fisher family for whom Pauline Breedlove works. Klotman acknowledges Pauline's complicity: 'Pauline even begins to see her own daughter through the acquired astigmatism of the Fishers' world' (124). However, she relates this complicity only to Pauline's relationship with the Fishers and not with Morrison's critique of the processes of education evident in her parody of the reading primer. I would suggest that the retrospective narrative of Pauline's life demonstrates that her acquisition of these 'white' values dates back much further than her relationship with the Fishers. As I explained above, Klotman does align the first version of the reading primer with the Fishers, so there is an implied connection with the reading primer. Chikwenye Okonjo Ogunyemi makes the black community's degree of complicity with the 'white American ideal of the family unit' described in the reading primer more explicit by aligning the first version of the reading primer with Geraldine:

> Geraldine, the symbol of what Hernton calls the 'old black bourgeoisie', with her clean house belongs to the only black family in the novel that draws near this ideal, but she is not happy, and her brutal son perpetrates violence on her pet cat. (112–13)

However, Ogunyemi sees the relationship between the reading primer and Pecola's family as one of contrast. He does note the similar family structure:

> The Mother-Father-Dick-Jane concept is finally transmuted to the Mrs. Breedlove-Cholly-Sammy-Pecola situation. The transmutation is Morrison's indirect criticism of the white majority for the black family's situation and for what is taught to the black child in school, as evidenced by the primer paragraph, that in no way relates to the child's reality. The black man is attacked emotionally from childhood, living in two impossible worlds: the fairy tale

world of lies when he is in contact with the white world and the equally incredible, grim world of black life. (113)

[30] The cat is killed when she attempts to stop Junior from swinging it around by its tail, causing him to fall and let go of it in full swing. Soaphead Church sets her up to kill the dog with poisoned meat.

[31] John Duvall argues that
> *The Bluest Eye* marks the absent site of authenticity as the African-American agrarian community. Until the death of his Aunt Jimmy, Cholly is nurtured by his rural Georgia community, just as Pauline is the product of a black agrarian community in Kentucky. Morrison's mother and father, from Alabama and Georgia respectively, seem coded in the novel's invocation of the rural as the surest site of authentic black identity. (44)

[32] Duvall suggests: 'What spells the beginning of the end of the Breedlove's happier moment...is Cholly's decision to move his bride north for the economic opportunities represented by industrial jobs' (44). Susan Willis implicitly agrees: 'Migration to the North signifies more than a confrontation with (and contamination by) the white world. It implies a transition in social class. Throughout Morrison's writing, the white world is equated with the bourgeois class – its ideology and life-style' (309).

[33] 'Pink' is 'a pale red colour.' Morrison is again playing with similarity and difference here. Pecola and the Fisher girl are both wearing the same colour but it is called different things.

[34] The fact that Pecola is at the Fisher house to collect the laundry contrasts her work with Jane's play in the reading primer. She is washing dishes when Cholly rapes her.

[35] Emma Parker's essay '"Apple Pie" Ideology and the Politics of Appetite in the Novels of Toni Morrison' is again relevant here, offering a brief but helpful reading of this scene (620).

[36] As Michael Awkward explains:
> The convention that Morrison revises here is that of the authenticating document, usually written by whites to confirm a genuine Black authorship of the subsequent text. The white voice of authority – a William Lloyd Garrison in the case of Frederick Douglass' *Narrative*, a William Dean Howells in the case of Paul Laurence Dunbar's *Lyrics of a Lowly Life* – has traditionally authenticated the black voice in Afro-American literature. (62)

Awkward reads Morrison's refunctioning of this convention as part of the novel's wider rejection of 'white standards':
> Morrison returns to an earlier practice – of the white voice introducing the black text – to demonstrate,...her refusal to allow white standards to arbitrate the success or failure of the Afro-American experience. Her manipulation of the primer is meant to suggest, finally, the inappropriateness of the white voice's attempt to authorize or authenticate the Afro-American text or to dictate the contours of Afro-American art. (63)

[37] Toni Morrison argues that this assumption of a white audience is a very important factor in the formation of the American literary canon:
> For reasons that should not need explanation here, until very recently, and regardless of the race of the author, the readers of virtually all American

150   *Notes*

fiction have been positioned as white. I am interested to know what that assumption has meant to the literary imagination. (*Playing in the Dark* xii)

[38] Critics have found it difficult to identify exactly who does tell the story. As Carl Malmgren says, 'The novel is not only multitextual, it is also polyphonic. The seasonal sections are in the first person, but even they are double-voiced, aware of the difference between the experiencing "I" and the narrating "I"' (251–2). Malmgren identifies that 'the critical consensus seems to be that there are two main speakers, Claudia in the seasonal sections, and an authorial persona elsewhere' (253). He actually argues against this consensus, suggesting instead 'that strong evidence, textual and biographical, exists to suggest that a single narrator, Claudia MacTeer, has composed the texts and created the voices' (253). Linda Dittmar, in contrast, focuses on the many different frames and voices in the novel and concludes that:

> The overall effect of this complexly structured work is to foreground the authorial project of orchestrating a fluid, multi-voiced novel, where the parts sometimes jostle against one another, sometimes complement or blend with each other, and at all times project a dense sense of the multiplicity of narration. Since the function of the story-telling act is, as Claudia puts it, to explain, Morrison's juxtaposition of diverse voices asserts that understanding is collective. In this respect, *The Bluest Eye*'s design supplements its thematic focus on communities as sites of meaning, for it posits that meanings get constructed dialogically. (141)

Chapter 2

[39] Lessing, preface to *The Golden Notebook* (9).

[40] See Suzette Henke's 'Reading Doris Lessing's *The Golden Notebook* as Feminist Trauma Narrative' in *Doris Lessing Studies* 27.1&2 (11–16) for an exploration of trauma and writing in *The Golden Notebook*.

[41] In her autobiography, *Walking in the Shade*, Lessing describes how conscious she was of needing to change at this point in her life:

> The genesis of *The Golden Notebook* was not lengthy, but it was complex, not only because of what went into it but because of my state at the time. I really was at a crossroads, a turning point; I was in the melting pot and ready to be remade. I knew I was – nothing unconscious about it. For one thing, I was determined my emotional life would from now on be different. For another, there was politics, the collapse of communism as a moral force. (334)

Lessing stresses the role of *The Golden Notebook* in bringing about the changes she needed:

> Writing *The Golden Notebook* changed me. Writing any book changes you: this has to be so, if you think about it. On the lowest level, if you are thinking hard about a subject, information and insights on that subject seem to come in from everywhere; books arrive in your life, you hear it on the radio, in conversations, and on television. This is a fact, it is true, you can rely on it – and there is no 'scientific' explanation for it. Yet. But I am not talking about this kind of rapid information-getting. Writing that novel changed the way I thought and

more fundamentally than thinking. When I began it, while I had thrown out communism, all of the mind-sets of communism remained. (346)

42 Alvin Sullivan expresses this view when he states, '[o]ne of the self-evident features of Doris Lessing's work is an abrupt change of form, beginning with *The Golden Notebook*' (71). 'What is significant in Lessing's work after *The Golden Notebook*,' he goes on to argue, 'is the freedom from conventional generic forms, as evidence that the writing of this one novel was a liberating discovery' (76).

43 This reading is famously expressed by Betsy Draine in *Substance Under Pressure: Artistic Coherence and Evolving Form in the Novels of Doris Lessing*: 'Seemingly overnight, the caterpillar becomes butterfly – the traditional novelist becomes not merely modern novelist, but a postmodern novelist. In this new and powerful identity, Lessing reshapes the form of the novel, giving it a postmodern order' (70). Similarly, Magali Michael argues that Lessing moves towards a 'postmodern notion of the subject as a dynamic set of culturally constructed positions' (84) in *The Golden Notebook*. Tonya Krouse's 'Freedom as Effacement in *The Golden Notebook*: Theorizing Pleasure, Subjectivity, and Authority' positions the novel 'betwixt and between modernist and postmodernist conceptions of the subject' (40). In *Walking in the Shade*, Lessing indicates her dislike of deconstructionist readings of the novel: 'Now the most bizarre of *The Golden Notebook*'s many lives. It became a text for deconstructionists. This book, born directly out of so much blood, sweat, and particularly tears, a little intellectual game? You have to laugh: there's nothing else to be done' (346). Clearly, Lessing feels that deconstructionist readings do not account sufficiently for the important category of experience that Lessing perceived as the source for the novel.

44 There is some controversy over whether Lessing did actually experience a writer's block similar to Anna's. Lessing has fuelled the controversy by stating in some interviews that she did and in others that she did not. In her interview with Jonah Raskin in 1969, she describes having 'put myself in a damned cage' while writing the *Children of Violence* series, and that having 'heaved the rules out' helped her (*Putting the Questions Differently* 13). In that interview, she also expresses a great deal of anxiety over writing about politics which mirrors the anxiety Anna experiences at the end of *The Golden Notebook*:

I am intensely aware of, and want to write about, politics, but I often find I am unable to embody my political vision in a novel. I want to write about Chinese peasants, the Algerians in the FLN, but I don't want to present them in false situations. I don't want to leave them out either. I find it difficult to write about politics.... I'm tormented by the inadequacy of the imagination. I've a sense of the conflict between my life as a writer and the terrors of our time. (15)

In contrast, however, when François-Olivier Rousseau asks her in 1985: 'In *The Golden Notebook* your heroine who has some of your characteristics and is made famous by a novel set in Africa during the last war suffers from writer's block. Is that a situation which you too have experienced?' Lessing replies: 'No, but the idea seemed interesting to me. For a time I was analyzed by a psychoanalyst specializing in artists suffering from "blocks". She would have loved to see me "blocked". I always disappointed her about it' (*Putting the Questions Differently* 149).

45 For example, see Vivien Leonard's '"Free Women" as Parody: Fun and Games in *The Golden Notebook*'.
46 Magali Michael describes it as a
> novel that is readable and yet subversive, a novel that presents recognizable characters and yet disrupts established aesthetic forms for depicting characters and notions of fixed identity, a novel that draws its readers into a conventional narrative and then explodes that narrative, a novel that is very structured and yet resists form, a novel that tells a story and yet challenges the very conventions by which stories have been told within Western culture. (95)
47 Seán Burke offers a brief and helpful account of how the 'strong act of rewriting' by poststructuralist critics resulted in the claim by some poststructuralists that 'criticism itself has become the primary discourse' (159):
> And this notion commands a certain respect, for the weakening of boundaries between creative and critical is not only a development within criticism, but also a powerful and necessary extension of modernism in general. As the literary text becomes more self-reflexive, as its artifices and narratological structures come to dominate the foreground, as the work of fiction becomes autocritical, autodeconstructive even, it is entirely concinnous that the critical text should become increasingly creative, interpretable, and like the work of Wilde and Mallarmé, a realm with charms, mazes, and mysteries of its own. (159–60)
48 Molly Hite offers a helpful analysis of how the notion of a framing narrative is disrupted by feminist metafiction in her article '(En)gendering Metafiction: Doris Lessing's Rehearsals for *The Golden Notebook*':
> Metafiction seems an important kind of writing for this project [of finding a feminist critical practice] because in its more radical manifestations it is not only fiction *about* fiction but fiction that makes the whole notion of 'about' problematic, so that the relations between frame and embedded stories – between dominant and subordinate, container and contained – become slippery, unstable, even liable to reverse themselves. Clearly these same relations between dominant and subordinate, container and contained, are essential to the construction of gender categories as well as to the construction of coherent traditional narratives, inasmuch as the conventionally masculine subsumes and circumscribes the conventionally feminine. (482)
49 Marie Danziger similarly argues that
> the reader needs to cope with two Tommys – similar in many ways, but very definitely not the same young man. The obvious impulse is to try to determine which is the 'real' Tommy, which text is the 'corrected' version. Each has its arguable advantages. The *Free Women* account, although it borders on embarrassing melodrama, demonstrates an inner logic that ties together several crucial narrative strands. (58)
50 'Anna meets her friend Molly in the summer of 1957 after a separation...' (25)
'*Two Visits, some telephone calls and a Tragedy*' (233)
'*Tommy Adjusts Himself to Being Blind While the Older People Try to Help Him*' (329)
'*Anna and Molly influence Tommy, for the better. Marion leaves Richard. Anna does not feel herself.*' (445)
'*Molly Gets Married and Anna Has an Affair*' (561)

[51] It is interesting to note that when Sprague rewrites this article for the chapter on *The Golden Notebook* in *Rereading Doris Lessing*, she edits out this enormous problem of readership that she identifies here. See page 66 of *Rereading Doris Lessing*.

[52] Sprague commences her chapter on *The Golden Notebook* in *Rereading Doris Lessing* by noting that, 'It took a while to recognize Anna Wulf's role as Anna-editor or Anna-writer or Anna-scriptwriter, or to accept Free Women as fiction, or to question the "truth" of the notebooks' (165).

[53] Schweickart argues (in 1985) that 'the "argument" written in the "shape" of the novel remains largely unread' because

> in spite of the obtrusiveness, the structure of the novel is easy to circumvent. We can appreciate the novel – be moved by it, be impressed by its perspicacious commentary on reality, be drawn into the experience it portrays – without coming to terms with the odd arrangement of the text. In addition, an experienced reader can read through the structure of the novel with minimal difficulty. For example, the plot is easily recovered. (263–4)

Schweickart captures the paradoxical nature of *The Golden Notebook* when she states: 'Thus, the structure of the novel is both obtrusive and self-effacing, necessary and gratuitous, essential and extraneous' (265). Schweickart's reading closely echoes Michael's quoted above. Michael describes it as a

> novel that is readable and yet subversive, a novel that presents recognizable characters and yet disrupts established aesthetic forms for depicting characters and notions of fixed identity, a novel that draws its readers into a conventional narrative and then explodes that narrative, a novel that is very structured and yet resists form, a novel that tells a story and yet challenges the very conventions by which stories have been told within Western culture. (95)

[54] This is a quotation from Doris Lessing which Barbara Ellen takes as the title of her article based on her interview with Lessing in 2001.

[55] Betsy Draine also emphasizes Lessing's control of the novel's paradoxically highly organized yet seemingly chaotic structure. In the 'new and powerful identity' of a 'postmodern novelist,' Draine claims that 'Lessing reshapes the form of the novel, giving it a postmodern order' (70).

[56] Claire Sprague, for example, argues that Lessing's presence is erased from the novel:

> The opening line is not Doris Lessing's line. It is written by Saul Green, who gives it to Anna, who gives it to the reader. Anna writes Free Women with Saul's help. Saul says: 'I'm going to give you the first sentence then. There are the two women you are, Anna. Write down: 'The two women were alone in the London flat' (639). Doris Lessing's presence is nearly obliterated. (*Rereading Doris Lessing* 67)

Jeanette King, arguing along similar lines, suggests that

> it is no longer possible to locate with any certainty the originator of either the Notebooks or *Free Women*, since either could be the product of a fictive Anna, rather than any 'real' Anna. And since the author of *Free Women* is so elusive, it is equally difficult to determine the relationship of Doris Lessing to the narrator, to determine where or when the assumptions of the narrative command authorial assent. If there is no single originator of meaning, there is no fixity of meaning, and no hierarchy of discourses – no privileging of one narrative 'voice' over another. (53)

57 Lessing's own statement suggests far more presence than Sprague implies, and a clearer, more singular meaning than King identifies, but far less authority than Fuoroli and Draine argue for.
58 Anna's use of her own experience to help her interpret this text is important – 'I searched my memory and rooted out certain fantasies of my own,' she tells us. This shared experience is the basis for her ability to correctly interpret whether this text is parodic or not. See my discussion of discursive communities below.
59 Note how the awkward hyphenated words draw attention to themselves – 'hard-drinking,' 'money-loving,' 'politics-mad.'
60 See the first page of Ellen's article for a brief account of the different public speaking occasions at which Lessing has asserted her disassociation from feminism.
61 Katherine Fishburn makes a similar argument concerning the relationship between 'Free Women' and the chaotic notebooks:

> After using several pages (from 331 to 368 in the paperback edition) to describe this day [15 September], Anna scores out the entire passage and replaces it with a single terse paragraph in which she condenses the day's events into nine sentences (p. 368). (On a less obvious plane, this is what she does throughout the novel when she alternates the four notebooks with the 'Free Women' sections). (88)

62 As Danziger says of the first account of 15 September: 'It's a masterful melange of realistic detail, meaningful dialogue, stream of consciousness, political and philosophical musings – all the trappings of first-rate conventional storytelling. All but the most cynical reader would be entirely seduced by this narrative tour-de-force' (57).
63 Danziger views this scene in which Tommy reads Anna's notebooks as the novel's 'primal scene,' arguing that '[w]hen Molly's son Tommy presumes to read her notebooks without asking, this act of male aggression is, in my reading, a symbolic rape, arguably the novel's most resonant event' (47). While Danziger overemphasizes the scene's 'overtly sexual implications,' her perception that this scene highlights Anna's fear of her reader(s) is very helpful. As Danziger says, the 'confrontation between writer and reader' is

> the arena where all the gritty basic conflicts get played out: fear, humiliation, aggression and submission, self-hatred, and the will to overpower and replace one's forerunners. By freighting the act of reading – and in particular of being read – with such loaded meaning, Lessing exposes a highly sensitive subject that is taboo for most writers and handled only with extreme caution or indirection by others. (48)

64 John Leonard notes Lessing's attempt to control readings of her work, when he states, 'Ever since she gave up on realism, she has been explaining herself in prefaces and afterwords, as if to bully the reader' ('The Spacing Out of Doris Lessing' 205). Margaret Moan Rowe dedicates the whole final chapter of her book on Lessing to '"The Battle of the Books": Lessing and the Critics.' She points out that 'While never succumbing to Charlotte Brontë's direct overture to her "Dear Reader", Doris Lessing has been canny in ways of trying to shape the reader's response to her fiction' (111) and that

> Lessing's call for a 'serious criticism' in 'The Small Personal Voice' was the first important instance of what has become a cottage industry for her:

admonishing critics (usually academic) and directing readers. The admonitions and directions find their way into attachments, prefaces and afterwords, to many of her novels and interviews with critics (mostly academic). (112)

Rowe reads the preface to *The Golden Notebook* as the 'most striking example' of Lessing's 'attempt at control': 'Lessing's most interesting gambit [...] is to turn herself into her own critic, whether "real" or "perfect", and analyse *The Golden Notebook* for her ideal reader' (114). Eve Bertelsen offers an insightful analysis of how Lessing attempts to control interpretations of her work in the course of an interview in her article, 'Who is It Who Says "I"?: The Persona of a Doris Lessing Interview.' Bertelsen examines what she terms 'Lessing's strenuous intervention: her insistence on retaining control of the meaning of her texts in opposition to the troublesome scenario of an interviewer who seeks to discover some of the historical, literary, and political determinants of her writing practices' (170).

[65] As Tonya Krouse argues,

as the Annas of the text write themselves into being, they also engage in repeated cancellations of the self through writing. In fact, as the Annas of the text write themselves into being, they seem to do so in order to facilitate subsequent self-cancellation or self-erasure. (44)

Chapter 3

[66] In order to designate the novel-within-the-novel, I use inverted commas. Thus, 'The Blind Assassin' refers to Iris/Laura's previous publication. *The Blind Assassin* refers to Atwood's novel as a whole.

[67] Smith points out that although slave narratives are an example of marginalized and unauthorized autobiographical subjects speaking out in this genre before the twentieth century, the 'slave narrative was consigned to obscurity for over one hundred years. It went unread, perhaps because it was, precisely, unreadable' (61). She argues that the growing instability in the genre of autobiography and the increased number of previously marginalized peoples speaking out in the form are two mutually dependent factors which were both causes and effects of each other and resulted in the complexity and diversity of the genre as we know it today.

[68] I believe Atwood's model of subjectivity undergoes significant revision between *Surfacing* in 1972 and *Lady Oracle* in 1976. I explore the differences between the two models of subjectivity Atwood presents in these novels later in this chapter. The model of subjectivity evident in *The Blind Assassin* is very similar to that presented in *Lady Oracle* despite the obvious difference in tone between the two novels.

[69] There is considerable overlap between Rao's chapter on *Lady Oracle* in her book *Strategies for Identity: The Fiction of Margaret Atwood* and her article on *Lady Oracle* entitled 'Margaret Atwood's *Lady Oracle*: Writing Against Notions of Unity.'

[70] Roxanne Fand is another critic who focuses on Joan's multiplicitous identity. In *The Dialogic Self: Reconstructing Subjectivity in Woolf, Lessing, and Atwood*, Fand

does not read the ending of *Lady Oracle* as particularly positive because she feels that Joan fails to accept her own dialogic identity. In contrast to Fand, Molly Hite offers a positive reading of Joan's subjectivity. In her study entitled *The Other Side of the Story: Structures and Strategies of Contemporary Feminist Narrative* she reads Joan's excess as a subversive strategy. I share Hite's interest in the 'excess' with which Joan describes herself. Kim L. Worthington offers an excellent reading of Joan's narrative self in *Self as Narrative: Subjectivity and Community in Contemporary Fiction*. Although Worthington shares the above critics' interest in Joan's multiplicity and textuality, she is concerned throughout her book with the issue of agency. My understanding of the self owes a great deal to her model of subjectivity:

> I suggest that the construction of a subject's sense of selfhood should be understood as a creative narrative process achieved within a plurality of intersubjective communicative protocols. In the act of conceptualizing one's selfhood, one writes a narrative of personal continuity through time. That is, in thinking myself, I remember myself: I draw together my multiple members – past and other subject positions – into a coherent narrative of selfhood which is more or less readable by myself and others. Understanding personhood in this way, I argue, leaves open the possibility of revision of one's conceptions of self, and also acknowledges the potential for misreading and misinterpretation of the narratives of self and others. At the same time it recognizes that a narrative of self provides the human subject with a sense of self-continuity and coherence that enables the projection of desire and intention towards an imagined future. In short, it allows the subject to function as a purposive, morally responsible agent. (13)

Ellen McWilliams also discusses models of subjectivity in *Margaret Atwood and the Female Bildungsroman*. Her study looks at how food imagery and the idea of ingestion are related to writing in Atwood's *The Edible Woman* and *Lady Oracle*.

[71] Cynthia Kuhn's study of *Self-Fashioning in Margaret Atwood's Fiction: Dress, Culture, and Identity* provides a helpful context for Atwood's use of a clothing image – 'ready-to-wear' – to describe her not 'fitting' language.

[72] For example, Sonia Mycak sees Joan's rejection of her *mother*'s judgments as central to her development into a free adult. Thus, although Mycak does explore Joan's relationships with men in her analysis, the success of Joan's 'struggle for subjectivity' (119) is determined by her final 'separation from the maternal' (118). Joan's textual and sexual experiences all relate to her relationship with her mother, in Mycak's reading:

> *Lady Oracle* ends with a resolution of Joan's relationship with her mother, a relationship that has been expressed as a preoccupation with death, a divided sense of self, a number of fractured identities, and a problematic relationship with food and with the body. It is a relationship that has been imaged in familial networks, bodily drives, sexual relations, and textual practices. (119)

[73] Critics have pointed to the fact that Joan passes her story on to a male journalist who will write it for her as a signal that Joan does not escape the maze. Furthermore, her own admission that 'there is something about a man in a bandage' (*Lady Oracle* 345) is an ironic echo of the nurse novels written by Mavis Quilp (the Polish Count) which inspired Joan's own literary career as a Costume Gothic Romance writer. In his study, *Margaret Atwood: A Feminist Poetics*, Frank

Davey makes a strong argument for Joan's continued entrapment in her Gothic plots. Although Davey acknowledges that Joan does see her own psycho-drama being played out in the maze of her fiction 'Stalked By Love,' and that her attack with the Cinzano bottle is an action, he goes on to question whether these actions constitute a change for Joan:

> But are these actions really new? Her attack with the Cinzano bottle is merely another instance of her fantasizing a man to be a Gothic villain; her decision to stay with and help her victim seems based not on a new sense of self but on the 'nurse' fantasy which patterned the novels of her first lover Paul.... (76)

74 I use the term 'refunctioning' as Margaret Rose does in *Parody: Ancient, Modern and Post-Modern*. She uses it in her definition of parody: 'the comic refunctioning of preformed linguistic or artistic material.' She defines 'refunctioning' as 'referring to the new set of functions given to parodied material in the parody and may also entail some criticism of the parodied work' (52). Joan's 'refunctioning' of Arthur's word 'mess' certainly entails criticism.

75 See, for example, Susan Jaret McKinstry in 'Living Literally by the Pen: The Self-Conceived and Self-Deceiving Heroine-Author In Margaret Atwood's *Lady Oracle*.' McKinstry argues that it is Joan's guilt over murdering her past self that returns when she buries her clothes in the Italian garden but feels like she was 'getting rid of a body, the corpse of someone I'd killed' (*Lady Oracle* 16): 'The body is not real, but the imagined – and dreaded – corpse of the old, fat Joan is indeed a murdered victim that returns to haunt its killer, the Joan who revised her past and deleted that self' (63). Molly Hite argues that the ghost of Joan's past overweight self is displaced into her image of the Fat Lady on the tight rope which shows how the female body is frequently excessive in this novel:

> They are indicative of a tendency on the part of the female body in this novel to turn up unexpectedly and inexplicably, to transgress the limits that have been set for it, to refuse to stay in its place. Another important manifestation of this tendency is the Fat Lady, who is at first, at least apparently, an imaginative construct based on the memory of too much flesh, which haunts Joan as a sort of ghostly residue of her overweight childhood. (137–8)

76 L. M. Montgomery's *The Blue Castle* may be a particular intertext for *Lady Oracle* as Atwood seems to hint at a parallel by calling her protagonist Joan Foster after the author of the nature books Valancy reads – John Foster – in Montgomery's novel.

77 When used in reference to parody, 'derivative' has generally been viewed as a negative word. As Hutcheon says in *A Theory of Parody*: '[Parody] has need of defenders. It has been called parasitic and derivative. Leavis's famous distaste, not to say contempt, for parody was based on his belief that it was the philistine enemy of creative genius and vital originality' (3–4). Here I use 'derivative' simply to indicate the fact that parody bases itself on a 'target text' rather than to imply that it lacks originality.

78 Alex in *The Blind Assassin* also makes lists of jargon to help him with his science fiction novels.

79 For Ellen McWilliams, the fact '[t]hat Joan thinks of her life fictions as "flabby" is very suggestive as it makes a direct link between the two modes of consumption that influence her development as a woman and, more particularly, as a woman writer' – her consumption of food and fiction (85).

80. It is an amusing irony and a 'victory' for Joan that it is Marlene's excess – her addition of the non-existent life saver which she claimed to have thrown to Joan – which puts Marlene in jail. Marlene was the image of all that Arthur admired but she proves unsuccessful as an accomplice in Joan's careful plot.
81. I will fully explore the difference between these novels' models of the self later, but it is interesting to put a parallel quotation from *Lady Oracle* alongside this one from *Surfacing*. In *Lady Oracle,* Joan argues for the disassociation of the fragments of her self: 'If I brought the separate parts of my life together (like uranium, like plutonium, harmless to the naked eye, but charged with lethal energies) surely there would be an explosion' (218).
82. Such as Julia Kristeva, Luce Irigaray and Hélène Cixous.
83. As the Surfacer admits at the end of the novel, it is unclear whether she actually is pregnant:
    > But I bring with me from the distant past five nights ago the time-traveller, the primaeval one who will have to learn, shape of a goldfish now in my belly, undergoing its watery changes. Word furrows potential already in its proto-brain, untravelled paths. No god and perhaps not real, even that is uncertain; I can't know yet, it's too early. (185)
84. Worthington helpfully summarises the huge cost of such a model of female identity and escape:
    > At the end of *Surfacing*, then, Atwood seems to reject the enticement of the exclusionist feminism which promises freedom from dismembering patriarchal discourse at the cost of the loss of readable selfhood. Excommunication, escape from (patriarchal) communicative rationality, fails utterly to procure meaningful self-identity and (self-) constitutive agency for female subjects: it does nothing at all to diminish, but in fact panders to, the perception of women as silent or irrational and incapable of serious constitutional engagement. (279–80)
85. 'American' in this novel is used to signify the abuses of the contemporary mechanised world. The 'Americans' kill birds, fill the lakes with the noise of their motorised boats, destroy the environment, and are made up of desires superimposed upon them by consumer society. The fact that it is actually Canadians who kill the bird and have a motorised boat does not change the symbolic import of how Atwood uses the term 'American' in this novel. The irony does, however, build a metafictional warning against national generalisations into Atwood's nationalistic use of 'American.'
86. Jane Flax lists a 'transparent medium of expression (language)' as one of the eight 'major themes and characters' of Enlightenment thought which postmodernism tries to 'reveal the internally contradictory nature of.' 'Enlightenment philosophers,' she explains, 'posit or presume a realist or correspondence theory of language in which objects are not linguistically or socially constructed; they are merely made present to consciousness by naming or by the right use of language' (31). Thus, the surfacer expresses a postmodern suspicion of language, but actually uses language in a way that presumes a 'realist or correspondence theory of language.'
87. Joan admits at the end of the narrative that she 'didn't tell any lies. Well, not very many. Some of the names and a few other things, but nothing major' (344).

[88] Molly Hite bases her entire book length study of women's contemporary narrative strategies on this notion of 'the Other Side.'
[89] Notice Joan's extensive postal activities despite her supposed 'exile' and 'silence.' She sends a postcard to Arthur and checks the post office repeatedly for mail.
[90] For Robert Phiddian the potential for satire is what differentiates parody from deconstructive critique.
[91] Eleanora Rao also identifies this moment in the text as marking the transition from purely playful, comic parody to deconstructive, critical parody:
> However, when Joan Foster's romance *Stalked by Love* is approaching the supposedly happy ending of the heroine Charlotte's adventures, Joan realises she cannot elaborate it any more, and refuses to obey the laws of the genre. At this point *Lady Oracle* deconstructs the kind of fiction it is parodying. ('Margaret Atwood's *Lady Oracle*' 138)

[92] As Jacques Derrida states in 'The Law of Genre,'
> As soon as the word *genre* is sounded, as soon as it is heard, as soon as one attempts to conceive it, a limit is drawn. And when a limit is established, norms and interdictions are not far behind: 'Do', 'Do not', says 'genre', the word *genre*, the figure, the voice or the law of genre. (224)

Of course, Derrida goes on to disrupt the law of genre by asking, 'What if there were, lodged within the heart of the law itself, a law of impurity or a principle of contamination?' (225).
[93] See also Sandra Gilbert and Susan Gubar's reading of *Jane Eyre* in *The Madwoman in the Attic* (336–71).
[94] For a more extensive consideration of postmodernism's politics, see Hutcheon's *The Politics of Postmodernism*.
[95] This strangely inappropriate image is another example of how Joan's use of language marks her increasing critical distance from the Gothic Romance.
[96] Susanne Becker also terms the reader Joan's 'accomplice.' She bases her justification for this reading on Joan's use of the Gothic tradition of complicity with the reader:
> it is tempting to read the opening of *Lady Oracle* also as a parody of the reader's position when reading the romance: Joan, too, has staged a 'disappearing act,' escaped from her chaotic life to Italy (!) to now look at it – and tell it – 'from the other side'. This recalls the opening of *Jane Eyre*: simultaneously being alienated from the family by her surrogate mother's interdiction and alienating herself by withdrawing beyond the drawing- and breakfast-rooms into the window-seat, the 'spoken subject' Jane (Silverman 1983, 47), as we have seen, is introduced in complicity with the reader (Spivak 1989, 180). Similarly, in Joan Foster's exile, the reader becomes her accomplice in recreating her life-story. Thus the gothic narrative move for inclusion of the reader is 'repeated,' and the intertextual complicity with a feminine gothic classic displays the reinforcing function of the reverential parody: it *continues* this tradition of women's writing. (156)

[97] Iris makes a similarly ironic comment about working women's lack of representation when discussing her father: 'He couldn't bear to throw his men out of work. He owed them allegiance, these men of his. Never mind that some of them were women' (167).

98 Leigh Gilmore offers a useful summary of the importance of the signature in early theories of autobiography. See the chapter entitled 'Technologies of Autobiography' in her *Autobiographics: A Feminist Theory of Women's Self-Representation*:

> Another 'father figure' in autobiography studies is Philippe Lejeune whose early formulation of autobiography's contractual basis focused on the guarantee offered by the signature. For Lejeune, the title page functioned as a signed document attesting to the historically truthful representation of the coherent self of an actual person. (75–6)

In moving the signature from the title page to the front cover and including the subtitle 'A History,' Benjamin Chase attempts to emphasize that his text is a 'historically truthful representation.' It is interesting that in his influential essay 'Conditions and Limits of Autobiography,' Georges Gusdorf identifies the most common motive for writing an autobiography to be that of 'providing a sort of posthumous propaganda for posterity that otherwise is in danger of forgetting them or of failing to esteem them properly' (36). This type of autobiography that is 'devoted exclusively to the defence and glorification of a man, a career, a political cause' is described as 'limited almost entirely to the public sector of existence' (36). Interestingly, Jane Marcus notes that in contrast, famous women often withdraw from public discourse in order to write their more private and personal autobiographies (Marcus 114). Indeed, the very title – *The Private Self* – which Shari Benstock chose for the collection of essays on women's autobiography she edited in 1988 highlights this difference between the traditional, masculine, public autobiography and a more private, female model.

99 Marta Dvorak's discourse analysis of this passage in her article 'The Right Hand Writing and the Left Hand Erasing in Margaret Atwood's *The Blind Assassin*' is helpful here:

> Ostensibly an objective, official record, the passage is suffused with overlapping resonances in which markers affirming power are overlaid with markers of ideological distancing. The paratactic enumeration of transitive verbs is meant to signal power, as is the book cover itself, green leather onto which not only the title but also the grandfather's heavy signature are stamped in gold. The seriation verbs in the anaphoristic mode gives sole agency to the industrialist in a demonstration of the triumphant control reigning in this age of nascent Canadian capitalism. Yet it is overlaid by the voice of the narrator, which in turn overlaps with the authorial voice organising the discourse. (61–2)

100 In order to designate the novel-within-the-novel, I use quotation marks. Thus, 'The Blind Assassin' refers to Iris/Laura's previous publication. *The Blind Assassin* refers to Atwood's novel as a whole. My assumption is that the newspaper articles, the copies of 'The Blind Assassin' and Iris's later autobiographical account are all left in the trunk by Iris for Sabrina.

101 This contrast in materials is also historical. The high quality materials used for *The Chase Industries: A History* reflect the prosperity of the period. The 'tawdry' dust jacket and cheap paper used for 'The Blind Assassin' are signs of the economic difficulties of 'the years just after the war' (285). It is ironic that *The Chase Industries: A History* survives time passing, but the actual Chase Industries go bankrupt and are shut down by Richard.

102 The echo of Banquo's uninvited visit to Macbeth's dinner table is highly appropriate. Iris never overcomes her guilt that she was in effect Laura's 'blind assassin.'

103 Hepburn does not offer any comments on the more sinister manifestation of the hand image in Winifred's threatening promise to Iris: 'I'll take you in hand' (234).

104 This is Diana Postlethwaite's complaint about this novel: 'such a triple-decker explication felt like *way* too much work to this fatigued reader' (162). She develops an amusingly ironic system of labelling *The Blind Assassin* and 'The Blind Assassin' BA_1 and BA_2 in order to exaggerate and critique this text's complications.

105 I do not wish to suggest that discomfort over the split between the private self and the public persona is exclusively a female experience. For example, when Iris's father, Norval Chase, can no longer fulfil his public role as owner of Chase Industries because he can no longer afford to retain '*his* men,' he also experiences a split between his private sympathy and regret, and his public demonization: 'Father, rendered in cardboard and wearing a top hat and smoking a cigar – not things he ever did – was burned in effigy, to loud cheering' (207). The top hat and cigar emphasize how his public image has become alienated from his private self.

106 Ruth Parkin-Gounelas uses post-Freudian psychoanalysis to explore the 'link between vision and violence' (2) in this novel in her article '"What Isn't There" in Margaret Atwood's *The Blind Assassin*: The Psychoanalysis of Duplicity.'

107 My reading echoes J. Brooks Bouson's analysis of the private and public. See, for example, her argument that 'Iris's memoir dialogically contests the public and official family version of events and tells the unofficial and secret version of family history, revealing the personal and cultural traumas Iris and her sister, Laura, suffer under a patriarchal system' (2). Our readings of Atwood's use of the feminist memoir differ in that my reading emphasizes Iris's 'textual revenge,' whereas Bouson focuses on Iris's writing as a means to purge her of guilt and to memorialize the sisters' traumas.

Chapter 4

108 Nicole King's reading is rather different. She reads Kiki's decision to sell the painting not as resistance to Carlene's ideas about the painting but as an ongoing demonstration of the goddess Erzulie's transformative function (273).

109 See Daniel Born's 'Private Gardens, Public Swamps: *Howards End* and the Revaluation of Liberal Guilt' for an analysis of Forster's sources for the notion of the 'abyss' in *Howards End* (147–50).

110 Ulka Anjaria comes close to the kind of analysis that relates *On Beauty*'s formal inheritance from Forster with the authors' thematic concerns when she suggests that

> a genealogical approach to *Howards End* that approaches it via the thematic concerns of *On Beauty* reveals that Forster's novel is also structured over a series of binaries from which canons of aesthetic value are questioned for their normalizing hold on the individual. (39)

[111] Philip Tew also places Zadie Smith's comments alongside David James' 'The New Purism' in *Zadie Smith*.
[112] See, for example, Sharon Raynor's 'From the Dispossessed to the Decolonized: From Samuel Selvon's *The Lonely Londoners* to Zadie Smith's "Hanwell in Hell"' and Éric Tabuteau's 'Marginally Correct: Zadie Smith's *White Teeth* and Sam Selvon's *The Lonely Londoners*' for readings of Smith's relatedness to Selvon.
[113] This strategy works for a period of time, but Leonard and Jacky are still put out of their flat for not paying the rent.
[114] In her brief overview of the reception of *White Teeth* in her Continuum Contemporaries study of Smith's first novel, Claire Squires notes: 'The Rushdie and Kureishi connection was widely mentioned' (75) and Corinne Fowler comments that 'Salman Rushdie's early review of *White Teeth* probably guaranteed the novel's commercial success' (79).

Chapter 5

[115] As Atwood explains, 'To get even a crumb fallen from the literary movable feast, you'd have to publish outside the country, and that meant you would have to write something that might snare you a foreign publisher' (68).
[116] Given producer Kate McKerrell's statement in the DVD extras for *Lost in Austen* that the production was consciously aiming for a younger audience, the similarity of these opening credits to the graphic novels by Hilary Burningham (illustrated by Rachel Phillips) and the Marvel Comic book by Nancy Butler and Hugo Petrus is pertinent as they are also marketed as introductions to Jane Austen for younger audiences.
[117] Haslett argues:
> Visitors to Chawton House, or Lyme Park, are confirmed in the sense that the series' image of England is 'real', rather than a way of seeing. Of course Lyme Park is a 'real' place in a way which Pemberley is not, but one of the consequences of the television dramatizations is to make Pemberley real, to naturalize it as an image of Regency England. This is not a false image, but it is a partial one, and the tendency of the film versions of Jane Austen is to make this particular way of seeing Regency England the historical or representative one. (204)

[118] In her chapter for *The Cambridge Companion to Jane Austen*, Jan Fergus helpfully presents the evidence that contradicts Henry Austen's claim about his sister that '[n]either the hope of fame nor profit mixed with her early motives' (qtd by Fergus 12). Fergus shows how commercial considerations were always present in the production and distribution of Austen's texts.
[119] Handwritten titles and/or authors' names, pencil drawings, 'feminine colours' such as pastels and pink and stylized images of the central female and (occasionally) male characters are all common features of 'chick lit' covers.
[120] See pages 71–2 for Ferriss's description of the ways in which Fielding is indebted to Austen and the rest of her chapter (71–84) for the ways in which the film version strengthened its ties to Austen.
[121] See Diana Wallace on ventriloquism (*The Woman's Historical Novel: British Women Writers, 1900–2000*, 217–19 and 223–4 in particular). Wallace references

A. S. Byatt's use of the word 'ventriloquism' in *On Histories and Stories* (43–7). Ellen McWilliams also uses the notion of ventriloquism in *Margaret Atwood and the Female Bildungsroman* (114–18).

[122] Castle, Terry. 'Sister-Sister.' Rev. of *Jane Austen's Letters*, ed. Deirde Le Faye. *London Review of Books* 17.5 (3 August 1995): 3–6. See Claudia L. Johnson's 'The Divine Miss Jane: Jane Austen, Janeites, and the Discipline of Novel Studies' for a very helpful analysis of the Terry Castle review and reactions to it and Roger Rosenblatt's famous attack on Eve Kosofsky Sedgwick's MLA paper 'Jane Austen and the Masturbating Girl.' Johnson argues for a queer reading of Austen and suggests it has a long history:

> To listen to the readers who attacked Sedgwick and Castle, we might imagine that no one had *ever* doubted Austen's normativity before. This is so far from the case that the wonder is rather that Austen's normality itself now appears beyond question to so many. (147)

[123] The time travel romantic comedy has, of course, been done repeatedly before. In terms of Amanda Price's desires and nostalgia, *Kate and Leopold* emerges as a helpful parallel. Indeed, Kate's secretary – a character who loves romance novels, in contrast to Kate's cold attitude to romance – is called Darcy which hints at Austen. Like Amanda, Kate (played by Meg Ryan) lives in a world without romance. What causes Kate to travel back in time is her love for Leopold, an immigrant English duke who accidentally followed Kate's ex-boyfriend through time into contemporary New York. In his director's comments to the film, James Mangold dismisses criticisms of the film for having depicted an idealized version of New York – both in the past and present. In contrast to Dan Zeff, Mangold is keen to emphasize the elements of fantasy in the time travel romantic comedy. Both films display nostalgia for the English gentleman. See Christine Berberich's *The Image of the English Gentleman in Twentieth-Century Literature: Englishness and Nostalgia* for an examination of what qualities the 'gentleman' embodies.

[124] See Claudia L. Johnson's 'The Divine Miss Jane: Jane Austen, Janeites, and the Discipline of Novel Studies' for a historical analysis of this positioning of Austen as escape, refuge or redemptive (154–5).

[125] James Mangold's director's commentary for *Kate and Leopold* seems similarly confused about the causes of Kate's emotional bankruptcy. He hints that perhaps it is a downside of the Women's Movement but then immediately jumps to praise the achievements of the Movement. He fails to engage critically with late capitalism itself in his commentary despite the ways in which the actual content of the film implies that critique.

[126] Linda Berdoll quotes Charlotte Brontë's criticism in her preface and suggest that her novel will 'right this wrong' of Austen's lack of passion.

[127] My point here is to identify the fear of negative judgements that *Lost in Austen* demonstrates by listing the kinds of negative language that reviewers have used previously. Many critics have developed Stam's work. Indeed, John Wiltshire suggests that it has become so very common for academic film critics to 'disparage the notion of "fidelity"' (160) that it might actually be helpful to bring back greater consideration of the relationship between an adaptation and its 'original' source. Wiltshire suggests that one negative effect of the movement against 'fidelity' in adaptation theory is that it 'disenfranchise[s] precisely that audience which shares knowledge with the script writer and director – knowledge of and familiarity with the original "classic" texts' (160).

128. This is where *Lost in Austen* contrasts with the idealized past presented in *Kate and Leopold*. This is partly because most of *Lost in Austen* is set in the past whereas most of the action in *Kate and Leopold* occurs in the contemporary time frame so we get much less detail regarding the past in that film.
129. Pirhana replies, 'I'm black.' She then returns us to the series' more comic tone by stating that she cannot live without toilet roll or chocolate even for ten minutes.
130. This phrase awkwardly echoes Amanda's earlier description of her 'standard pubic topiary' as being that of a 'landing strip.'
131. Foster appropriates this term 'pimp' from popular culture without examining the gender politics of some of its other various popular meanings.
132. Whelehan does revise her reading of *Bridget Jones's Diary* somewhat in *The Feminist Bestseller* by placing it in a longer tradition of popular feminist fiction. See also her *Helen Fielding's* Bridget Jones's Diary: *A Reader's Guide.*

Bibliography

Abbey, Sharon and Andrea O'Reilly, eds. *Redefining Motherhood: Changing Identities and Patterns*. Toronto: Second Story P, 1998. Print.

Altman, Marsha. *The Darcys and the Bingleys: A Tale of Two Gentlemen's Marriages to Two Most Devoted Sisters*. Naperville, Illinois: Sourcebooks-Landmark, 2008. Print.

Anderson, Linda, ed. *Plotting Change: Contemporary Women's Fiction*. Stratford-Upon-Avon Studies Second Ser. London: Edward Arnold, 1990. Print.

—. 'The Re-Imagining of History in Contemporary Women's Fiction.' Anderson 129–41.

Anjaria, Ulka. '*On Beauty* and Being Postcolonial: Aesthetics and Form in Zadie Smith.' Walters 31–55. Print.

Atkinson, Yvonne. 'Language That Bears Witness: The Black English Tradition in the Works of Toni Morrison.' Conner 12–30.

Atwood, Margaret. *The Blind Assassin: A Novel*. Toronto: McClelland & Stewart, 2000. Print.

—. *Bodily Harm*. 1981. London: Vintage, 1996. Print.

—. *Cat's Eye*. 1988. London: Virago, 1990. Print.

—. *The Edible Woman*. 1969. Toronto: McClelland & Stewart, 1989. Print.

—. *The Handmaid's Tale*. 1985. London: Virago, 1987. Print.

—. 'Haunted by Their Nightmares.' Bloom, *Toni Morrison* 143–7. Print.

—. 'If You Can't Say Something Nice, Don't Say Anything At All.' Shields and Anderson 133–48.

—. *Lady Oracle*. Toronto: McClelland & Stewart; Seal, 1976. Print.

—. *Murder in the Dark*. Toronto: McClelland & Stewart, 1983. Print.

—. *Negotiating With the Dead: A Writer on Writing*. The Empson Lectures. Cambridge: Cambridge UP, 2002. Print.

—. *Oryx and Crake*. Toronto: McClelland & Stewart, 2003.

—. *Payback: Debt and the Shadow Side of Wealth*. London: Bloomsbury Publishing, 2008. Print.

—. *The Penelopiad: The Myth of Penelope and Odysseus*. Toronto: Knopf, 2005.

—. *Second Words: Selected Critical Prose*. Toronto: Anansi, 1982. Print.

—. *Selected Poems: 1966–1984*. Toronto: Oxford UP, 1990. Print.

—. *Surfacing*. 1972. London: Virago, 1979. Print.

—. *Wilderness Tips*. London: Virago, 1991. Print.

Austen, Jane. *Pride and Prejudice*. 1813. London: Headline, 2006. Print.

Awkward, Michael. *Inspiring Influences: Tradition, Revision, and Afro-American Women's Novels*. New York: Columbia UP, 1989. Print.

Baker, Houston A. Jr. *Blues, Ideology, and Afro-American Literature: A Vernacular Theory*. Chicago: Chicago UP, 1984.

Bakhtin, Mikhail. *The Dialogic Imagination: Four Essays*. Trans. Caryl Emerson and Michael Holquist. Ed. Michael Holquist. Austin: Texas UP, 1981. Print.
—. *Rabelais and His World*. 1965. Trans. Hélène Iswolsky. Bloomington: Indiana UP, 1984. Print.
Baraka, Amiri. 'The "Blues Aesthetic" and the "Black Aesthetic": Aesthetics as the Continuing Political History of a Culture.' *Black Music Research Journal* 11.2 (1991): 101–9. *JSTOR*. Web. 12 May 2010.
Barry, Brian. *Culture and Equality*. Cambridge: Polity Press, 2001. Print.
Barth, John. *The Friday Book: Essays and Other Nonfiction*. Toronto: General Publishing Co., 1984. Print.
Barthes, Roland. *Image, Music, Text*. Trans. Stephen Heath. London: Fontana-HarperCollins, 1977. Print.
Becker, Susanne. *Gothic Forms of Feminine Fiction*. Manchester: Manchester UP, 1999. Print.
Beitchman, Philip. *I Am a Process with No Subject*. Gainesville: University of Florida Press, 1988. Print.
Belsey, Catherine. *Critical Practice*. London: Routledge, 1980. Print.
Belsey, Catherine, and Jane Moore. eds. *The Feminist Reader*. Basingstoke: Macmillan, 1989. Print.
Benhabib, Seyla. *Situating the Self: Gender, Community and Postmodernism in Contemporary Ethics*. Cambridge: Polity, 1992. Print.
Benstock, Shari, ed. *The Private Self: Theory and Practice of Women's Autobiographical Writings*. Chapel Hill: University of North Carolina Press, 1988. Print.
Bentley, Nick. 'Doris Lessing's The Golden Notebook: An Experiment in Critical Fiction.' Ridout and Watkins. 44–60.
—. 'Re-writing Englishness: Imagining the Nation in Julian Barnes's *England, England* and Zadie Smith's *White Teeth*.' *Textual Practice* 21.3 (2007): 483–504. *JSTOR*. Web. 20 Jan. 2010.
Berberich, Christine. *The Image of the English Gentleman in Twentieth-Century Literature: Englishness and Nostalgia*. Aldershot: Ashgate, 2007. Print.
Berdoll, Linda. *Mr Darcy Takes a Wife: a Novel*. Naperville, Illinois: Sourcebooks-Landmark, 2004. Print.
Bertelsen, Eve. 'Who Is It Who Says "I"?: The Persona of a Doris Lessing Interview.' Kaplan and Rose, *Doris Lessing* 169–82.
Bjork, Patrick Bryce. *The Novels of Toni Morrison: The Search for Self and Place Within the Community*. American University Studies. 31. New York: Peter Lang, 1992. Print.
Bloom, Harold. *The Anxiety of Influence: A Theory of Poetry*. Oxford: Oxford UP, 1973. Print.
—. ed. *Doris Lessing*. Modern Critical Views. New York: Chelsea House Publishers, 1986. Print.
—. ed. *Frederick Douglass's* Narrative of the Life of Frederick Douglass. Modern Critical Interpretations. New York: Chelsea House, 1988. Print.
—. ed. *Toni Morrison*. Modern Critical Views. New York: Chelsea House, 1990. Print.
Bordo, Susan. 'Feminism, Postmodernism and Gender-Scepticism.' Linda Nicholson 133–56.

Born, Daniel. 'Private Gardens, Public Swamps: *Howards End* and the Revaluation of Liberal Guilt.' *Novel: A Forum on Fiction* 25.2 (1992): 141–59. *JSTOR.* Web. 24 Apr. 2010.
Boschman, Robert. 'Excrement and "Kitsch" in Doris Lessing's *The Good Terrorist.*' *ARIEL* 25.3 (1994): 7–27. Print.
Bouson, J. Brooks. *Brutal Choreographies: Oppositional Strategies and Narrative Design in the Novels of Margaret Atwood.* Amherst: Massachusetts UP, 1993. Print.
—. '"A Commemoration of Wounds Endured and Resented:" Margaret Atwood's *The Blind Assassin* as Feminist Memoir.' *Critique: Studies in Contemporary Fiction* 44.3 (2003): 251–69. *JSTOR.* Web. 26 Apr. 2010.
—. *Quiet as It's Kept: Shame, Trauma and Race In the Novels of Toni Morrison.* SUNY Ser in Psychoanalysis and Culture. Albany: State U of New York P, 2000. Print.
Boym, Svetlana. *The Future of Nostalgia.* New York: Basic Books, 2001. Print.
Bradbury, Malcolm, ed. *The Novel Today: Contemporary Writers on Modern Fiction.* 2nd ed. London: Fontana, 1990. Print.
Bradshaw, David, ed. *The Cambridge Companion to E. M. Forster.* Cambridge: Cambridge UP, 2007. Print.
—. '*Howards End.*' Bradshaw 151–72.
Bridget Jones's Diary. Screenplay by Helen Fielding, Andrew Davies and Richard Curtis. Dir. Sharon Maguire. Perf. Renée Zellweger, Hugh Grant and Colin Firth. Miramax and Universal, 2001. Film.
Brontë, Charlotte. *Jane Eyre.* 1847. Oxford: Oxford UP, 1998. Print.
Brownmiller, Susan. 'Best Battles Are Fought by Men and Women Together.' Sprague and Tiger 218–21.
Brownstein, Rachel M. '*Northanger Abbey, Sense and Sensibility, Pride and Prejudice.*' Copeland and McMaster 32–57.
Bruss, Elizabeth W. *Autobiographical Acts: The Changing Situation of a Literary Genre.* Baltimore: Johns Hopkins UP, 1976. Print.
Bucknell, Brad. 'Henry Louis Gates Jr. and the Theory of "Signifyin(g)."' *ARIEL* 21.1 (1990): 65–84. Print.
Burke, Seán. *The Death and Return of the Author: Criticism and Subjectivity in Barthes, Foucault and Derrida.* Edinburgh: Edinburgh UP, 1992.
Burningham, Hilary. Illus. Rachel Phillips. *The Graphic Novel Series: Pride and Prejudice by Jane Austen.* London: Evans Brothers, 2004.
Butler, Judith. *Gender Trouble: Feminism and the Subversion of Identity.* London: Routledge, 1990. Print.
Butler, Nancy and Hugo Petrus. *Pride and Prejudice: Adapted from the Novel by Jane Austen.* New York: Marvel, 2009. Print.
Byatt, A. S. *On Histories and Stories: Selected Essays.* 2000. London: Vintage, 2001. Print.
Byerman, Keith E. 'Beyond Realism.' Gates and Appiah 100–25.
Cameron, Deborah. *Feminism and Linguistic Theory.* 2nd ed. London: Macmillan, 1985. Print.
Caponi, Gena Dagel, ed. *Signifyin(g), Sanctifyin,' and Slam Dunking: A Reader in African-American Expressive Culture.* Amherst: U of Massachusetts P, 1999. Print.
Castle, Terry. 'Sister-Sister.' Rev. of *Jane Austen's Letters,* ed. Deirde Le Faye. *London Review of Books* 17.5 (3 Aug. 1995): 3–6. Web. 30 Oct. 2009.

Chatman, Seymour. 'Parody and Style.' *Poetics Today* 22.1 (2001): 25–39. *EBSCO*. Web. 24 Apr. 2010.

Cheng, Anne Anlin. 'Wounded Beauty: An Exploratory Essay on Race, Feminism, and the Aesthetic Question.' *Tulsa Studies in Women's Literature* 19.2 (2000): 191–217. *JSTOR*. Web. 26 Apr. 2010.

Childs, Peter. *Contemporary Novelists: British Fiction since 1970*. Basingstoke: Palgrave-Macmillan, 2005. Print.

Christian, Barbara T. 'Layered Rhythms: Virginia Woolf and Toni Morrison.' Peterson 19–36.

Cohen, Stanley, and Laurie Taylor. *Escape Attempts: The Theory and Practice of Resistance to Everyday Life*. Rev. ed. London: Routledge, 1992. Print.

Conner, Marc C., ed. *The Aesthetics of Toni Morrison: Speaking the Unspeakable*. Jackson: UP of Mississippi, 2000. Print.

Conrad, Joseph. *Heart of Darkness*. 1902. London: Penguin, 1995. Print.

—. *The Secret Agent*. 1907. London: Everyman, 1997. Print.

Cooke, Nathalie. *Margaret Atwood: A Biography*. Toronto: ECW, 1998. Print.

Copeland, Edward and Juliet McMaster, eds. *The Cambridge Companion to Jane Austen*. Cambridge: Cambridge UP, 1997. Print.

Corse, Sandra. *Operatic Subjects: The Evolution of the Self in Modern Opera*. Madison, Teaneck: Fairleigh Dickinson UP, 2000. Print.

Coward, Rosalind. 'The True Story of How I Became My Own Person.' Belsey and Moore 35–47.

Crapanzano, Vincent. 'The Postmodern Crisis: Discourse, Parody, Memory.' *Cultural Anthropology* 6.4 (1991): 431–46. *JSTOR*. Web. 14 Apr. 2010.

Crown, Sarah. 'Doris Lessing Wins Nobel Prize.' *The Guardian*. 11 Oct. 2007. *www.guardian.co.uk*. Web. 10 May 2010.

Curie, Mark, ed. *Metafiction*. Harlow: Longman, 1995. Print.

Dane, Joseph A. *Parody: Critical Concepts Versus Literary Practices, Aristophanes to Sterne*. Norman: U of Oklahoma P, 1988. Print.

Danziger, Marie A. *Text/Countertext: Postmodern Paranoia in Samuel Beckett, Doris Lessing, and Philip Roth*. New York: Peter Lang, 1996. Print.

Davey, Frank. *Margaret Atwood: A Feminist Poetics*. Vancouver: Talonbooks, 1984. Print.

Davidson, Arnold E. and Cathy N. Davidson, eds. *The Art of Margaret Atwood: Essays in Criticism*. Toronto: Anansi, 1981. Print.

Davies, Carole Boyce. *Black Women, Writing and Identity: Migrations of the Subject*. London: Routledge, 1994. Print.

Dawkins, Jane. *Letters from Pemberley: The First Year*. Naperville, Illinois: Sourcebooks-Landmark, 2007. Print.

De Beauvoir, Simone. *The Second Sex*. 1949. London: Picador, 1988.

Dentith, Simon. *Parody*. The New Critical Idiom. New York: Routledge, 2000. Print.

Derrida, Jacques. *Acts of Literature*. Ed. Derek Attridge. London: Routledge, 1992. Print.

Dibble, Elizabeth. *The Unresolvable Plot: Reading Contemporary Fiction*. London: Routledge, 1988. Print.

Dittmar, Linda. '"Will the Circle Be Unbroken?": The Politics of Form in *The Bluest Eye*.' *Novel: a Forum on Fiction* 23 (1990): 137–55. Print.

Doty, Mark, ed. *Open House: Writers Redefine Home*. Graywolf Forum 5. Saint Paul, Minnesota: 2003. Print.

Douglas, Christopher. 'What *The Bluest Eye* Knows about Them: Culture, Race, Identity.' *American Literature* 78.1 (2006): 141–68. *JSTOR*. Web. 26 Apr. 2010.

Douglass, Frederick. *Narrative of the Life of Frederick Douglass*. Oxford: Oxford UP, 1999. Print.

Draine, Betsy. 'Nostalgia and Irony: The Postmodern Order of *The Golden Notebook*.' *Modern Fiction Studies* 26 (1980): 31–48. Print.

—. *Substance Under Pressure: Artistic Coherence and Evolving Form in the Novels of Doris Lessing*. Madison: University of Wisconsin Press, 1983. Print.

Du Plessis, Rachel Blau. *Writing Beyond the Ending: Narrative Strategies of Twentieth-Century Women Writers*. Bloomington: Indiana UP, 1985. Print.

Duvall, John N. *The Identifying Fictions of Toni Morrison: Modernist Authenticity and Postmodern Blackness*. New York: Palgrave-St. Martin's, 2000. Print.

Dvorak, Marta. 'The Right Hand Writing and the Left Hand Erasing in Margaret Atwood's *The Blind Assassin*.' *Palimpsests. Commonwealth Essays and Studies* 25.1 (2002): 59–68. Print.

Eagleton, Mary. *Figuring the Woman Author in Contemporary Fiction*. Basingstoke: Palgrave, 2005. Print.

Eakin, Paul John. *How Our Lives Become Stories: Making Selves*. Ithaca: Cornell UP, 1999. Print.

Ebert, Teresa L. *Ludic Feminism and After: Postmodernism, Desire, and Labor in Late Capitalism*. Critical Perspectives on Women and Gender. Michigan: Michigan UP, 1996. Print.

Elam, Diane. *Feminism and Deconstruction: Ms. En Abyme*. London: Routledge, 1994. Print.

Elbaz, Robert. *The Changing Nature of the Self: A Critical Study of the Autobiographical Discourse*. London: Croom Helm, 1988. Print.

Eliot, T. S. *Collected Poems: 1909–1962*. London: Faber and Faber, 1963. Print.

Ellen, Barbara. '"I have nothing in common with feminists. They never seem to think that one might enjoy men."' *The Observer*. 9 Sept. 2001. *guardian.co.uk*. Web. 24 Apr. 2010.

Elliott, Jane. 'The Currency of Feminist Theory' in *PMLA* 121.5 (2006): 1679–703. Print.

Ellis, John. 'The Literary Adaptation.' *Screen* 23.1 (May-June 1982): 3–5. Print.

Evans, Mari, ed. *Black Women Writers (1950–1980)*. New York: Anchor, 1984. Print.

Fand, Roxanne J. *The Dialogic Self: Reconstructing Subjectivity in Woolf, Lessing, and Atwood*. Selinsgrove: Susquehanna UP, 1999. Print.

Felski, Rita. *Beyond Feminist Aesthetics: Feminist Literature and Social Change*. Cambridge, MA: Harvard, UP, 1989. Print.

Fergus, Jan. 'The Professional Woman Writer.' *The Cambridge Companion to Jane Austen*. Copeland and McMaster 12–31.

Ferriss, Suzanne and Mallory Young, eds. *Chick Lit: The New Woman's Fiction*. London: Routledge, 2006. Print.

Ferriss, Suzanne. 'Narrative and Cinematic Doubleness: *Pride and Prejudice* and *Bridget Jones's Diary*.' Ferriss and Young 71–84.

Fetterley, Judith. *The Resisting Reader: A Feminist Approach to American Fiction*. Bloomington: Indiana UP, 1978. Print.

Fielding, Helen. *Bridget Jones's Diary*. London: Picador, 1996. Print.

Fischer, Susan Alice. '"A Glance from God": Zadie Smith's *On Beauty* and Zora Neale Hurston.' *Changing English* 14.3 (2007): 285–97. *JSTOR*. Web. 20 Jan. 2010.

Fishburn, Katherine. 'Teaching Doris Lessing as a Subversive Activity: A Response to the Preface to *The Golden Notebook*.' Kaplan and Rose, *Doris Lessing* 81–92.

Fitzgerald, F. Scott. *The Great Gatsby*. 1926. London: Penguin, 1950. Print.

Flax, Jane. 'Postmodernism and Gender Relations in Feminist Theory.' Linda Nicholson 39–62.

—. *Thinking Fragments: Psychoanalysis, Feminism, and Postmodernism in the Contemporary West*. Berkeley: U of California P, 1990. Print.

Forster, E. M. *Howards End*. 1910. London: Penguin, 2000. Print.

—. *Two Cheers for Democracy*. 1951. Harmondsworth: Penguin, 1974.

Foster, Brandy. 'Pimp My Austen: The Commodification and Customization of Jane Austen.' *Persuasions On-Line* 29.1 (2008) *JSTOR*. Web. 17 Dec. 2009.

Fowler, Corinne. 'A Tale of Two Novels: Developing a Devolved Approach to Black British Writing.' *The Journal of Commonwealth Literature* 43.3 (2008): 75–94. *JSTOR*. Web. 20 Jan. 2010.

Fox, Robert Elliot. Rev. of *Figures in Black: Words, Signs, and the 'Racial Self,'* by Henry Louis Gates Jr. *Black American Literature Forum* 22 (1988): 841–8. Print.

Fraser, Nancy, and Linda J. Nicholson. 'Social Criticism without Philosophy: An Encounter Between Feminism and Postmodernism.' Linda Nicholson 19–38.

Friedman, Susan Stanford. 'Women's Autobiographical Selves: Theory and Practice.' Benstock 34–62.

Fullbrook, Kate. *Free Women: Ethics and Aesthetics in Twentieth-Century Women's Fiction*. New York: Harvester Wheatsheaf, 1990. Print.

Fuoroli, Caryn. 'Doris Lessing's "Game": Referential Language and Fictional Form.' *Twentieth Century Literature* 27 (1981): 146–65. Print.

Furman, Jan. *Toni Morrison's Fiction*. Understanding Contemporary American Lit. Columbia: U of South Carolina P, 1996. Print.

Fuss, Diana. *Essentially Speaking: Feminism, Nature and Difference*. New York: Routledge, 1989. Print.

Garber, Marjorie. *Quotation Marks*. New York: Routledge, 2003. Print.

Genette, Gérard. *Paratexts: Thresholds of Interpretation*. 1987. Trans. Jane E. Lewin. Cambridge: Cambridge UP, 1997. *Google Books*. Web. 10 May 2010.

Gibson, Donald B. 'Text and Countertext in *The Bluest Eye*.' Gates and Appiah 159–74.

Gasiorek, Andrzej. *Post-War British Fiction: Realism and After*. London: Edward Arnold, 1995. Print.

Gates, Henry Louis Jr. *Figures in Black: Words, Signs, and the 'Racial' Self*. New York: Oxford UP, 1987. Print.

—. *Loose Canons: Notes on the Culture Wars*. New York: Oxford UP, 1992. Print.

—. *The Signifying Monkey: A Theory of Afro-American Literary Criticism*. New York: Oxford UP, 1988. Print.

—. '"What's Love Got To Do With It?": Critical Theory, Integrity, and the Black Idiom.' *New Literary History* 18 (1987): 345–62. Print.

Gates, Henry Louis Jr., and K. A. Appiah, eds. *Toni Morrison: Critical Perspectives Past and Present*. Amistad Literary Ser. New York: Amistad, 1993. Print.

Gibson, Graeme. ed. *Eleven Canadian Novelists: Interviewed By Graeme Gibson*. Toronto: Anansi, 1973. Print.

Gilbert, Sandra M., and Susan Gubar. *The Madwoman in the Attic: The Woman Writer and the Nineteenth-Century Literary Imagination.* New Haven: Yale, 1979. Print.

Gillan, Jennifer. 'Focusing on the Wrong Front: Historical Displacement, the Maginot Line, and *The Bluest Eye.*' *African American Review* 36.3 (2002): 283–98. *JSTOR.* Web. 26 Apr. 2010.

Gillis, Stacy, Gillian Howie and Rebecca Munford, eds. *Third Wave Feminism: A Critical Exploration.* 2nd ed. Basingstoke: Palgrave, 2007.

Gilmore, Leigh. *Autobiographics: A Feminist Theory of Women's Self-Representation.* Reading Women Writing Ser. Ithaca: Cornell UP, 1994. Print.

Goldman, Jane. 'Forster and Women.' Bradshaw 120–37.

Gordon, Jan B. 'The Third Cheer: "Voice" in Forster.' *Twentieth Century Literature* 31.2/3 (1985): 315–28. *JSTOR.* Web. 20 Jan. 2010.

Grace, Sherrill. 'Gender as Genre: Atwood's Autobiographical "I."' Colin Nicholson 189–203.

Graglia, Carolyn F. *The Housewife as Pariah: Contemporary Feminism's War on the Family.* London: Institute of United States Studies, 1997. Print.

Grange, Amanda. *Mr. Darcy's Diary.* Naperville, Illinois: Sourcebooks-Landmark, 2007. Print.

Greene, Gayle. 'Bleak Houses: Doris Lessing, Margaret Drabble and the Condition of England.' *Forum for Modern Language Studies* 28.4 (1992): 304–19. Print.

—. *Doris Lessing: The Poetics of Change.* Ann Arbor: University of Michigan Press, 1994. Print.

—. 'Feminist Fiction and the Uses of Memory.' *Signs* 16.2 (Winter 1991): 290–321. *JSTOR.* Web. 17 Dec. 2009.

Guerrero, Ed. 'Tracking "The Look" in the Novels of Toni Morrison.' Middleton 27–41.

Guignon, Charles and David R. Hiley, eds. *Richard Rorty.* Contemporary Philosophy in Focus. Cambridge: Cambridge UP, 2003. Print.

Gurr, Andrew. *Writers in Exile: The Identity of Home in Modern Literature.* Harvester Studies in Contemporary Literature and Culture. Brighton: Harvester, 1981. Print.

Gusdorf, Georges. 'Conditions and Limits of Autobiography.' Ed. and trans. James Olney. *Autobiography: Essays Theoretical and Critical.* Princeton: Princeton UP, 1980. 28–48. Print.

Hanoosh, Michele. 'The Reflexive Function of Parody.' *Comparative Literature* 41 (1989): 113–27. *JSTOR.* Web. 24 Apr. 2010.

Haslett, Moyra. *Marxist Literary and Cultural Studies.* London: Macmillan Press, 2000. Print.

Heilbrun, Carolyn G. *Women's Lives: The View from the Threshold.* Alexander Lectures. Toronto: U of Toronto P, 1999. Print.

Heilmann, Ann and Mark Llewellyn, eds. *Metafiction and Metahistory in Contemporary Women's Writing.* Basingstoke: Palgrave, 2007. Print.

Heinze, Denise. *The Dilemma of 'Double-Consciousness': Toni Morrison's Novels.* Athens, Georgia: U of Georgia P, 1993. Print.

Henke, Suzette. 'Reading Doris Lessing's *Golden Notebook* as Feminist Trauma Narrative.' *Doris Lessing Studies* 17.1&2 (2008): 11–16. Print.

Hepburn, Allan. 'Fiction High and Low.' *Essays on Canadian Writing.* 72 (2000): 131–7. Print.

Heydt-Stevenson, Jill. '"Slipping into the Ha-Ha": Bawdy Humor and Body Politics in Jane Austen's Novels.' *Nineteenth Century Literature* 55.3 (2000): 309–39. *JSTOR.* Web. 17 Dec. 2009.

Hite, Molly. '(En)Gendering Metafiction: Doris Lessing's Rehearsals for *The Golden Notebook.*' *Modern Fiction Studies* 34 (1988): 481–500. Print.

—. *The Other Side of the Story: Structures and Strategies of Contemporary Feminist Narrative.* Ithaca: Cornell UP, 1989. Print.

—. 'Subverting the Ideology of Coherence: *The Golden Notebook* and *The Four-Gated City.*' Kaplan and Rose, *Doris Lessing* 61–9.

Hodge, Merle. *Crick Crack, Monkey.* 1970. Oxford: Heinemann, 2000. Print.

Holstein, James A. and Jaber F. Gubrium. *The Self We Live By: Narrative Identity in a Postmodern World.* Oxford: Oxford UP, 2000. Print.

House, Elizabeth B. 'Artists and the Art of Living: Order and Disorder in Toni Morrison's Fiction.' *Modern Fiction Studies* 34 (1988): 27–44. Print.

Howells, Coral Ann. '*Cat's Eye*: Elaine Risley's Retrospective Art.' Colin Nicholson. 204–18. Print.

—. *Contemporary Canadian Women's Fiction: Refiguring Identities.* Basingstoke: Palgrave, 2003. Print.

Humm, Maggie. *Border Traffic: Strategies of Contemporary Women Writers.* Cultural Politics Ser. Manchester: Manchester UP, 1991. Print.

Hurston, Zora Neale. 'Characteristics of Negro Expression.' Caponi 293–308. Print.

—. *Their Eyes Were Watching God.* 1937. New York: Harper, 1990. Print.

Hutcheon, Linda. Afterword. *The Edible Woman.* By Margaret Atwood. Toronto: McClelland & Stewart, 1989. 313–19. Print.

—. *Irony's Edge: The Theory and Politics of Irony.* London: Routledge, 1994. Print.

—. *A Poetics of Postmodernism: History, Theory, Fiction.* London: Routledge, 1988. Print.

—. *The Politics of Postmodernism.* London: Routledge, 1989. Print.

—. 'Theorizing – Feminism and Postmodernism: A Conversation with Linda Hutcheon.' By Kathleen O'Grady. *Rampike* 9.2 (1998): 20–2. *Canadian Writers Athabasca University.* Web. 2 Sept. 2002.

—. *A Theory of Adaptation.* New York: Routledge, 2006.

—. *A Theory of Parody: The Teachings of Twentieth-Century Art Forms.* London: Routledge, 1985. Print.

Jacobs, Harriet A. *Incidents in the Life of a Slave Girl: Written by Herself.* Eds. L. Maria Child, and Jean Fagan Yellin. Cambridge, Massachusetts: Harvard UP, 2000. Print.

James, David. 'The New Purism.' *Textual Practice* 21.4 (2007): 687–714. *Taylor and Francis Routledge Journals Online.* Web. 24 Apr. 2010.

James, Henry. *The House of Fiction: Essays on the Novel.* Ed. Leon Edel. London: Rupert Hart-Davis, 1957. Print.

Jensen, Robert. *Getting Off: Pornography and the End of Masculinity.* Cambridge, MA: South End Press, 2007. Print.

Joannou, Maroula. *Contemporary Women's Writing: From* The Golden Notebook *to* The Color Purple. Manchester: Manchester UP, 2000. Print.

Johnson, Claudia L. 'Austen Cults and Cultures.' Copeland and McMaster 211–26.
—. 'The Divine Miss Jane: Jane Austen, Janeites, and the Discipline of Novel Studies.' *boundary 2*. 23.3 (1996): 143–63. *JSTOR*. Web. 17 Dec. 2009.
Jones, Ann Rosalind. 'Writing the Body: Toward an Understanding of *l'Écriture féminine*.' *The New Feminist Criticism*. Ed. Elaine Showalter. London: Virago, 1986. 361–77. Print.
Joyce, Joyce A. 'The Black Canon: Reconstructing Black American Literary Criticism.' *New Literary History* 18 (1987): 335–44. Print.
—. 'A Tinker's Damn: Henry Louis Gates Jr. and "The Signifying Monkey" Twenty Years Later.' *Callaloo* 31.2 (2008): 370–80. *Callaloo Online Archive*. Web. 26 Apr. 2010.
—. '"Who the Cap Fit": Unconsciousness and Unconscionableness in the Criticism of Houston A. Baker, Jr. and Henry Louis Gates, Jr.' *New Literary History* 18 (1987): 371–84. *JSTOR*. Web. 14 Apr. 2010.
Kaplan, Carey and Ellen Cronan Rose, eds. *Approaches to Teaching Lessing's* The Golden Notebook. MLA Approaches to Teaching World Literature. New York: MLA, 1989. Print.
—. *Doris Lessing: The Alchemy of Survival*. Athens: Ohio UP, 1988. Print.
Kaplan, Sydney Janet. *Feminine Consciousness in the Modern British Novel*. Urbana: U of Illinois P, 1975. Print.
Kate and Leopold. Screenplay and Dir. James Mangold. Perf. Meg Ryan and Hugh Jackman. Miramax Films, 2001. Film.
Kemp, Peter. Review of Zadie Smith's *On Beauty*. *The Times*. 4 September 2004. *www.timesonline.co.uk*. Web. 19 July 2010.
Kerby, Anthony Paul. *Narrative and the Self*. Bloomington: Indiana UP, 1991. Print.
Kesselman, Amy, Lily D. McNair and Nancy Schniedewind. eds. *Women: Images and Realities: A Multicultural Anthology*. London: Mayfield Publishing Co., 1995. Print.
Kilson, Martin. 'Master of the Intellectual Dodge: A Reply to Henry Louis Gates.' *West Africa Review* 1.2 (2000): 7pp. Web. 18 Aug. 2002.
King, Jeanette. *Doris Lessing*. Modern Fiction Ser. London: Edward Arnold, 1989. Print.
King, Nicole. 'Creolisation and *On Beauty*: Form, Character and the Goddess Erzulie.' *Women: a Cultural Review* 20.3 (2009): 262–76. *JSTOR*. Web. 20 Jan. 2010.
Kiremidjian, G. D. 'The Aesthetics of Parody.' *The Journal of Aesthetics and Art Criticism* 28.2 (1969): 231–42. *JSTOR*. Web. 14 Apr. 2010.
Klotman, Phyllis. 'Dick-and-Jane and the Shirley Temple Sensibility in *The Bluest Eye*.' *Black American Literature Forum* 13 (1979): 123–5. Print.
Knapp, Mona. *Doris Lessing*. New York: Frederick Ungar Publishing, 1984. Print.
Kroetsch, Robert. *The Lovely Treachery of Words: Essays Selected and New*. Studies in Canadian Literature. Toronto: Oxford UP, 1989. Print.
Krouse, Tonya. 'Freedom as Effacement in *The Golden Notebook*: Theorizing Pleasure, Subjectivity, and Authority.' *Journal of Modern Literature* 19.3 (2006): 39–56. *JSTOR*. Web. 10 May 2010.
Kuester, Martin. *Framing Truths: Parodic Structures in Contemporary English-Canadian Historical Novels*. Theory / Culture. Toronto: Toronto UP, 1992. Print.
Kuhn, Cynthia G. *Self-Fashioning in Margaret Atwood's Fiction: Dress, Culture, and Identity*. Series XXVII: Feminist Studies. New York: Peter Lang, 2005. Print.

Ladino, Jennifer. 'Longing for Wonderland: Nostalgia for Nature in Post-Frontier America.' *Iowa Journal of Cultural Studies* 5. (2004): 88–110. Web. 30 Oct 2009.
Laing, R. D. *The Divided Self*. Harmondsworth: Penguin, 1960. Print.
LeClair, Thomas. 'The Language Must Not Sweat: A Conversation with Toni Morrison.' Taylor-Guthrie 119–28. Print.
Lee, Alison. *Realism and Power: Postmodern British Fiction*. London: Routledge, 1990. Print.
Lee, Dorothy H. 'The Quest for Self: Triumph and Failure in the Works of Toni Morrison.' Evans 346–60.
Leonard, John. 'The Spacing Out of Doris Lessing.' Sprague and Tiger 204–9.
Leonard, Vivien. '"Free Women" as Parody: Fun and Games in *The Golden Notebook*.' *Perspectives on Contemporary Literature* 6 (1980): 20–7. Print.
Lessing, Doris. *Alfred and Emily*. London: Fourth Estate-HarperCollins, 2008.
—. *The Four-Gated City*. Children of Violence 5. 1969. London: Panther-Granada, 1972. Print.
—. *The Golden Notebook*. 1962. London: Flamingo-Harper, 1972. Print.
—. *The Good Terrorist*. 1985. London: Flamingo-Harper, 1993. Print.
—. *The Grass is Singing*. 1950. London: Flamingo-Harper, 1994. Print.
—. *Martha Quest*. Children of Violence 1. 1952. London: Panther-Granada, 1966. Print.
—. *Memoirs of a Survivor*. 1974. London: Picador-Pan, 1976. Print.
—. *Prisons We Choose to Live Inside*. New York: Harper & Row, 1987. Print.
—. *Putting the Questions Differently: Interviews with Doris Lessing, 1964–1994*. Ed. Earl G. Ingersoll. London: Flamingo-Harper, 1996. Print.
—. *A Small Personal Voice: Essays, Reviews, Interviews*. Ed. Paul Schlueter. London: Flamingo-Harper, 1994. Print.
—. *The Sweetest Dream*. London: Flamingo-Harper, 2001. Print.
—. *Under My Skin: Volume One of My Autobiography, to 1949*. London: Flamingo-Harper, 1995. Print.
—. *Walking in the Shade: Volume Two of My Autobiography 1949 to 1962*. New York: HarperCollins, 1997. Print.
Lewis, Paul. *Comic Effects: Interdisciplinary Approaches to Humor in Literature*. Albany: State U of New York P, 1989. Print.
Lorde, Audre. 'The Master's Tools Will Never Dismantle the Master's House.' *Writings by Radical Women of Color*. Eds. Cherríe Moraga and Gloria Anzaldua. New York: Kitchen Table/Women of Color Press, 1981. 98–101. Print.
Lost in Austen. Screenplay by Guy Andrews. Dir. Dan Zeff. Perf. Jemima Rooper and Elliot Cowan. ITV-Mammoth Screen, 2008. Television.
Lurie, Alison. 'Bad Housekeeping.' Bloom, *Doris Lessing* 201–8.
Lyotard, Jean-Francois. *The Postmodern Condition: A Report on Knowledge*. Trans. Geoff Bennington and Brian Massumi. Theory and History of Lit. 10. Manchester: Manchester UP, 1984. Print.
Mainardi, Pat. 'The Politics of Housework.' Kesselman, McNair and Schniedewind 162–5.
Malmgren, Carl D. 'Texts, Primers, and Voices in Toni Morrison's *The Bluest Eye*.' *Critique* 41 (2000): 251–62. Print.
Marcus, Jane. 'Invincible Mediocrity: The Private Selves of Public Women.' Benstock 114–46.

Marder, Herbert. 'The Paradox of Form in *The Golden Notebook*.' *Modern Fiction Studies* 26 (1980): 49–54. Print.
Marx, John. 'The Feminization of Globalization.' *Cultural Critique* 63 (Spring 2006): 1–32. *JSTOR*. Web. 20 Jan. 2010.
Maslen, Elizabeth. *Doris Lessing*. Writers and Their Work. Plymouth: Northcote House Publishers, 1994. Print.
Matthews, Glenna. *'Just a Housewife': The Rise and Fall of Domesticity in America*. Oxford: Oxford UP, 1987. Print.
Matus, Jill. *Toni Morrison*. Contemporary World Writers. Manchester: Manchester UP, 1998. Print.
May, Brian. 'Neoliberalism in Rorty and Forster.' *Twentieth Century Literature* 39.2 (1993): 185–207. *JSTOR*. Web. 20 Jan. 2010.
Mazrui, Ali A. 'Millennium Letter to Henry Louis Gates Jr.: Concluding a Dialogue?' *West Africa Review* 1.2 (2000): 6 pp. Web. 18 Aug. 2002 .
McBride, Dwight A. 'Speaking the Unspeakable: On Toni Morrison, African-American Intellectuals, and the Uses of Essentialist Rhetoric.' Peterson 131–52.
McDermott, Sinead. 'Memory, Nostalgia, and Gender in "A Thousand Acres."' *Signs* 28.1 (2002): 389–407. *JSTOR*. Web. 17 Dec. 2009.
McDowell, Deborah E. '"The Changing Same": Generational Connections and Black Women Novelists.' *New Literary History* 18 (1987): 281–302. Print.
—. '"The Self and the Other": Reading Toni Morrison's *Sula* and the Black Female Text.' Bloom, *Toni Morrison* 149–63.
McKay, Nellie Y., ed. *Critical Essays on Toni Morrison*. Boston: G. K. Hall, 1988. Print.
McKee, Patricia. 'Spacing and Placing Experience in Toni Morrison's *Sula*.' Peterson 37–62.
McKinstry, Jaret Susan. 'Living Literally by the Pen: The Self-Conceived and Self-Deceiving Heroine-Author in Margaret Atwood's *Lady Oracle*.' Mendez-Egle 58–70.
McNall, Sally Allen. *Who Is In the House?: A Psychological Study of Two Centuries of Women's Fiction in America, 1795 to the Present*. New York: Elsevier, 1981. Print.
McRobbie, Angela. *The Aftermath of Feminism: Gender, Culture and Social Change*. London: Sage, 2009. Print.
McWilliams, Ellen. *Margaret Atwood and the Female Bildungsroman*. Farnham: Ashgate, 2009. Print.
Meaney, Gerardine. *(Un)Like Subjects: Women, Theory, Fiction*. London: Routledge, 1993. Print.
Meindl, Dieter. 'Gender and Narrative Perspective in Margaret Atwood's Stories.' Colin Nicholson 219–29.
Mendez-Egle, Beatrice, ed. *Margaret Atwood: Reflection and Reality*. Living Author Ser. 6. Edinburg, Texas: Pan American UP, 1987. Print.
Michael, Magali Cornier. *Feminism and the Postmodern Impulse: Post-World War II Fiction*. Albany: State U of New York P, 1996. Print.
Middleton, David L., ed. *Toni Morrison's Fiction: Contemporary Criticism*. Critical Studies in Black Life and Culture. 30. New York: Garland Publishing, 1997. Print.
Miner, Madonne M. 'Lady No Longer Sings the Blues: Rape, Madness, and Silence in *The Bluest Eye*.' Pryse, and Spillers 76–91.

Mitchell, W. J. T., ed. *On Narrative*. Chicago, Chicago UP, 1981. Print.
Mitchell-Kernan, Claudia. 'Signifying, Loud-Talking and Marking.' Caponi 309–30.
Moi, Toril, ed. *French Feminist Thought: A Reader*. Trans. Sean Hand and Roisin Mallaghan. Oxford: Blackwell, 1987. Print.
—. '"I am not a woman writer": About Women, Literature and Feminist Theory Today.' *Eurozine*. www.eurozine.com. 12 June 2009. Web. 5 Mar. 2010.
Monaghan, David, Ariane Hudelet and John Wiltshire. *The Cinematic Jane Austen: Essays on the Filmic Sensibility of the Novels*. Jefferson: McFarland, 2009. Print.
Montgomery, L. M. *The Blue Castle*. 1926. Toronto: Bantam, 1989. Print.
Morey, Peter. 'Postcolonial Forster.' Bradshaw 254–73.
Mori, Aoi. *Toni Morrison and Womanist Discourse*. Modern American Lit. 16. New York: Peter Lang, 1999. Print.
Morrison, Toni. *Beloved*. Harmondsworth: Plume-Penguin, 1997. Print.
—. *The Bluest Eye*. 1970. Harmondsworth: Plume-Penguin, 1994. Print.
—. *A Mercy*. New York: Knopf, 2008.
—. Interview with Zia Jaffrey. 'The Salon Interview.' www.salon.com. 2 Feb. 1998. Web. 10 May 2010.
—. Interview with *Time Magazine* Readers. YouTube.com. 15 May 2008. Web. 10 May 2010.
—. *Jazz*. 1992. Harmondsworth: Plume-Penguin, 1993. Print.
—. *Playing in the Dark: Whiteness and the Literary Imagination*. William E. Massey Sr. Lectures in the History of American Civilization. 1990. New York: Vintage-Random, 1992. Print.
—. 'The Site of Memory.' 1987. *The Norton Anthology of African American Literature*. Eds. Henry Louis Gates Jr. and Nellie Y. McKay. 2nd ed. New York: Norton, 2004. 2290–2299. Print.
—. *Song of Solomon*. Harmondsworth: Plume-Penguin, 1977. Print.
—. *Sula*. 1973. Harmondsworth: Plume-Penguin, 1982. Print.
—. 'Unspeakable Things Unspoken: The Afro-American Presence in American Literature.' Bloom, *Toni Morrison* 201–30.
Moses, Cat. 'The Blues Aesthetic in Toni Morrison's The Bluest Eye.' *African American Review* 33.4 (1999): 623–37. *JSTOR*. Web. 26 Apr. 2010.
Moynihan, Patrick. *The Negro Family: The Case for National Action*. United States Department of Labour. March 1965. http://www.dol.gov/oasam/programs/history/webid-meynihan.htm. Web. 15 April 2010.
Mullen, Bill. 'Breaking the Signifying Chain: A New Blueprint for African-American Studies.' *Modern Fiction Studies* 47 (2001): 145–63. Print.
Mullen, John. 'Interview with Doris Lessing.' *Nobelprize.org*. 14 April 2008. Web. 18 Jan. 2010.
Munro, Alice. *Selected Stories*. London: Penguin, 1996. Print.
Mycak, Sonia. *In Search of the Split Subject: Psychoanalysis, Phenomenology, and the Novels of Margaret Atwood*. Toronto: ECW P, 1996. Print.
Nagel, Thomas. *The View from Nowhere*. Oxford: Oxford UP, 1986. Print.
Nalbantian, Suzanne. *Aesthetic Autobiography: From Life to Art in Marcel Proust, James Joyce, Virginia Woolf and Anais Nin*. Basingstoke: Macmillan P, 1994. Print.
Naylor, Gloria. 'A Conversation: Gloria Naylor and Toni Morrison.' Taylor-Guthrie 188–217.

Negra, Diane. *What a Girl Wants?: Fantasizing the Reclamation of Self in Postfeminism*. London: Routledge, 2009. Print.
Neisser, Ulric and Robyn Fivush, eds. *The Remembering Self: Construction and Accuracy in the Self-narrative*. Cambridge: Cambridge UP, 1994. Print.
Nicholson, Colin. ed. *Margaret Atwood: Writing and Subjectivity*. London: St. Martin's, 1994. Print.
Nicholson, Linda J., ed. *Feminism/Postmodernism*. London: Routledge, 1990. Print.
Nissan, Axel. 'Form Matters: Toni Morrison's *Sula* and the Ethics of Narrative.' *Contemporary Literature* 40.2 (1999): 263–85. *JSTOR*. Web. 24 Apr. 2010.
O'Grady, Kathleen. 'The Empire Strikes Back.' *Women's Review of Books*. 18.1 (2000): 19–20. *EBSCO*. Web. 24 Apr. 2010.
Ogunyemi, Chikwenye Okonjo. 'Order and Disorder in Toni Morrison's *The Bluest Eye*.' *Critique* 19.1 (1977): 112–20. Print.
Olney, James, ed. *Autobiography: Essays Theoretical and Critical*. Princeton: Princeton UP, 1980. Print.
Outka, Elizabeth. 'Buying Time: *Howards End* and Commodified Nostalgia.' *Novel: A Forum on Fiction* 36.3 (2003): 330–50. *JSTOR*. Web. 24 Apr. 2010.
Palmer, Paulina. *Contemporary Women's Fiction: Narrative Practice and Feminist Theory*. London: Harvester Wheatsheaf, 1989. Print.
Parker, Emma. '"Apple Pie" Ideology and the Politics of Appetite in the Novels of Toni Morrison.' *Contemporary Literature* 39.4 (1998): 614–43. *JSTOR*. Web. 26 Apr. 2010.
Parkin-Gounelas, Ruth. '"What Isn't There" in Margaret Atwood's *The Blind Assassin*: The Psychoanalysis of Duplicity.' *Modern Fiction Studies* 50.3 (2004): 681–701. *Project Muse*. Web. 26 Apr. 2010.
Peach, Linden. *Toni Morrison*. 2nd ed. London: Macmillan, 2000. Print.
—, ed. *Toni Morrison*. New Casebooks. New York: St. Martin's, 1998. Print.
Pearce, Lynne. *Reading Dialogics*. Interrogating Texts Ser. London: Arnold, 1994. Print.
Pecora, Vincent P. *Self and Form in Modern Narrative*. Baltimore: John Hopkins UP, 1989. Print.
Peel, Ellen. 'The Self is Always an Other: Going the Long Way Home to Autobiography.' *Twentieth Century Literature* 35 (1989): 1–16. Print.
Peterson, Nancy J., ed. *Toni Morrison: Critical and Theoretical Approaches*. Baltimore: Johns Hopkins UP, 1997. Print.
Phiddian, Robert. 'Are Parody and Deconstruction Secretly the Same Thing?' *New Literary History* 28.4 (1997): 673–96. *JSTOR*. Web. 14 Apr. 2010.
Pickering, Jean. 'Marxism and Madness: The Two Faces of Doris Lessing's Myth.' *Modern Fiction Studies* 26 (1980): 17–30. Print.
Piersen, William D. 'A Resistance Too Civilized to Notice.' Caponi 348–70.
Postlethwaite, Diana. Rev. of *When We Were Orphans*, *The Blind Assassin* and *Affinity*. *Yale Review* 89.2 (2001): 159–70. Print.
Powell, Timothy B. 'Toni Morrison: The Struggle to Depict the Black Figure on the White Page.' Middleton 45–60.
Pride and Prejudice. Screenplay by Andrew Davies. Dir. Simon Langton. Perf. Jennifer Ehle and Colin Firth. BBC1, 1995. Television.
Pryse, Marjorie, and Hortense J. Spillers, eds. *Conjuring: Black Women, Fiction, and Literary Tradition*. Bloomington: Indiana UP, 1985. Print.

Pucci, Suzanne R. and James Thompson, eds. *Jane Austen and Co.: Remaking the Past in Contemporary Culture.* New York: SUNY, 2003. Print.
Rao, Eleonora. 'Margaret Atwood's *Lady Oracle*: Writing Against Notions of Unity.' Colin Nicholson 133–52.
—. *Strategies for Identity: The Fiction of Margaret Atwood.* Writing About Women Feminist Literary Studies Ser. New York: Peter Lang, 1993. Print.
Raynor, Sharon. 'From the Dispossessed to the Decolonized: From Samuel Selvon's *The Lonely Londoners* to Zadie Smith's "Hanwell in Hell."' Walters 141–55. Print.
Rhys, Jean. *Wide Sargasso Sea.* Harmondsworth: Penguin, 1966. Print.
Rich, Adrienne. 'When We Dead Awaken: Writing as Re-Vision.' 1971. *On Lies Secrets and Silence: Selected Prose 1966–1978.* London: Virago, 1980. 33–49. Print.
Ridout, Alice and Susan Watkins, eds. *Doris Lessing: Border Crossings.* London: Continuum, 2009. Print.
Rigler, Laurie Viera. *Confessions of a Jane Austen Addict.* London: Bloomsbury, 2009.
Rigney, Barbara Hill. *Margaret Atwood.* Women Writers Series. London: Macmillan, 1987. Print.
—. *The Voices of Toni Morrison.* Columbus: Ohio State UP, 1991. Print.
Roberts, Adam. 'Jane Austen and the Masturbating Critic' Crusie 51–62.
Rorty, Richard. *Contingency, Irony, and Solidarity.* Cambridge: Cambridge UP, 1989. Print.
Rose, Margaret. *Parody: Ancient, Modern and Post-Modern.* Literature, Culture, Theory. Cambridge: Cambridge UP, 1993. Print.
Rosner, Victoria. 'Home Fires: Doris Lessing, Colonial Architecture, and the Reproduction of Mothering.' *Tulsa Studies in Women's Literature* 18.1 (1999): 59–89. *JSTOR.* Web. 2 May 2010.
Rosowski, Susan. 'Margaret Atwood's *Lady Oracle*: Fantasy and the Modern Gothic Novel.' *Critical Essays on Margaret Atwood.* Ed. Judith McCombs. New York: G. K. Hall & Co, 1988. Print.
Rowe, Margaret Moan. *Doris Lessing.* Women Writers. London: MacMillan, 1994. Print.
Rubenstein, Roberta. *Home Matters: Longing and Belonging, Nostalgia and Mourning in Women's Fiction.* Basingstoke: Palgrave, 2001. Print.
—. *The Novelistic Vision of Doris Lessing: Breaking the Forms of Consciousness.* Urbana: University of Illinois Press, 1979. Print.
Ryan, Allan J. 'Postmodern Parody: A Political Strategy in Contemporary Canadian Native Art.' *Art Journal* 51.3 (1992): 59–65. *JSTOR.* Web. 14 Apr. 2010.
Safer, Elaine B. 'The Essay as Aesthetic Mirror: John Barth's "Exhaustion" and "Replenishment."' *Studies in American Fiction* 15 (1987): 109–17. Print.
Sage, Lorna. *Doris Lessing.* Contemporary Writers. London: Methuen, 1983. Print.
—. *Women in the House of Fiction: Post-War Women Novelists.* Basingstoke: Macmillan, 1992. Print.
Samuels, Wilfred D., and Clenora Husdon-Weems. *Toni Morrison.* Twayne's United States Authors Ser. New York: Twayne-Macmillan, 1990. Print.
Sanders, Julie. *Adaptation and Appropriation.* The New Critical Idiom. London: Routledge, 2006. Print.
Saxton, Ruth and Jean Tobin, eds. *Woolf and Lessing: Breaking the Mold.* New York: St. Martin's, 1994. Print.
Scanlan, Margaret. 'Language and the Politics of Despair in Doris Lessing's *The Good Terrorist.*' *Novel: a Forum on Fiction* 23.2 (1990): 182–98. Print.

Scarry, Elaine. *On Beauty and Being Just*. 2000. London, Duckworth, 2006. Print.
Schlueter, Paul. *The Novels of Doris Lessing*. Carbondale: Southern Illinois UP, 1973. Print.
Schweickart, Patrocinio P. 'Reading a Wordless Statement: The Structure of Doris Lessing's *The Golden Notebook*.' *Modern Fiction Studies* 31 (1985): 263–79. Print.
Scott, Virginia. 'Doris Lessing's Modern Alice in Wonderland: *The Good Terrorist* as Fantasy.' *International Fiction Review* 16.2 (1989): 123–7. Print.
Sedgwick, Eve Kosofsky. 'Jane Austen and the Masturbating Girl.' *Critical Inquiry* 17.4 (Summer 1991): 818–37. *JSTOR*. Web. 17 Dec. 2009.
Selvon, Sam. *The Lonely Londoners*. 1956. London: Penguin, 2006. Print.
Shields, Carol and Marjorie Anderson, eds. *Dropped Threads: What We Aren't Told*. Toronto: Vintage-Random, 2001. Print.
Showalter, Elaine. *A Literature of Their Own: from Charlotte Brontë to Doris Lessing*. Rev. ed. London: Virago, 1982. Print.
Smith, Sidonie. *Subjectivity, Identity and the Body: Women's Autobiographical Practices in the Twentieth Century*. Bloomington: Indiana UP, 1993. Print.
Smith, Zadie. *Changing My Mind: Occasional Essays*. London: Penguin, 2009. Print.
—. 'Love, Actually.' *The Guardian* 1 Nov. 2003. guardian.co.uk. Web. 24 Apr. 2010.
—. 'On the Beginning.' *The Guardian* 15 July 2006. guardian.co.uk. Web. 24 Apr. 2010.
—. *On Beauty*. London: Penguin, 2005. Print.
—. *White Teeth*. London: Penguin, 2000. Print.
Spacks, Patricia Meyer. 'Free Women.' Bloom, *Doris Lessing* 95–101.
Spender, Dale. *Man Made Language*. London: Routledge, 1980. Print.
Spikes, Michael P. *Understanding Contemporary American Literary Theory*. Understanding Contemporary American Lit. Columbia: U of South Carolina P, 1997. Print.
Sprague, Claire and Virginia Tiger, eds. *Critical Essays on Doris Lessing*. Boston: G. K. Hall, 1986. Print.
Sprague, Claire. 'Doubletalk and Doubles Talk in *The Golden Notebook*.' *Papers on Language and Literature* 18 (1982): 181–97. Print.
—. '*The Golden Notebook*: In Whose or What Great Tradition?' Kaplan and Rose, *Approaches* 78–83.
—, ed. *In Pursuit of Doris Lessing: Nine Nations Reading*. Basingstoke: Macmillan, 1990. Print.
—. *Rereading Doris Lessing: Narrative Patterns of Doubling and Repetition*. Chapel Hill: U of North Carolina P, 1987. Print.
Squires, Claire. *Zadie Smith's* White Teeth: *A Reader's Guide*. Continuum Contemporaries. London: Continuum, 2002. Print.
Stam, Robert. *Literature through Film: Realism, Magic, and the Art of Adaptation*. Oxford: Blackwell, 2005. Print.
Steedman, Carolyn. *The Tidy House: Little Girls Writing*. London: Virago, 1982. Print.
Stein, Karen F. 'A Left-Handed Story: *The Blind Assassin*.' Wilson 135–53.
Stepto, Robert. 'Intimate Things in Place: A Conversation with Toni Morrison.' 1976. Taylor-Guthrie 10–29.
—. 'Narration, Authentication, and Authorial Control.' Bloom, *Frederick Douglass's Narrative* 45–57.
Stern, Frederick C. 'Doris Lessing: The Politics of Radical Humanism.' Kaplan and Rose, *Doris Lessing* 43–60.

Stern, Katherine. 'Toni Morrison's Beauty Formula.' Conner 77–91.
Stetz, Margaret D. *British Women's Comic Fiction, 1890–1990.* Aldershot, England: Ashgate, 2001. Print.
Stewart, Kathleen. 'Nostalgia – A Polemic.' *Cultural Anthropology* 3.3 (1988): 227–41. *JSTOR*. Web. 17 Dec. 2009.
Sturrock, John. *The Language of Autobiography: Studies in the First Person Singular.* Cambridge: Cambridge UP, 1993. Print.
Sullivan, Alvin. 'Ideology and Form: Decentrism in *The Golden Notebook, Memoirs of a Survivor,* and *Shikasta.*' Kaplan and Rose, *Doris Lessing* 71–9.
Sutcliffe, Thomas. 'Last Night's TV: *Lost in Austen,* ITV1 and *God on Trial,* BBC2.' *The Independent* 4 September 2008. Web. 30 Oct 2009.
Swendson, Shanna. 'The Original Chick-Lit Masterpiece.' Crusie 63–9.
Tabuteau, Éric. 'Marginally Correct: Zadie Smith's *White Teeth* and Sam Selvon's *The Lonely Londoners.*' *Cities on the Margin; on the Margin of Cities: Representations of Urban Space in Contemporary Irish and British Fiction.* Eds. Philippe Laplace and Éric Tabuteau. Besançon: Presses Universitaires Franc-Comtoises, 2003. 81–96. http:books/google.co.uk. Web. 15 July 2010.
Tasker, Yvonne and Diane Negra, eds. *Interrogating Post-feminism: Gender and the Politics of Popular Culture.* Durham: Duke UP, 2007.
Taylor, Jenny, ed. *Notebooks, Memoirs, Archives: Reading and Rereading Doris Lessing.* London: Routledge, 1982. Print.
Taylor-Guthrie, Danille, ed. *Conversations with Toni Morrison.* Jackson: UP of Mississippi, 1994. Print.
Teeman, Tim. Rev. of *Lost in Austen. Times Online* 25 Sept. 2008. Web. 30 Oct. 2009.
Tennant, Emma. *Pemberley Revisited: Pemberley* and *An Unequal Marriage.* 2nd ed. London: Maia Press, 2005. Print.
Tew, Philip. *Zadie Smith.* New British Fiction. Basingstoke: Palgrave-Macmillan, 2010. Print.
Tew, Philip and Rod Mengham, eds. *British Fiction Today.* London: Continuum, 2006. Print.
Thiong'o, Ngugi wa. *Decolonising the Mind: The Politics of Language in African Literature.* London: J. Currey, 1986. Print.
Tirrell, Lynne. 'Storytelling and Moral Agency.' Middleton 3–25.
Tolan, Fiona. 'Identifying the Precious in Zadie Smith's *On Beauty.*' Tew and Mengham 128–38. Print.
Turner, Henry S. 'Empires of Objects: Accumulation and Entropy in E. M. Forster's *Howards End.*' *Twentieth Century Literature* 46.3 (2000): 328–45. *JSTOR*. Web. 20 Jan. 2010.
Tynan, Maeve. '"Only Connect": Intertextuality and Identity in Zadie Smith's *On Beauty.*' Walters 73–89. Print.
Vevaina, Coomi S. *Re/Membering Selves: Alienation and Survival in the Novels of Margaret Atwood and Margaret Laurence.* Creative New Literatures Series 11. New Delhi: Creative P, 1996. Print.
Voiret, Martine. 'Books to Movies: Gender and Desire in Jane Austen's Adaptations.' Pucci and Thompson 229–45. Print.
Wagner, Linda W. 'Toni Morrison: Mastery of Narrative.' *Contemporary American Women Writers: Narrative Strategies.* Eds. Catherine Rainwater, and William J. Scheick. Lexington, Kentucky: UP of Kentucky, 1985. 191–205. Print.

Walker, Alice. *In Search of Our Mothers' Gardens: Womanist Prose*. New York: Harvest-Harcourt, 1983. Print.
Walker, Nancy A. *Feminist Alternatives: Irony and Fantasy in the Contemporary Novel by Women*. Jackson: UP of Mississippi, 1990. Print.
—. '"Wider Than the Sky": Public Presence and Private Self in Dickinson, James, and Woolf.' Benstock 272–303.
Wall, Kathleen. 'Ethics, Knowledge, and the Needs for Beauty: Zadie Smith's *On Beauty* and Ian McEwan's *Saturday*.' *University of Toronto Quarterly* 77.2 (Spring 2008): 757–88. *JSTOR*. Web. 5 Apr. 2010.
Wallace, Diana. *The Woman's Historical Novel: British Women Writers, 1900–2000*. 2nd ed. Basingstoke: Palgrave, 2008. Print.
Walls, Elizabeth MacLeod. '"A Little Afraid of the Women Today": The Victorian New Woman and the Rhetoric of British Modernism.' *Rhetoric Review* 21.3 (2002): 229–46. *JSTOR*. Web. 20 Jan. 2010.
Warren, Kenneth. Rev. of *The Signifying Monkey* by Henry Louis Gates Jr. *Modern Philology* 88.2 (1990): 224–6. *JSTOR*. Web. 26 Apr. 2010.
Waters, Sarah. *Affinity*. London: Virago, 1999. Print.
—. *Fingersmith*. London: Virago, 2002. Print.
Watkins, Susan. *Twentieth-Century Women Novelists: Feminist Theory Into Practice*. Basingstoke: Palgrave-St. Martin's, 2001. Print.
Walters, Tracey L. *Zadie Smith: Critical Essays*. New York: Peter Lang, 2008. Print.
Waters, Sarah. Introduction. *Dancing with Mr Darcy: Stories Inspired by Jane Austen and Chawton House*. Dinas Powys: Honno, 2009. Print.
Watson, Daphne. *Their Own Worst Enemies: Women Writers of Women's Fiction*. London: Pluto Press, 1995. Print.
Waugh, Patricia. *Feminine Fictions: Revisiting the Postmodern*. London: Routledge, 1989. Print.
—. *Harvest of the Sixties: English Literature and it Background 1960 to 1990*. Oxford: Oxford UP, 1995. Print.
—. *Metafiction: The Theory and Practice of Self-Conscious Fiction*. 1984. London: Routledge, 1988. Print.
—. *Practising Postmodernism / Reading Modernism*. London: Edward Arnold, 1992. Print.
Webster, Emma Campbell. *Lost in Austen: Create Your Own Jane Austen Adventure*. New York: Riverhead Books, 2007. Print.
Werrlein, Debra T. 'Not so Fast, Dick and Jane: Reimagining Childhood and Nation in *The Bluest Eye*.' *MELUS* 30.4 (2005): 53–72. *JSTOR*. Web. 26 Apr. 2010.
Whelehan, Imelda. *The Feminist Bestseller*. Basingstoke: Palgrave, 2005. Print.
—. *Helen Fielding's* Bridget Jones's Diary*: A Reader's Guide*. London: Continuum, 2001. Print.
—. *Overloaded: Popular Culture and the Future of Feminism*. London: Women's Press, 2000. Print.
Whittaker, Ruth. *Doris Lessing*. Macmillan Modern Novelists. Basingstoke: Macmillan, 1988. Print.
—. 'Doris Lessing and the Means of Change.' Anderson 1–16.
Williams, Lisa. *The Artist as Outsider in the Novels of Toni Morrison and Virginia Woolf*. Contributions in Women's Studies. 181. Westport, Connecticut: Greenwood P, 2000. Print.

Willis, Susan. 'Eruptions of Funk: Historicizing Toni Morrison.' Bloom, *Toni Morrison* 309–25.
Wilson, Sharon Rose. ed. *Margaret Atwood's Textual Assassinations: Recent Poetry and Fiction*. Columbus: Ohio State UP, 2003. Print.
Wiltshire, John. 'Afterword: On Fidelity.' Monaghan, Hudelet and Wiltshire 160–70.
Wood, Michael. *Children of Silence: Studies in Contemporary Fiction*. London: Pilmico-Random, 1998. Print.
Woolf, Virginia. 'Professions for Women.' *A Bloomsbury Group Reader*. Ed. S. P. Rosenbaum. Oxford: Blackwell, 1993. 274–9. Print.
—. *A Room of One's Own*. London: Penguin, 1928. Print.
—. 'Women and Fiction.' *Collected Essays: Volume 2*. London: Hogarth Press, 1966. 141–8. Print.
—. *A Woman's Essays*. Ed. Rachel Bowlby. London: Penguin, 1992. Print.
Worthington, Kim L. *Self as Narrative: Subjectivity and Community in Contemporary Fiction*. Oxford: Clarendon, 1996. Print.
Yaeger, Patricia. *Honey-Mad Women: Emancipatory Strategies in Women's Writing*. New York: Columbia UP, 1988. Print.

Index

adaptation ix, 12, 106, 123, 125–8, 130, 133–6, 141, 163fn., 164fn.
affect theory 136–7
African 8, 19, 23, 24, 30, 59
African American 8, 10, 16–28, 30, 32, 35, 37, 42–3, 45, 64, 71, 75, 115, 145fn.,146fn., 149fn.
agency 27, 29–31, 43, 72–3, 76, 99, 126, 130, 140, 156fn., 158fn., 160fn.
Alabama 149fn.
Altman, Marsha 13, 141
America/American 1, 2, 8, 16, 21, 30, 34, 38, 40, 43, 53, 59, 79, 81, 104, 109, 115–17, 123, 144fn., 145fn., 147–9fn., 158fn.
American Revolution 2
Anderson, Marjorie 71, 73
'Angel in the House' 3
Anjaria, Ulka 161fn.
architecture 4, 144fn.
Arterton, Gemma 125
Atwood, Margaret vii, ix, 1–13, 15, 19, 54, 67, 69–101, 103, 116, 123, 124, 143, 155–61fn., 162fn., 163fn.
  Blind Assassin, The vii, ix, 3, 7, 11, 12, 15, 69–73, 89–102, 143, 155fn., 157fn., 160fn., 161fn.
  Lady Oracle vii, 5, 7, 11–12, 54, 69–78, 82–9, 96, 143, 155–9fn.
  Negotiating With the Dead 67, 124
  Payback 103
  Surfacing 1, 71–2, 74, 78–86, 88, 155fn., 158fn.
Auden, W. H. 131
Austen, Jane vii, viii, ix, 1, 2, 12, 13, 26, 123–42, 143, 162–4fn.
authorial control/power 58–9, 83
authorship viii, 32, 42, 46, 47, 58, 91, 93, 101, 127, 149fn.
autobiography 11, 52, 70–1, 89–99, 143, 150fn., 155fn., 160fn.
autodidact 112
automatic writing 69, 82

Awkward, Michael 149fn.
Ayatollah 119

Baker, Houston A. Jr 16, 23, 114–15
Baraka, Amiri 117
Barry, Brian 108, 120–1
Barth, John viii, 28
Barthes, Roland/Barthesian 65, 94
BBC 123, 125, 127
beauty 16, 32, 34–6, 41, 43, 87, 111, 113–16, 118, 126, 143
Beauvoir, Simone de 6, 31
Becker, Susanne 75, 77, 159fn.
belated/belatedness vii, viii, 28, 108, 143
Belsey, Catherine 53–4
Benstock, Shari 160fn.
Bentley, Nick 50, 52–4, 68
Berberich, Christine 138, 141, 163fn.
Berdoll, Linda 13, 123, 130, 141, 163fn.
Bertelsen, Eve 155fn.
Bikman, Minda 48
bildungsroman 92, 156fn., 163fn.
'Black Experience' 27, 45
'black is beautiful' 34
Bloom, Harold 13, 146fn.
blues aesthetic 112, 114, 116–17
Blues, Ideology, and Afro-American Literature 115
Bonneville, Hugh 133
border crossings 47, 52
Born, Daniel 111, 121–2, 161fn.
Bouson, J. Brooks 94, 101, 161fn.
Boym, Svetlana 23, 137–8
Brent, Linda 43–45
Bridget Jones's Diary 7, 123, 127, 138, 164fn.
Britain/British ix, 109, 110, 119–20, 123, 127, 163fn.
Brontë, Charlotte 4, 87, 131, 154fn., 163fn.
Brownmiller, Susan 62
Bucknell, Brad 145fn.
Burke, Séan 13, 152fn.
Burningham, Hilary 162fn.
Butler, Judith 30–1

Butler, Nancy 123, 162fn.
Byatt, A. S. 163fn.

Cambridge 13, 124, 162fn.
Canada/Canadian 8, 26, 62, 69, 85, 103, 124, 158fn., 160fn.
cannibalism 12, 66, 109
canon 2, 8, 18, 20, 53, 107, 109, 113, 119, 144–6fn., 149fn., 161fn.
capitalism 72, 106, 130, 135, 141, 142, 160fn., 163fn.
Castle, Terry 128, 163fn.
Cheng, Anne Anlin 35, 114
Chicago 24–5
chick lit 127, 162fn.
Cixous, Hélène 158fn.
Child, L. Maria 43, 44, 45
Christian/Christianity 34, 44, 112
Christian, Barbara 145fn.
comic/comedy 28, 33, 84–6, 89, 107, 109, 126, 128, 133, 157fn.,159fn.,162fn.,163fn., 164fn.
Communist Party/Communism 49, 65, 150–1fn.
complicit/complicity 9, 17–18, 21–2, 26–7, 29–30, 35, 40–1, 45, 51–2, 54, 56, 60, 67, 70, 86, 130, 148fn., 159fn.
Confessional 74–5, 97, 101
Congolese 109
Conrad, Joseph 4, 109
  Heart of Darkness 109
consumerism 40
Contingency, Irony, and Solidarity 121
Cosmopolitan magazine 130
costume 75–6, 85, 123, 125–9, 131, 136–7, 156fn.
counter-discourse/counter-discursive 11, 18–19, 21–2, 26–7, 38
Cowan, Elliot 125
Coward, Rosalind 97–9
Crick Crack, Monkey 33–4, 109
critical distance 9, 17, 30, 42, 56, 60, 65, 86, 159fn.
Critical Practice 53
Crown, Sarah 50
Culture and Equality 108, 121
Curie, Mark 52, 68, 92

Dane, Joseph 10
Danziger, Marie 65, 152fn., 154fn.
Davey, Frank 85–86, 157fn.
Davies, Andrew 125, 127
Dawkins, Jane 13, 141

Day, William Patrick 75
Dean, Michael 49–50, 52
Derrida, Jacques 159fn.
desire 7, 12, 20, 23, 30, 36, 40, 47, 71, 73, 74, 78, 85, 88, 94, 100, 109, 119, 130–1, 135, 137, 139, 147fn.,156fn.,158fn.,163fn.
diary 7, 53, 59, 123, 127, 138, 164fn.
Dick and Jane 17, 31, 35, 38–9, 42–3, 148fn.
Dickinson, Emily 94
discursive communities 11, 62–3, 154fn.
Dittmar, Linda 38, 42, 150fn.
doll 35, 42
domesticity 2–3, 6, 16
domestic space 2
Don Quixote 50, 53
Douglas, Christopher 24, 34, 37, 118
Douglass, Frederick 43–4, 149fn.
Draine, Betsy 151fn.,153–4fn.
Duvall, John 64, 144fn., 149fn.
Dvorak, Marta 160fn.

Eagleton, Mary ix, 52, 56, 75, 85
Ebert, Teresa 9, 142
ecocriticism 136
Eliot, George 4, 35
Eliot, T. S. 137
Ellen, Barbara 47, 62, 68, 153fn.
Elliott, Jane 12, 16, 29, 37, 108–9, 121, 141, 143
Ellis, John 135
England/English 8, 10, 13, 19, 30, 41, 109, 110, 119, 125, 127, 128, 131–5, 138, 140, 148fn.,162fn.,163fn.
Enlightenment/enlightenment 49, 108, 158fn.
Erzulie 103, 105, 111, 112, 118, 161fn.
Eskimoes 84
essentialism/essentialist 17, 23, 30, 37, 78, 146fn.
Esu-Elegbara 22, 24
European 19, 50, 145fn.
Eurozine 30, 47
excess/excessive 18, 36, 54, 60, 73–7, 85–6, 88–9, 156–8fn.
experience viii, ix, 2–4, 7–9, 11, 15–16, 27, 32, 36, 42, 43, 45, 48–50, 52–3, 55, 57, 59–60, 62–3, 65–71, 76–84, 87, 92, 95, 97, 99–101, 106, 111, 113–15, 117–18, 124, 129, 132, 134, 137, 145fn.,147fn.,149fn.,151fn., 153fn., 154fn., 156fn., 161fn.

Index

family ix, 3, 6, 7, 17, 25, 31–2, 34, 35, 38–41, 79, 104–5, 110–11, 113, 117, 124, 142, 146–8fn., 159fn., 161fn.
Fand, Roxanne 71, 82, 155–6fn.
father/grandfather 4, 5, 15, 17, 31, 33, 38, 41, 58, 78, 79–80, 89–90, 92–6, 99, 101, 103, 107, 112, 145fn., 148–9fn., 159–61fn.
feminism 5, 9, 16–17, 27, 29, 37, 62, 72, 108, 123, 129–31, 138–9, 141–2, 143, 154fn., 158fn.
  death of 17, 130
feminist viii, ix, 1–3, 5–6, 9, 11, 12, 15–16, 26–7, 30, 47, 50, 58, 60–2, 65–8, 72, 78–9, 87, 92–5, 97, 99, 101, 105, 108, 124, 129–30, 134–5, 139, 141–2, 150fn., 152fn., 156fn., 157fn., 160fn., 161fn., 164fn.
Fergus, Jan 124, 162fn.
Ferriss, Suzanne 127, 162fn.
Fetterley, Judith 66
Fielding, Helen 123, 127, 162fn., 164fn.
First World War 1
Firth, Colin 125–7
Fischer, Alice 105, 118
Fishburn, Katherine 154fn.
Flax, Jane 87, 158fn.
Florida 103
Forster, E. M. 9, 12–13, 104–9, 111–112, 120–2, 123, 161fn.
  Howards End 2, 12, 104–12, 117, 121–2, 144fn., 161fn.
Foster, Brandy 134, 164fn.
Fowler, Corinne 110, 123, 162fn.
Fox, Robert Elliot 145fn.
fragments/fragmented 32, 34, 38, 51, 59, 71, 74, 79, 87, 97, 109, 137, 147fn., 158fn.
frame 41, 43, 45, 51–2, 54, 65, 75, 118, 150fn., 152fn., 164fn.
Freud, Sigmund/Freudian 79, 85, 133, 161fn.
Fullbrook, Kate 49, 54
funk/funkiness 24, 37, 75, 147fn.
Fuoroli, Caryn 57–9, 154fn.
Fuss, Diana 23, 145fn., 146fn.

Garber, Marjorie 128
Garrison, Lloyd 44–5, 149fn.
Gates, Henry Louis Jr. 10, 16–30, 37–8, 51, 145–6fn.

gender 3, 8, 26, 30–1, 35, 40, 61, 67, 80, 130, 132, 140–2, 152fn., 164fn.
Genette, Gérard 46, 68
genre/generic 5, 7, 9, 11, 24, 50–3, 57, 68, 70, 72, 75, 86–7, 92–3, 97, 101, 106, 127, 135–7, 151fn., 155fn., 159fn.
gentleman 138, 140–1, 163fn.
Georgia 149fn.
Georgian 134, 140
ghost 75, 88, 145fn., 157fn.
Gibson, Donald 32–3, 43, 45, 147fn.
Gilbert, Sandra 4, 159fn.
Gillan, Jennifer 33, 39
Gilmore, Leigh 93, 160fn.
Gothic 54, 69, 72, 75–8, 82, 85–8, 157fn., 159fn.
Grange, Amanda 123
Greene, Gayle 3, 135–6, 141
Gubar, Susan 4, 159fn.
guilt 3, 69, 104, 121–2, 157fn., 161fn.
Gusdorf, Georges 71, 93, 160fn.

Haiti/Haitian 103–5, 111, 114, 117, 122
haunt/haunted 38, 88, 94, 95, 122, 136, 157fn.
Harewood House 125
Haslett, Moyra 125, 134, 141, 162fn.
Headline Book Publishing 127
Heart of Darkness 109
Heilbrun, Carolyn 6–7, 11–12, 15, 48, 144fn.
Henke, Suzette 150fn.
Hepburn, Allan 95, 102, 161fn.
heterosexual 131, 134–5, 139–140
Heydt-Stevenson, Jill 131
Hite, Molly 74, 88, 152fn., 156fn., 157fn., 159fn.
Hodge, Merle 33–4, 109
homage 13, 105, 109, 127
home 2–3, 5–6, 8, 12, 15, 23, 32, 34, 37, 39–40, 49, 55, 60, 69, 78, 110, 112, 116, 117, 129, 132, 135–7, 142, 144fn., 148fn.
homeless/homelessness 6, 93
homosexual/homosexuality 131
Houdini 88–89
house 2–8, 12–13, 15–17, 20, 31–32, 35–41, 66, 70, 76, 78–79, 81, 84, 89, 98, 104–5, 109, 116–17, 122, 125–6, 134, 141, 144fn.
'house of fiction' 2, 4, 6, 8, 10, 12, 70, 143, 144fn.

housewife/housewives 3, 5–6, 13, 69, 141–2
housework/housekeeping 3, 5, 16, 39, 40
Howards End 2, 12, 104–12, 117, 121–2, 144fn., 161fn.
humour 9, 28–9, 76
husband 3, 12, 39, 60, 73–4, 85, 88, 92, 104, 111, 112, 117
Hurston, Zora Neale 18, 105, 107, 116, 118, 145fn.
Hutcheon, Linda ix, 9, 17–18, 21, 26–7, 29, 51, 53, 61–2, 72, 128, 133, 135, 144fn., 157fn., 159fn.
Hyppolite, Hector 103, 111, 117, 122

identity politics 64, 109
imitation 18–21, 26, 74, 83
indebtedness 12, 22, 103, 105–6, 125–6
Independent, The 129
India 119
Indian rock drawings/paintings 78, 81
inheritance/inherited vii, 1–2, 7, 12–13, 22, 103–8, 111, 116–17, 122, 143
intention (authorial) 47, 54, 58–59, 61–2, 66–67, 106, 143, 156fn.
intertextual 9, 12, 17, 38, 77, 105, 107, 110, 127, 128, 159fn.
Irigaray, Luce 158fn.
irony/ironic iii, viii, 1–2, 9, 11, 12, 13, 15, 26, 28, 32, 33, 40–1, 42, 44, 46, 47, 52, 55–6, 58–63, 72, 75, 78, 82, 86, 89, 90, 93, 95, 99, 103, 107, 108, 111, 119, 121, 128, 130, 133, 138, 140, 148, 156, 158–61fn.
Islam 119
ITV 12, 125–7, 133, 138

Jacobs, Harriet 43–4
Jaffrey, Zia 38
James, Alice 94
James, David 13, 107, 122, 143, 162fn.
James, Henry 4, 6
Jenkins, Roy 119
Jensen, Robert 129, 139, 140
Johnson, Claudia L. 131, 137, 163fn.
Jones, Ann Rosalind 79
Joyce, Joyce Ann 16, 22, 145fn.

Kate and Leopold 136, 163–4fn.
Kemp, Peter 109
Kentucky 149fn.
Kilson, Martin 145fn.
Kimball, Roger 131

King, Jeanette 153–4fn.
King, Nicole 105, 161fn.
Kiremidjian, G. D. 7, 50, 53, 58, 68
Klotman, Phyllis 147–8fn.
Kristeva, Julia 158fn.
Krouse, Tonya 151fn., 155fn.
Kuhn, Cynthia 156fn.
Kureishi, Hanif 162fn.

Lacan, Jacques/Lacanian 79, 94
Ladino, Jennifer 135–136, 141
Lady Chatterley's Lover/Lady Chatterley Trial 118–20
Laing, R. D./Laingian 49
LeClair, Thomas 32
Lee, Dorothy 148fn.
Lejeune, Philippe 160fn.
Leonard, John 154fn.
Leonard, Vivien 152fn.
lesbian 20, 93, 97, 128, 134
Lessing, Doris vii, viii, 1–2, 4–5, 7–13, 19, 25, 26, 46, 47–68, 69, 139, 143, 144fn., 150–5fn.
  Alfred and Emily 1
  The Golden Notebook vii, viii, 1, 5, 7, 11–12, 25–6, 46, 47–68, 69, 139, 143, 144fn., 150–5fn.
  Nobel Speech 13
  Under My Skin 55
  Walking in the Shade 150fn., 151fn.
Lewis, Paul 28–29
Lexington YMHA 62
liberal/liberalism 55, 72, 106, 108, 114, 118–22, 143, 161fn.
liminality 6–7, 11, 48–9, 58, 68
literary tradition 8, 20, 25, 28, 94, 109
London 1, 7, 55–6, 110–11, 122, 125, 127, 134–5, 137, 144fn., 153fn., 163fn.
Lonely Londoners, The 110, 162fn.
Lorain, Ohio 39
Lorde, Audrey 16, 20, 22
Lost in Austen ix, 12, 125–42, 143, 162–4fn.
love 15, 36, 41, 42, 76, 84, 86, 88, 92, 104–6, 109, 109, 111, 114, 115, 128–9, 132–5, 140, 151fn., 157fn., 159fn., 163
Lyme Park 125, 162fn.

mad/madness 2, 6, 41, 60, 66, 87, 110, 141, 154fn., 159fn.
Mainardi, Pat 3
Maîtresse Erzulie 103, 105, 111–12, 118, 161
Mallarmé, Stéphane 14, 152fn.
Malmgren, Carl 146fn., 148fn., 150fn.

Manchester 123
Mangold, James 163fn.
Marcus, Jane 160fn.
margin/marginal/marginalized 7, 26, 70, 98, 119, 155fn., 162fn.
marriage/marry 6, 38–40, 54, 65, 77–8, 97, 99, 101, 104, 105, 111, 117, 126, 134, 138, 140–1, 152fn.
Marx/Marxist/Marxism 50, 125, 141
mask 11, 106
Matthews, Glenna 2–3
May, Brian 108
maze 14, 74–5, 88, 152fn., 156fn., 157fn.
Mazrui, Ali 145
McBride, Dwight A. 146fn.
McDermott, Sinead 136
McKay, Nellie Y. 16
McKerrell, Kate 162fn.
McKinstry, Susan Janet 157fn.
McRobbie, Angela 130
McWilliams, Ellen 69, 92, 156–8fn., 163fn.
Mehlman, Jeffrey 93
memoir 95, 101, 161fn.
mess 3, 35, 37, 41, 50, 54, 58, 73, 75–8, 84, 89, 106, 157fn.
metafiction/metafictional 13–14, 50, 52, 54, 57, 59, 68, 92, 99, 143, 152fn., 158fn.
Michael, Magali 51, 151–3fn.
mimetic/mimesis 18, 53, 57–8, 67, 81, 106
mimic/mimicry 18, 26, 37
Mitchell-Kernan, Claudia 24–6, 28
modernism/Modernism 13, 28, 152fn.
Moi, Toril 30–1, 47
Mobile 37
Montgomery, L. M. 157fn.
Morrison, Toni vii, viii, 1–2, 4–10, 12–13, 15–46, 47, 64, 67, 75, 109, 114–16, 118, 140, 143, 144–50fn.
  The Bluest Eye vii, viii, 1, 5–7, 10, 12, 13, 15–17, 22, 24, 27, 31–46, 47, 67, 75, 109, 115–16, 118, 140, 143, 149–50fn.
  A Mercy 1
  Playing in the Dark 8, 150fn.
Moses, Cat 115, 117
mother/grandmother 2, 3, 8, 11, 12, 16, 25, 31, 36–8, 41–2, 79–80, 83, 85, 89, 92, 93–6, 98, 104–105, 107, 112, 116–17, 122, 127, 129, 140–1, 144fn., 145fn., 148–9fn., 156fn., 159fn.
Moynihan, Patrick/Moynihan Report 34, 39
Mozart, Wolfgang 112–13

Mullen, John 54
multiculturalism 34, 37, 108, 110, 118, 120
Mycak, Sonia 156fn.

nation/national 2, 8, 34, 118–19, 123, 158fn.
Negra, Diane 130, 138
neoliberalism 108
New Literary History 16
New York 62, 163fn.
Nobel Prize 13, 50, 68
nostalgia vii, viii, ix, 1–3, 12, 23, 53, 71, 106, 108, 117, 123, 129, 134–42, 143, 144fn., 163fn.
novel 1, 3–8, 11–13, 17, 24, 27–8, 32–4, 37, 39, 41–3, 45–6, 47–65, 67–78, 81–93, 95, 97–101, 104–10, 112–16, 118–19, 121–2, 123–39, 141–2, 143, 144fn., 147–58fn., 160–3fn.
novelist 2, 5–6, 48, 52–3, 108, 109, 151fn., 153fn.

obituary 96, 98–9, 110
Obscene Publications Act, The 119
Odysseus 135
O'Grady, Kathleen 26
Ogunyemi, Chikwenye Okonjo 147–8fn.
Ohio 39
Olney, James 93
original/originality 7, 13, 18, 21–2, 31, 37, 38, 40, 74, 107, 122, 127, 135, 143, 157fn., 163fn.
Outka, Elizabeth 108

paradox/paradoxical 8, 9, 20, 49–52, 54, 57, 59, 69, 88, 92, 129, 153fn.
paratext 46, 68
Parker, Emma 147fn., 149fn.
Parkin-Gounelas, Ruth 161fn.
parody/parodic vii, 1–2, 4, 7–13, 15, 17–19, 21–33, 35–6, 38, 40, 42–7, 49–64, 67–9, 71–8, 85–6, 90, 94–6, 98–100, 105–7, 110, 119, 122, 132, 138, 143, 144–fn., 148fn., 152fn., 154fn., 157fn., 159fn.
  definition of 9, 17
patriarchy 11, 130, 142
peak oil viii
Pemberley 2, 13, 123, 125, 141, 162fn.
Pemberton, Joe 123
Penelope 1, 135
Penguin Classic 127
Petrus, Hugo 123, 162fn.
Phiddian, Robert 29, 57–8, 106–7, 119, 159fn.

Phillips, Rachel 162fn.
Phillips, Wendall 43
picaresque 6
plagiarism 21, 105
Plato 35
'playing the dozens' 24–5, 28–9
pleasure 9, 13, 35, 77, 89, 93, 118, 121, 122, 126, 130, 132–3, 143, 151fn.
poet/poetry/poetic 4–5, 8, 13, 82, 84, 113, 122
polyphony/polyphonic 74, 150fn.
pornography/pornographic 118, 129–31, 138–41
postfeminist 94
Postlethwaite, Diana 161fn.
postmodernism/postmodernist/postmodernity viii, 9–10, 17, 26–8, 49, 52, 72, 87–8, 144fn., 151fn., 158–9fn.
poststructuralist/poststructuralism 9, 13, 16–17, 23, 30, 146fn., 152fn.
Powell, Timothy 22, 42, 147–8fn.
Pride and Prejudice 2, 4, 13, 123, 125, 127–9, 132–4, 138, 141–2
primer, reading 10, 17, 27, 31–36, 38–44, 47, 115, 147–9fn.
Pucci, Suzanne R. 123–4, 126, 137

quotation marks 125, 128, 160fn.

race 1, 8, 19–20, 23, 30–1, 33–4, 104, 117, 145fn., 146fn., 149fn.
racism/racist 16, 18, 23–4, 33–4, 37, 40, 44, 134, 145fn.
Rao, Eleanora 72–73, 155fn., 159fn.
rape 12, 41, 149fn., 154fn.
Raskin, Jonah 151fn.
Raynor, Sharon 162fn.
reader ix, 6, 8–11, 13–14, 32, 34, 38, 42–6, 47, 49, 51–68, 70–2, 77, 89, 90–2, 95–7, 99, 101, 104, 106–7, 112–14, 119, 123, 125–6, 132, 134, 137–8, 141–2, 147–9fn., 152–5fn., 159fn., 161fn., 163fn., 164fn.
realism 48–50, 52, 54–7, 67–8, 75, 94, 107, 154fn.
'refunctioning' 44, 73, 75, 149fn., 157fn.
Regency 125–9, 131, 134–5, 138, 162fn.
repetition/repetitive 9, 17–19, 21–2, 27, 29–30, 32, 38, 46, 51–2, 56, 59–60, 67, 76, 86, 133–5, 146–8fn.
Requiem 112
retellings viii, 1–2, 7, 12–14, 17, 22, 108, 122, 123–5, 138–9, 143

Rhodesia 1
Rhys, Jean 87, 107
Rigler, Laurie Viera 127, 138
Rigney, Barbara 41
Roberts, Adam 132–133, 138
Romantic/Romanticism/romantic 23, 74, 99, 111, 115, 119, 135, 140, 163fn.
Room of One's Own, A/'room of one's own' 6, 117, 124
Rooper, Jemima 125
Rorty, Richard 108, 121–2
Rose, Margaret 28, 144fn., 157fn.
Rosenblatt, Roger 131, 163fn.
Rosner, Victoria 144fn.
Rosowski, Susan 83
Rousseau, François-Olivier 151fn.
Rowe, Margaret Moan 154–5fn.
Rubenstein, Roberta 55–7, 136, 144fn.
Rushdie, Salman 118–20, 162fn.
Ruskin, John 111
Ryan, Meg 163fn.

Sage, Lorna 6, 48
Sanders, Julie 105, 125
sarcasm/sarcastic 54
Satanic Verses, The 119–20
satire 23, 86, 106, 159fn.
Scarry, Elaine 12, 114–15, 118, 143
Schweickart, Patrocinio 56, 153fn.
Second Wave Feminism 6, 108
Sedgwick, Eve Kosofsky 163fn.
self, the/selfhood vii, 4, 19–20, 29–32, 63–4, 69–74, 76–8, 80–3, 85–6, 88, 92–5, 109–10, 148fn., 155–8fn., 160–1fn.
Selvon, Sam 12, 110, 162fn.
Seton, Ernest Thompson 103
sexual/sexuality 8, 79, 88, 93, 97–8, 101, 112, 118, 119, 126, 128, 129–32, 134–5, 138–40, 154fn., 156fn.
Sexual Revolution 129, 140
Shakespeare/Shakespearean 6, 85
Shakur, Tupac 114
Shields, Carol 71
short story 5
Signet Classic 127
Signifying Monkey, The 16, 18–31, 38, 145–6fn.
silence/silenced 10–12, 19, 31, 41, 82, 85, 87, 91, 94–5, 97, 100–2, 118, 159fn.
slave narrative 1, 10, 19, 42–5, 155fn.
slavery 1, 16, 19, 22, 27, 43–4
Smith, Sidonie 70, 93, 96–8, 155fn.

Smith, Zadie vii, viii, 1–2, 12–13, 22, 35, 103–22, 123, 138, 143, 162fn.
 On Beauty vii, viii, 2, 7, 12, 22, 35, 103–22, 138, 143, 161fn.
 White Teeth 1, 107, 110, 162fn.
Spacks, Patricia Meyer 54
Spikes, Michael 145fn.
Sprague, Claire 55–57, 153–4fn.
Squires, Claire 110, 162fn.
Stam, Robert 133, 163fn.
stealing 103
Steedman, Carolyn 2, 147fn.
Stein, Gertrude 4
Stein, Karen 95
Stepto, Robert 5
subjectivity 22, 29, 32, 34, 70–1, 78, 80, 83, 85, 151fn., 155–6fn.
subvert/subversion/subversive 17, 18, 26–8, 35, 37, 49, 53, 60, 68, 72, 77, 87, 92, 95, 99, 135, 152–3fn., 156fn.
suicide/suicidal 54–5, 66, 73, 83
Sullivan, Alvin 151fn.
Sumner, Charles 43
survival viii, 16, 20, 71, 81, 86
Süssmayr 112–13
Sutcliffe, Thomas 129
Swendson, Shanna 127

Tabuteau, Éric 162fn.
target text 7, 27–8, 29–30, 157fn.
Taylor, Charles 120
Teeman, Tim 135
Tennant, Emma 13, 123, 141
Tew, Philip 162fn.
Thiong'o, Ngugi Wa 109
Third Wave Feminism/Feminist 108
Thompson, James 123–4, 126, 137
threshold 2, 6–8, 11–12, 15, 48, 53, 68, 70, 98, 116, 144fn.
Tilbury 110
Time Magazine 147
Times, The 110, 135
Tolan, Fiona 111
Tse-Tung, Mao 35
Tupac – see Shakur, Tupac

Turner, Henry S. 108
Tynan, Maeve 105–107, 109

UK 47, 50, 110, 130

ventriloquism 2, 12, 128, 162–3fn.
vernacular 20–1, 23–6, 37, 113, 115, 117, 145fn.
Victoria and Albert Museum 76
Victorian 76, 97, 99, 108, 120
Vintage Classic 127
Voiret, Martine 126, 129–30, 136–7
Voodoo 34, 105, 118

Walker, Nancy 11, 94–5, 97
Wallace, Diana 72, 123, 136–7, 142, 162fn.
Walters, Tracey 117
Warren, Kenneth 146fn.
Waste Land, The 137
Watkins, Susan ix, 47
Waugh, Patricia viii, ix, 49, 53, 118–20
Webster, Emma Campbell 126–7
West/Western 18–21, 23–4, 26, 42, 70, 107, 119, 130, 144–6fn., 152–3fn.
Whelehan, Imelda 6, 72, 124, 129, 131, 138–139, 141, 164fn.
Whittaker, Ruth 48
Wide Sargasso Sea 87, 107
wife (see also 'housewife') 13, 55, 60, 77, 87, 92, 96, 98, 104, 111, 123, 130, 140, 141
Wilde, Oscar 14, 152fn.
Willis, Susan 38–9, 147fn., 149fn.
Wiltshire, John 126, 163fn.
Windrush 110–111
Women's Liberation 47, 61–2, 64
Woolf, Virginia 3–4, 6, 15, 94, 124, 145fn., 155fn.
Worthington, Kim 29–31, 77, 79–80, 156fn., 158fn.

Yaeger, Patricia 45

Zeff, Dan 125, 128, 134, 163fn.

www.ingramcontent.com/pod-product-compliance
Lightning Source LLC
Chambersburg PA
CBHW070639300426
44111CB00013B/2167